Santa Clara County Library District

408-293-2326

Checked Out Items 3/5/2018 10:44
XXXXXXXXX7615

Item Title	Due Date
1. De-escalate : how to calm an angry person in 90 seconds or less 33305240505887	3/26/2018
2. Grass roots : the rise and fall and rise of marijuana in America 33305240199707	3/26/2018

No of Items: 2

24/7 Telecirc: 800-471-0991
www.sccl.org
Thank you for visiting our library.

Santa Clara County Library District
408-293-2326

Checked Out Items 3/5/2018 10:44
XXXXXXXXXX7615

Item Title	Due Date
1. De-escalate : how to calm an angry person in 90 seconds or less 33305240505887	3/26/2018
2. Grass roots : the rise and fall and rise of marijuana in America 33305240199707	3/26/2018

No of Items: 2

24/7 Telecirc: 800-471-0991
www.sccl.org
Thank you for visiting our library.

GRASS ROOTS

GRASS ROOTS

THE RISE AND FALL
AND RISE OF
MARIJUANA IN AMERICA

EMILY DUFTON

BASIC BOOKS

New York

Basic Books
Hachette Book Group
1290 Avenue of the Americas, New York, NY 10104
www.basicbooks.com

Printed in the United States of America
First Edition: December 2017

Published by Basic Books, an imprint of Perseus Books, LLC, a subsidiary of Hachette Book Group, Inc.

The Hachette Speakers Bureau provides a wide range of authors for speaking events. To find out more, go to www.hachettespeakersbureau.com or call (866) 376-6591.

The publisher is not responsible for websites (or their content) that are not owned by the publisher.

Print book interior design by Jeff Williams

Library of Congress Control Number: 2017956164
ISBNs: 978-0-465-09616-9 (hardcover), 978-0-465-09617-6 (ebook)

LSC-C

10 9 8 7 6 5 4 3 2 1

To Herr Professor Leo P. Ribuffo, EBD *père*,
and my beloved HDMs 4 and 5.
Thank you, always, for your support.

CONTENTS

INTRODUCTION

A Higher Calling

THE HISTORY OF marijuana in America is, to quote its chroniclers the Grateful Dead, a long, strange trip, involving tens of thousands of ordinary individuals who, along with corporations, federal officials, presidents, and first ladies, felt a personal stake in determining the future of pot. They are people who found a "higher calling" in the battle over marijuana rights in America—individuals whose dedication was so complete that they crafted careers out of fighting for or against the drug. But even for those who joined the movement for only a short time, marijuana, and the threat or promise it contains, has long been a powerful motivator, inspiring thousands of activists over the past fifty years to form into two opposing camps, either supporting or denouncing the use of the drug. These activists have worked for years to convince Americans that their view of marijuana is correct, and they've sought to counteract each other—as well as the dominant view of the drug at the time—by organizing political protests, national movements, large-scale conferences, and voting campaigns. This is the surprising power of marijuana: not since the battle over the federal prohibition of alcohol has a drug pushed so many to take action, and no other intoxicant in American history has inspired so many people to take to the streets.

But Prohibition ended in 1933 with alcohol's legality enshrined in a constitutional amendment, and few have questioned its legal status since. Marijuana is a different story. Through powerful arguments and even more powerful campaigns, grassroots activists and their supporters have transformed the reputation—and legal status—of marijuana three times, moving it from legality to illegality and back again. First pro-marijuana activists were responsible for launching the nation's first drive to decriminalize personal marijuana use in the 1970s, when they succeeded in making possession a civil misdemeanor in a dozen states. In response, concerned parents launched a booming anti-marijuana counterrevolution that demonized, and then outlawed, marijuana in the 1980s, reversing the earlier decriminalization trend. Now, today's current push for legalization is driven once again by pro-marijuana activists who are inspired by both the drug's medical utility and a concern for social justice and civil rights. Arguing that marijuana prohibition does more harm than good, modern activists have launched one of the most successful grassroots legalization efforts of all time: twenty-eight states now allow residents to use medical marijuana, while eight states and the District of Columbia have legalized recreational weed.

This history is what makes marijuana unique. Unlike cocaine and LSD, only marijuana has had the distinct ability to move back and forth at the state and local levels—between legality and illegality, acceptance and condemnation—while always remaining federally illegal. And the drug's rise, fall, and resurrection would have been impossible without the participation of thousands of grassroots activists, many of them everyday people who, over the past fifty years, have continually pushed the use of the drug into new realms.

Of course, marijuana use in America goes back much further than fifty years; it was only in the past five decades that grassroots activists made marijuana their cause. The culture that surrounds the drug stretches back to before the country's beginnings as an independent nation. Hemp—fiber made from the cannabis plant's stalk—is one of the strongest and most durable materials in nature, and it was used throughout early American history to manufacture, among other things, cloth, twine, rope, paper, and sails. In 1619, all Jamestown colonists were required by law to grow and maintain hemp, and George Washington, Thomas Jefferson, and Benjamin Franklin grew the plant on their plantations and farms for domestic use.[1]

By the late 1800s, the drug had come to prominence as a useful and widely available medicine and was popular in pain-relieving tinctures sold in local pharmacies. Cannabis was believed to be so safe that the drug was marketed to women through romantic postcard campaigns that showed concerned mothers applying a cannabis salve to soothe the gums of teething babies and relieve children's colds.[2] As a pain reliever, marijuana worked wonderfully. Delta-9-tetrahydrocannabinol, or THC, the principal psychoactive component found in the leaves of the female cannabis plant, is a mild analgesic and antiemetic that was used to treat the pain, cramps, nausea, and fatigue of everyone from nineteenth-century American children to Chinese peasants in the Zhou Dynasty (1046–256 B.C.) to Queen Victoria of England, who used it to relieve her menstrual cramps.[3]

Despite its popularity, however, marijuana's role in American medicine was short-lived. With the forces of Progressivism rallying around ideals of sobriety and the tide of Prohibition rising, Treasury Department officials lobbied to have marijuana added to the drugs covered by the Harrison Narcotics Tax Act, passed in December 1914. The act—sponsored by Representative Francis Burton Harrison of New York and one of the first federal drug control laws—didn't explicitly outlaw marijuana, but rather regulated and taxed the production, importation, and distribution of opiates and coca products. After the Harrison Act, along with the 1906 Pure Food and Drug Act, required drug producers to honestly label the contents of their tinctures, cannabis-based medicines slowly were either banned or replaced. Smokable marijuana didn't qualify as a narcotic, however, and remained in legal limbo until 1937, when the Marijuana Tax Act made the possession or transfer of cannabis illegal, while allowing states to enforce their own marijuana laws and to tax hemp and marijuana cultivation and distribution.

Once effectively outlawed, marijuana took on a second life. Recreational marijuana smoking had been introduced to Americans in the late 1800s by Mexican refugees fleeing the dictatorship of President Porfirio Díaz; as it slowly spread north from the border, the drug grew controversial, primarily because of the people associated with its use. A 1917 report from the Treasury Department noted that in Texas, only "Mexicans and sometimes Negroes and lower class whites" smoked marijuana for pleasure and warned that "drug-crazed" minorities could harm or assault upper-class white women—by far the report's chief concern.[4] Fears about its ability to induce violence would continue to haunt the debate over marijuana throughout the early twentieth century. For

instance, films like *Reefer Madness,* released in 1936, associated marijuana use with murder, miscegenation, and suicide as it showed the
transformation of a group of otherwise upstanding young white people
into a laughing cabal of maddened criminals.

Even with the drug's stigmatized reputation, however, marijuana
use spread across the country over the next few decades, and its popularity continued to grow. It was the subject of increased debate in the
1930s, when Harry Anslinger took control of the newly founded Federal Bureau of Narcotics and launched a campaign against marijuana
that would last the rest of his thirty-two-year career. It was Anslinger,
angered by the lack of federal action against the drug, who lobbied for
the passage of the Marijuana Tax Act of 1937. He also published a series of anti-pot articles in *The American Magazine.* In his most famous,
"Marijuana: Assassin of Youth," which appeared in July 1937, Anslinger
warned that the drug was "as dangerous as a coiled rattlesnake" and
declared that the number of "murders, suicides, robberies, criminal
assaults, holdups, burglaries, and deeds of maniacal insanity it causes
each year, especially among the young, can only be conjectured."[5]

In part because of its hyperbolically bad reputation, "smoking tea"
was celebrated in cities like Los Angeles and New York as the new way
to enjoy the Jazz Age or, alternatively, to forget Depression-era blues.
Manhattan-based swing violinist Stuff Smith and his Onyx Boys Club
summed up their enthusiastic feelings about pot in their 1936 song "If
You're a Viper," which explained how "a tea" could lighten the spirits of
a "viper" hip to marijuana, even in the midst of the Depression.[6] Even as
Prohibition was repealed and alcohol once again became increasingly
available, marijuana remained a popular drug among the urban avant-
garde and artistic elite, and, despite the 1937 act, it became easier than
ever to obtain.

The drug's ready availability changed in the 1940s, when World War
II transformed marijuana's doppelgänger, hemp, into a patriotic and
necessary crop. By 1942, with hemp from the South Pacific squarely
under the control of the Japanese, the US Navy needed additional supplies. In response, the US Department of Agriculture released the film
Hemp for Victory!, which encouraged "patriotic farmers" to grow up to
50,000 acres of hemp over the next year to supply the US forces battling
the Axis powers abroad. "Hemp for mooring ships; hemp for tow lines;

hemp for tackle and gear; hemp for countless naval uses both on ship and shore . . . hemp for victory," the film proclaimed as the camera captured American battleships sailing proudly out to sea.[7]

When the war ended, however, hemp was no longer in demand and marijuana was controversial again. By the 1950s, amid fears of juvenile delinquency, the perceived threat of oversexualized rock and roll, and the rise of footloose teenagers, marijuana sparked terror in adults. Its use, and unavoidable abuse, were themes in numerous "social guidance" films, such as 1951's *The Terrible Truth*, which warned young people that "most teenagers start off with marijuana. Then they decide to see if heroin has any kick. It does. Sometimes it takes only a few days to find out they can't leave it alone. . . . There are practically no happy endings when you fool with drugs."[8] Unlike the days of *Reefer Madness*, when the fear was that marijuana would drive users insane, this era was in the grip of a larger social fear that made such warnings about marijuana's immediate effects pale in comparison. Now the fear was that marijuana would unavoidably lead to other, harder drug use, and this element of the "gateway drug" theory would be endorsed by anti-marijuana activists for decades to come.

But even if the fears about the drug in the 1950s echoed the fears of the 1930s, in many ways it was a golden age for marijuana. Quarantined primarily to circles of artists and musicians in urban areas like San Francisco and New York, marijuana developed a cultish fan base that celebrated the drug's mysterious and ethereal effects. Beat writers Allen Ginsberg and Jack Kerouac penned paeans to its liberating potential, and it was shared in the smoky back rooms of jazz clubs in Harlem, inspiring performances from musicians like Charlie Parker, Mezz Mezzrow, and Miles Davis.[9] Kerouac credited the increased sensitivity and insight he gained from smoking pot for driving his "wild form," a new kind of writing that combined jazz with his desire "to catch the fresh dream, the fresh thought," as though he were "a fisherman of the deep with old, partially useful nets."[10]

After a brief period of underground popularity in the '50s, everything changed in the 1960s, when marijuana was transformed from an avant-garde trend into a national phenomenon led, like many things during that decade, by young people. As trafficking routes from South and Central America solidified and Americans' taste for the drug increased, marijuana migrated across the nation, its use centering primarily on college campuses. There it found a receptive audience among young people who were terrified of the draft, sympathetic to the civil rights movement, enamored of the free speech movement, and tired of the previous decade's stunting conventionality. Disgusted by the wastefulness and conformity driving America's consumer culture and devastated by the wars raging at home for civil rights and abroad in Vietnam, young pot smokers of the 1960s embraced the drug as a signifier of protest, a visible representation of the generational break. Smoking pot in the sixties symbolized rebellion against everything "straight" in American culture: it meant being against the war, against capitalism, against racism and sexism, and, most importantly, against the hawkish, Vietnam-supporting adults who used and often abused alcohol as their drug of choice.

This transformation in drug preference is telling. The more philosophical marijuana smokers of the sixties argued that their drug use was not just a way to alleviate boredom or pain, but represented a deeper cultural shift, an awakening of public consciousness to the injustices of the world. To the hippies for whom the drug was a communal sacrament, marijuana use represented a new take on the American Dream— one that came, according to one hippie, "without the phoniness and hierarchy, the profit and power, the processed food and the three-piece suits, the evening news and the suburban ranch house."[11] The humble weed offered "heads" (a colloquial term for pot smokers) an alternative America, one that emphasized community, authenticity, and a return to nature. Although marijuana use was perhaps the most visible sign of the counterculture, many hippies resisted the media's urge to collapse the two: as one University of Utah student explained, the movement was "not a beard. It is not a weird, colorful costume, it is not marijuana. The hippie movement is a philosophy, a way of life."[12]

Marijuana also quickly became a natural extension, and prominent feature, of the protests that defined the era. At antiwar and free speech gatherings, smoking marijuana became an inherently political act, comparable to other stances that activists were taking and often just as potentially dangerous. Like marching on the Pentagon or occupying university administration buildings, using and possessing marijuana could get activists thrown in jail. Arrests for possession of the drug became increasingly common as authorities cracked down on social rebellion and national leaders, especially Richard Nixon, associated the drug with a broader criminal threat. In some states, marijuana quickly became the drug that authorities targeted the most. In California, marijuana accounted for only 27 percent of all drug arrests in 1960, but by 1967, the year of the "Human Be-In" and the "Summer of Love," that number had escalated to 61 percent. And whereas only about 5,000 people were arrested annually for marijuana in California at the beginning of the decade, by 1967 that number had grown to 37,514.[13]

As marijuana became central to antiwar protests and free speech gatherings, the drug itself also became a focus of civil protest. After the first official protest advocating for legalization, launched in San Francisco in August 1964, activists began to see the criminalization of marijuana as one of many things that authorities insisted—incorrectly—were necessary, like segregation and the war in Vietnam. Recognizing that segregation was unnatural and the Vietnam War unwinnable, young people protested them. In the same vein, recognizing that marijuana didn't cause the criminal insanity, murderous rage, or direct line to heroin addiction that officials and teachers had been warning about for years, young people also began protesting the country's oppressive marijuana laws. For many, marijuana became one of the clearest signs that the government could lie to its citizens, and they saw in protesting marijuana laws the potential to correct decades of misinformation. As the early activist Kenneth Rice told the underground newspaper *The Berkeley Barb* in April 1966, "If we can organize all the people who know the truth about marijuana, in all different classes and areas of society, we'll be able to legalize it."[14]

Although he probably hoped that this transformation would happen more quickly than it did, Rice foretold many of the trends that would shape marijuana activism—both for and against the drug—in the years to come. By working to, as Rice put it, tell the "truth" about marijuana, activists have influenced voters and politicians to transform marijuana laws three times. The first change was inspired by the activism of the 1960s: between 1973 and 1978, legalization supporters, modeling the social protests of the previous decade, defended an adult's right to privacy and sparked the passage of decriminalization laws in a dozen states. In response, concerned parents from across the country formed a national movement in the late 1970s and early 1980s to overturn those laws, arguing that decriminalization had increased adolescent use of marijuana and the drug was too dangerous to warrant only a fine. This movement led to the second major change in marijuana laws, when the Reagan administration oversaw nationwide recriminalization of marijuana and inspired a wider cultural and legal crackdown on drug use. Most recently, activists working to help patients suffering from diseases like cancer, glaucoma, and HIV/AIDS, as well as activists working to correct decades of systemic and racial injustice resulting from the country's punitive drug war, have launched ballot initiatives to legalize marijuana for medicine and recreation. These initiatives, which represent the third major shift in the country's marijuana laws, have been enormously successful, and many proponents claim that, with nearly 70 million people living in states where the drug is legal, legalization is here to stay.

That effect remains to be seen, but through each of these historical twists and turns, grassroots activists have been the ones who have led the fight for changes in local and national marijuana laws. Working with politicians and inspiring voters, generations of marijuana protesters have become some of the most powerful activists in American history, doing more to repeatedly change drug laws than any group of advocates since Prohibition. More importantly, these activists have strengthened their case, not by immediately influencing top political leaders, but by going directly to the American people and organizing on the local level until their movements draw national strength. By making powerful, and often sympathetic, claims about the people whom marijuana laws affect the most, these activists have consistently been able to sway public opinion, ultimately transforming political opinion as well. And their influence has been profound. Rarely in the past fifty years have politicians themselves started the process of changing drug laws; instead, they have jumped on the bandwagon only after activists made the shift both popular and politically safe. We tend to associate major changes in the drug war with powerful figures like presidents and first ladies, but in fact it has always been grassroots activists who have led the way.

Grass Roots tells these activists' stories, from the first protest in 1964 until today. It highlights each movement's most powerful members and offers their history as both a warning to current activists (hint: even a friendly presidential administration can make an imperfect ally) as well as a source of inspiration (appealing directly to voters works). Furthermore, *Grass Roots* shows how important marijuana has been for over five decades of American history. The battle over the drug has always been about much more than whether individuals have the right to smoke, eat, or vape it for effect. Instead, questions about marijuana have long been tied to ideas about freedom and liberty, safety and security, and the rights of an individual versus the collective good—themes that are at the core of many other major historical debates. The nation's ongoing battle over marijuana also highlights Americans' core concerns over how involved the government should be in citizens' private lives, whether we should privilege public safety and sobriety over individuals' ability to do what they want, and who deserves to be punished, or protected, for committing drug crimes. These questions have never been fully answered, and it is marijuana activists who have kept up the debate, continually shifting how Americans talk about the drug and which groups are most affected by changing drug laws.

Most of all, however, *Grass Roots* shows that, when it comes to marijuana, nothing is certain. Legalization activists today celebrate the passage of recreational use laws and argue that, because of their expansion, the battle is over and legal marijuana is here to stay. But the history of marijuana activism shows that voters are fickle, and that attitudes toward the drug can rapidly change. By exploring the impact of grassroots activists—as well as the roots of "grass" in America—we can see that the discourse on marijuana has always moved in cycles, shifting repeatedly between acceptance and condemnation. Despite what seems like a strong trend toward legalization today, if major problems emerge in states where marijuana has been legalized, or if the Trump administration decides to challenge the new laws, everything could swiftly change, just as happened in the 1970s when parent activists overturned decriminalization laws, or in the 1990s when "Just Say No" was replaced by support for medical—and now recreational—marijuana use.

In short, the story of marijuana in America is far from over, and many new chapters are undoubtedly yet to come. Still, the continuing debate over the merits and dangers of legalization can only be enriched by acknowledging the grassroots activists whose decades-long work to change the country's marijuana laws has brought us to this moment today. Their history has long gone untold, but by bringing the effects of their activism to light, *Grass Roots* tells their story, and ours.

1

"FORWARD, ALL SMOKERS!"

AUGUST 16, 1964, was a quiet Sunday in San Francisco. The Giants were set to play the Milwaukee Braves in Candlestick Park that afternoon, while the city prepared to host the Beatles, scheduled to arrive two days later for the start of their first North American tour. Occupied by the arrival of the Fab Four, the police were taken by surprise when twenty-eight-year-old Lowell Eggemeier walked into the city's Hall of Justice, lit up a joint, and politely asked to be arrested for smoking pot. "I am starting a campaign to legalize marijuana smoking," he told the stunned cops who watched him take a drag. "I wish to be arrested." At the time, it was a felony to smoke marijuana in California, and Eggemeier was quickly hauled off to jail.[1]

Beyond this initial act, not much is known about Eggemeier, the nation's first grassroots marijuana activist. Reports have called him a peacenik and a hippie, but "hippie" was a loosely formed idea in 1964, one year before thousands of sandal- and bead-wearing youth would descend upon the Haight-Ashbury district and Golden Gate Park. And Eggemeier, a lifelong Californian who wore his hair short and preferred to wear T-shirts and jeans, was not a typical counterculture activist. A quiet, bearded man who enjoyed spending time with his dogs, Eggemeier didn't realize that his time in the San Francisco Hall of Justice would launch a revolution that would last fifty more years. After serving nearly a year in prison for his act, he returned to his quiet life, abandoning any association with marijuana activism or the people who would continue to fight for his cause.

But for the thousands of young people who followed in Eggemeier's footsteps, the battle for legalization had only begun. Eggemeier's action coincided with the rise of a national counterculture, when young people abandoned en masse the strictures and constraints of modern American life and sought to create a new, bohemian approach to living that emphasized peace, creativity, and a willingness to experiment with mind-altering drugs. The hippies who gathered in San Francisco shortly after Eggemeier's arrest were emblematic of this shift, and when Eggemeier's lawyer unearthed old government reports that lauded marijuana's beneficial effects, the hippies were quick to accept his claims. For the thousands of people experimenting with the drug, knowing that the government had once recognized marijuana's benefits—even if reports on those benefits were over fifty years old—made the contemporary antidrug laws seem like a hoax, and the rising arrest rates an attack on personal freedom.

With support from the poet Allen Ginsberg, marijuana activism soon spread across the country, inspiring protests, garnering followers, and challenging authority along the way. But pro-marijuana activism didn't stay exclusively focused on the drug for long. The battle for legalization arrived in the United States just as protests were starting in earnest against the Vietnam War, and marijuana activism was quickly subsumed into the burgeoning national antiwar movement. By 1967, when up to 35,000 young men were being drafted each month, the antiwar effort was growing at a rapid rate, with protests taking place everywhere from California to New York to Washington, DC. Given marijuana's prominence in the counterculture, activists brought the drug to antiwar protests and rallies across the country, merging the act of smoking pot with the cause of protesting the war. Marijuana became a common sight as activists marched on the National Mall and movement leaders promised to "levitate the Pentagon" and exorcise it of its deadly ghosts.

Though rallies for legalization fell to the wayside as the war demanded increased attention, marijuana hardly disappeared from these events. Instead, marijuana's presence at antiwar rallies had surprising benefits for the legalization cause. Introduced to a far larger crowd at these rallies, the drug quickly became something—and sometimes the only thing—that diverse factions of antiwar protesters had in common.

Though certainly not every antiwar activist smoked pot, those who did found common ground, both in their interest in opposing the war and the legal peril in which their marijuana use placed them. As the activist Jerry Rubin remembered, "You started to see more and more people actually high at demonstrations. Now everybody got stoned—everywhere you looked, people would be passing the joint, like a peace pipe. Besides opposition to the war, it was the single most important unifying cultural activity."[2]

By 1968, marijuana was no longer simply, as Allen Ginsberg once put it, "fun." Instead, pot had become fiercely political. The first four years of marijuana activism—from the first legalization protest in 1964 to the national antiwar rallies in 1968—were some of the most tumultuous in the history of the country, and of the drug. Transformed from a "gentle, beautiful thing," as one pro-pot activist put it in 1964, into one of the most ubiquitous and powerful aspects of protests against the war, marijuana came to signal a shared suspicion of authority. And the activists who emerged from the Vietnam era became some of the most effective organizers of the subsequent legalization campaign, because they understood both the power of collective action and the symbolic power of the drug. Armed with the lessons they learned in the antiwar movement, they were prepared to wage what would become a fifty-year battle for legalization. Even as the American war in Vietnam drew to a close, the battle for marijuana rights had only begun.

•

Lowell Eggemeier's attorney, James R. White III, was not terribly familiar with "smoking grass." A well-known conservative civil libertarian who once described himself as "to the right of Barry Goldwater," White had built his career on arguing for the rights of those whom he felt the government had abused in some way. Though White had never before worked with a defendant arrested for drugs, there was something about Eggemeier's claims that compelled him to take the case.[3]

After Eggemeier's arrest, White immediately filed a petition with the California Supreme Court for a writ of habeas corpus demanding his client's release. Then, after some initial research, he defended Eggemeier's actions based on his readings of the Eighth and Fourteenth Amendments. White argued that marijuana's status as an illegal narcotic, along with the state's increasing crackdown on pot smokers, deprived its users of due process, thus violating the Fourteenth Amendment, while the lengthy prison sentences handed out for marijuana crimes violated the Eighth Amendment's constitutional ban on cruel and unusual punishment.

In defense of his claims, White cited evidence in his brief from numerous, if antiquated, reports—namely, those of the Indian Hemp Drugs Commission of 1894, the Panama Canal Zone Commission of 1925, and the 1944 La Guardia Committee—that found marijuana to be less toxic and habit-forming than tobacco or alcohol, and thus less worthy of a legal ban. A diligent researcher, White found that, in the almost fifty-year-old Panama Canal Zone report, the committee had agreed that "there is no evidence that marijuana is a 'habit-forming' drug in the sense in which the term is applied to alcohol, opium, cocaine, etc., or that it has any appreciably deleterious influence on the individual using it." Given the relative safety of the drug, as well as the American government's previous recognition of that fact, White argued that its prohibition as a narcotic was unconstitutional in the extreme, and that Eggemeier did not deserve to be jailed for its possession or use.[4]

Working pro bono, White raised money for Eggemeier's case by printing copies of his petition, decorating the slim booklets with a hand-drawn marijuana leaf, and selling them under the title *Marijuana Puff-In*. Copies of Eggemeier's defense quickly began circulating through the hands of the proto-hippies living in the San Francisco Bay Area, bringing government-issued reports on the relative banality of marijuana into public view for the first time in decades. In coffee shops like the Blue Unicorn, where bohemians often washed dishes to pay for their meal, people gathered to play chess, listen to music, and discuss what White had found.

White became dedicated to Eggemeier's cause because, as a libertarian, he saw the state's marijuana laws as inherently infringing on individual rights. As part of his defense strategy, and in acknowledgment of the growing interest in his claims among many San Franciscans, White founded the first organization in the country dedicated to overturning marijuana prohibition. Four months after Eggemeier launched his protest, in December 1964, White held a rally in Union Square to introduce LEMAR (a contraction of LEgalize MARijuana) to the world.

White was quick to point out that his new group didn't explicitly advocate smoking pot. Instead, LEMAR supported "each person's right to smoke if he wants to"—a distinction that the libertarian and his followers saw as key. As White began hosting events throughout the city, smaller LEMAR outposts formed in coffee shops like the Blue Unicorn and on the nearby campus of University of California, Berkeley. Kenneth Rice, Berkeley LEMAR's spokesperson, promised the underground newspaper *The Berkeley Barb* that his group would "not try to change the law through any illegal or irresponsible method." Instead, the group's aim was to "raise money, educate the public, and gather signatures to change the laws." They were hoping to get 460,000 signatures to place the marijuana issue on the California ballot by 1966.[5]

Yet as LEMAR spread across the city, Eggemeier languished behind bars. Despite White's actions, an appeals court refused to hear Eggemeier's case, and he was convicted and sentenced to a year in prison. When finally released, Eggemeier quietly returned home, avoiding marijuana activism—and any connection to LEMAR—for the rest of his life. In a troubling twist of fate, just as the movement began to take off, the intense legal ramifications of smoking a single joint had caused its first activist to abandon the cause.

As Eggemeier departed, however, other activists were just beginning their campaigns. Nine years after Allen Ginsberg baptized marijuana—along with jazz bands, hipsters, and peyote—in the footnote to his famous 1955 poem *Howl*, the poet spent a year in Berkeley. Nearing forty and widely respected with numerous awards to his name, Ginsberg attended the first LEMAR rally that December, shortly before he planned to return to New York. Though he was familiar with marijuana, this was the first time Ginsberg had encountered people who were actively fighting to legalize its use, and the poet, who was already bridging the gap between the Beats of the 1950s and the burgeoning hippie movement of the 1960s, sought to bring the legalization movement with him when he returned to the East Coast.

Back in New York, Ginsberg went to the Peace Eye Bookstore, the city's gathering place for counterculture activists. Located in the East Village, the Peace Eye was owned by the poet and musician Ed Sanders, a wild-haired, mustached native of Kansas City who was so moved when he read *Howl* that he dropped out of the University of Missouri, hitchhiked to New York, and took on a new life as a counterculture leader. Sanders had known Ginsberg since 1961, and their mutual interests in poetry and protest made them obvious collaborators for LEMAR's first East Coast chapter.

They launched into action immediately. On December 27, Ginsberg and twenty-three other young men and women protested in front of the City Department of Welfare's headquarters at nearby Tompkins Square Park, under the watchful eyes of nine police. Posters printed by Sanders at the Peace Eye invited people to join the "Marijuana March" and outlined LEMAR's primary goals: to legalize the use of the drug; to legalize the sale and transportation of pot; and to free all prisoners arrested on marijuana charges.[6]

The *New York Times* and *The Village Voice* sent reporters to cover the event. "For three hours in a misty drizzle, the picketers marched with placards saying 'Smoke pot, it's cheaper and healthier than liquor,' 'Pot is harmless' and 'Repeal marijuana prohibition,'" the *Times* reported. A young woman named Kitty Politchevsky told the paper that marijuana was "a gentle, beautiful thing," and added that this was the first in a series of LEMAR demonstrations. *The Village Voice* reported that Ginsberg and his partner Peter Orlovsky played finger cymbals and led the group in chants of "Om Hari Namo Shiva," which, Ginsberg explained, was a meditation to Shiva, the Indian god of meditation and marijuana.[7]

During the protest, activists handed out copies of *The Marijuana Newsletter* to passersby. This small, hand-illustrated brochure was created by Sanders, along with Orlovsky, Randolfe Wicker, and C. T. Smith, and published, Sanders proudly proclaimed, by the Peace Eye "as a public service." Printed on pale pink paper, the *Newsletter* promised readers "the facts about marijuana, the gentle benevolent herb," along with position papers, medical information, and information about LEMAR's campaign. It also served as a call to arms, as evidenced by the editorial Sanders published the following month, in January 1965:

> Like liquor prohibition, pot prohibition violates personal liberty, promotes racketeering, and invites mass evasion of the law. . . . [Marijuana] is in *all* respects socially useful, gentle, benevolent, and absolutely *non*addictive.

Why should thousands of New Yorkers who smoke marijuana be harassed, freaked, arrested, maltreated, and even blackmailed? Down with prohibition! Forward, all smokers! Let's have a *Total Assault* against all those who would torture our minds and bodies with their creepy outmoded laws! Join the marijuana campaign! A carefully planned, intelligent, and energetic marijuana education program will free marijuana to those who want to use it for many generations.[8]

The Village Voice continued to follow Ginsberg and Sanders as they took their campaign to the streets. On January 10, a few weeks after their first protest, the poets led a march on the New York Women's House of Detention to protest the incarceration of several marijuana users. The day was cold, and a light snow fell on Ginsberg and others as they stood in the street. Fred McDarrah, a staff photographer for *The Voice* who chronicled the Beats and the burgeoning hippie generation, took a portrait of Ginsberg grasping a cup of coffee, a hand-lettered sign hanging around his neck reading, in large letters, POT IS FUN. The image of the famous poet advocating for marijuana quickly spanned the globe. "It made quite a splash at the time because it quickly became a worldwide image," Sanders recalled later. "This bearded poet with a gleam in his eye, carrying this sign in the snow. In a sense, that single image became like a shot heard around the world."[9]

Building on the popularity of McDarrah's image, Ginsberg published a pages-long pro-legalization article in *The Atlantic Monthly* in November 1966. "The Great Marijuana Hoax" excoriated the decades-long federal effort to marginalize and punish marijuana users and demanded justice for those incarcerated for the drug. "Hoax" is a long and sometimes meandering article that outlines everything from Ginsberg's own drug use and pot's effects on music and the arts to petty grievances (including the time a doctor called him "mad" for using the drug) and the history of cannabis use abroad. Most of the article is devoted, however, to Ginsberg's argument that the history of marijuana suppression is founded almost entirely on prejudice: marijuana prohibition allowed the police to target artists and counterculture activists, who were perceived as threats, and he noted that the "use of marijuana has always been widespread among the Negro population in this country, and suppression of its use . . . has been one of the major unconscious, or unmentionable, methods of suppression of Negro rights." His plan for the national future of the drug rested on two increasingly popular ideas: that the drug created positive, beneficial states of mind, and that the laws against it were deeply harmful to the populace—more harmful, Ginsberg argued, than the use of the drug itself.

Ginsberg's article made the case for "the end of prohibition of marijuana, and a total shift of treatment of actually addictive drugs to the hands of the medical profession," as well as "a total dismantling of the whole cancerous bureaucracy that has perpetuated this historic fuck-up on the United States." Marijuana prohibition was a government coverup, Ginsberg wrote, an "insane hoax on public consciousness" that had undoubtedly violated some "laws of malfeasance in public office." But Ginsberg was less concerned with those who perpetuated the laws than with those who had suffered because of them. He concluded by arguing that "some positive remuneration is required for those poor citizens" who had been arrested for marijuana. "For the inoffensive charming smokers who have undergone disgraceful jailings, money is due as a compensation," Ginsberg argued, making a claim that would be echoed, decades later, by legalization activists in the twenty-first century.[10]

Ginsberg's fame and support helped promote the burgeoning legalization campaign throughout the country. By 1966, artists, activists, and scholars had formed three more LEMAR chapters, in Detroit, Cleveland, and Buffalo, New York. Michael Aldrich, the first person to study marijuana myth and folklore in an academic context, started the group in Buffalo. The Detroit group was formed by John Sinclair, the jazz poet and founder of the White Panther Party, and d. a. levy, the visual poet and artist, formed the branch in his hometown in Ohio.

The movement didn't fare as well in the conservative Midwest as it had in New York, however. Ginsberg's international fame buffered him from prosecution, but Sinclair and levy would be heavily persecuted for their involvement with legalization efforts. In 1969, Sinclair was arrested for giving two joints to undercover agents and sentenced to ten years in prison, inspiring John Lennon's song "Ten for Two" and the John Sinclair Freedom Rally in 1971, where bands and speakers, including Ginsberg, performed and advocated for his release. Sinclair was eventually freed after twenty-nine months in prison, but levy, who supported legalization but was not a heavy smoker, was continually targeted by Ohio police, primarily for distributing "obscene" poetry to minors. The local paper ran editorials against his art, and he was repeatedly jailed for giving "weird and way out" poetry readings to underage youth. After two years of harassment for his art and LEMAR activism, levy committed suicide on November 24, 1968, shooting himself with a .22 rifle while seated in the lotus position in his East Cleveland apartment. He was twenty-six years old.[11]

Michael Aldrich, a young graduate student at the State University of New York (SUNY) in Buffalo, found greater success in bringing LEMAR to new audiences. A scholar of literature and myth, Aldrich was impressed by the acceptance of marijuana that he saw in India, where he studied for a year on a Fulbright scholarship. While pursuing his doctorate in English, he formed LEMAR's first student branch in 1966 with his adviser, the controversial, prize-winning literary critic Leslie Fiedler.[12] Though Aldrich remembered its beginnings as little more than "fifteen hippies in a room," LEMAR Buffalo grew quickly, becoming the philosophical center of the movement. Aided by his access to university resources, by 1968 the bespectacled, eloquent Aldrich also began publishing the *Marijuana Review,* a magazine dedicated "to all things cannabis," and was soon organizing campus "Dope Conferences," with guest speakers who included Timothy Leary and Ken Kesey. At these events, speakers would laud marijuana's beneficial effects and excoriate the federal government's attempts to restrict it, while encouraging their young audiences to take matters into their own hands by organizing their own legalization campaigns.[13] After four years of successful LEMAR activism, Aldrich finished his time on campus in 1970, earning the nickname "Dr. Dope" after successfully defending his 145-page dissertation on "Cannabis Myths and Folklore," the first academic publication on the drug.

Despite LEMAR's moderate success, publicly protesting marijuana's "creepy, outmoded laws" remained a highly suspicious activity in postwar America. The revolution that Ginsberg, Aldrich, levy, and Sinclair were leading was small, appealing primarily to those already familiar with the drug or tapped into the bohemian underground. And despite LEMAR's relatively rapid growth, erupting from a single act of protest in San Francisco to four additional chapters in just two years, membership in the group remained extremely small. It wasn't until marijuana joined the antiwar cause that legalization protests became truly potent. With "smoke-ins" bringing activists together and the drug birthing, in Jerry Rubin's words, "a new man," marijuana's affiliation with the antiwar movement built upon LEMAR's initial success and emboldened thousands of new smokers to take to the streets.

•

Before the arrival of the hippies, Don McNeill, a writer with *The Village Voice,* described Manhattan's Tompkins Square Park as "peaceful, if boring."[14] In the late 1950s and early '60s, the area was quiet and diverse, filled with immigrants from Italy, Hungary, Russia, Poland, and the Ukraine, as well as more recent additions of African Americans and Puerto Ricans. Together, residents had transformed the neighborhood's nineteenth-century tenement houses into a thriving community surrounding the ten-acre park, and complaints were mild: besides the era's ongoing fears of juvenile delinquency, elderly immigrants worried about youngsters playing handball, and there was evidence of growing, but relatively minor, racial tensions.

By 1967, lured by the neighboring Peace Eye Bookstore and the area's cheap rents, a growing number of young bohemians had made the park the center of New York's thriving counterculture, with hundreds of people playing bongos on "Hippie Hill" and listening to music at the band shell erected the year before. That summer, McNeill announced that the East Village had experienced a "hippie explosion," with "changes unprecedented in its constantly changing history."[15] Suddenly the park was host to thousands of young people whose be-ins and public art performances would be chronicled in underground papers like *The Village Voice* and the *East Village Other,* and on June 2 of that year, the park was also the site of the nation's first "smoke-in," when marijuana was used to ease racial tensions, inspiring a new form of counterculture activism.

For weeks tensions had been mounting between white hippies and a group of local Puerto Rican youth. The spring had been filled with fights and riots as hippies clashed with the police and the Puerto Ricans objected to the hippies' "takeover" of their park. After a riot between hippies and the police on Memorial Day that resulted in numerous injuries and forty-two arrests, the hippies battled again two days later, this time with a group of young Puerto Rican men who objected to a performance by the Grateful Dead, who played their first East Coast performance at the Tompkins Square band shell on June 1. After the concert ended at 10:00 P.M., the Puerto Ricans began to protest, and the hippies responded by starting a fight. In the space of an hour, half a dozen people were attacked and cars, motorcycles, and surrounding property were damaged and destroyed.[16]

That evening a small group of Puerto Ricans and hippies met together to prevent another riot. A concert was planned for the following day, and to avoid the need for police, whom neither group trusted, it was decided that a small group of volunteers would serve as "Serenos," or "peacekeepers," marked with white armbands. The Serenos would "link arms and surround any trouble," proving that the hippies and Puerto Ricans could settle their own disputes without interference from the law. It was also decided that the music featured would be more diverse and multicultural. The next night the band shell hosted acts like Mongo Santamaría and Len Chandler, while Chino Garcia emceed in Spanish. "Hippies and Puerto Ricans grooved together on the Latin music. And when the music stopped shortly before midnight, everyone held his breath," *The Voice* reported. "But there was no riot."[17]

One reason there was no riot was because nearly everyone in the park was getting peacefully, blissfully stoned. A young Peace Eye activist named Dana Beal had organized the country's first informal smoke-in during the concert. As the audience grooved to Latin beats, Beal handed out joints to the crowd. An hour later, the park was at peace, with people dancing on the site where, a day before, riots had broken out. Beal was amazed by how quickly and easily the drug brought disparate groups of people together. "Passing out pot refocused the energy," he remembered. "We weren't against each other anymore. Pot allowed hippies and Puerto Ricans to join together against the police."[18]

Recognizing the power of marijuana to bring people together, for the rest of July 1967, Beal hosted a smoke-in every Sunday in the park. Each session would start with the smoking of banana peels, a perfectly legal substance that earlier that year had acquired the false reputation of being a mild hallucinogen. A band would play while hippies gathered and police patrolled, and real marijuana had replaced bananas by the night's end. The scenes were surprisingly peaceful: hippies and Puerto

Ricans smoked and danced together, while the police, wanting to avoid a riot, let the revelers be.

By the end of the month, the gatherings were large enough to warrant coverage in the *New York Times*. "About 200 young people gathered between two gnarled trees and smoked marijuana for over three hours," the *Times* reported, noting that the event was sponsored by a group of "subversive dope fiends." Surprisingly, despite marijuana's continued illegality in New York and rising rates of marijuana arrests across the country, there wasn't a single arrest. One patrolman told the *Times* reporter that an arrest "would cause more trouble than it was worth," while another didn't believe the hippies were doing anything wrong. It "probably isn't pot," another cop, who clearly didn't understand the drug, told the reporter. "I don't know if you know how to smoke pot, but you can't smoke it in the open air. It's probably banana anyway."[19]

With marijuana bringing together counterculture activists in New York, Peace Eye activists began planning larger events, using marijuana to protest the Vietnam War. Antiwar protests had been occurring regularly since April 1965, but by the fall of 1967, as more young men were being drafted and President Lyndon Johnson was reiterating the importance of American involvement abroad, rallies were taking on a new and significantly more political turn.[20] A month later, on October 21, 1967, one of the largest such protests took place on the National Mall and, later that day, across the Potomac River at the Pentagon in Arlington, Virginia. The "March on the Pentagon to Confront the Warmakers" drew approximately 100,000 activists to Washington, and it was an extremely diverse gathering. *Time* magazine wrote that the crowd contained "all the elements of American dissent in 1967," including radicals and hippies, professors, black nationalists, conservationists, housewives, women's groups, and veterans returned from the war.[21]

The march was organized by the National Mobilization Committee to End the War in Vietnam (MOBE) and featured speakers and musicians like pediatrician Dr. Benjamin Spock and the trio Peter, Paul, and Mary. The MOBE's coordinator, the well-known pacifist David Dellinger, had appointed Peace Eye activist Jerry Rubin to organize the event and lead an additional march on the Pentagon once the rally at the Lincoln Memorial was complete. Dellinger, who was in his fifties at the time, wanted Rubin to make the march appealing to young people, and Rubin was the ideal candidate to do so. A political prankster and self-described "anti-capitalist comic of the 1960s," Rubin was committed to "the radical dream of transforming the system from the outside" and saw the rally as the perfect place to launch a new kind of political performance art, transforming an otherwise orderly event into the edgy, drug-infused activism that would become the trademark of both Rubin and his compatriot Abbie Hoffman.[22]

The rally on the Mall was fairly quiet and conventional, with limited clashes between protesters and the police. When it was over, however, Rubin, Hoffman, and Sanders switched gears, leading roughly half the crowd, accompanied by patrolmen on motorcycles and low-flying helicopters, across the Potomac. There, Rubin and Hoffman's promise to "levitate the Pentagon" would sear the protest into the memories of its participants.

According to Norman Mailer, who attended the rally and wrote his Pulitzer Prize–winning "nonfiction novel" *The Armies of the Night* about the event, Hoffman, Rubin, and Sanders planned to smoke marijuana and then "encircle the Pentagon with twelve hundred men in order to form a ring of exorcism sufficiently powerful to raise the Pentagon three hundred feet. In the air the Pentagon would then, went the presumption, turn orange and vibrate until all evil emissions had fled." As people sang and grasped hands, Sanders would call upon Zeus and Anubis, the god of the dead, to "raise the Pentagon from its destiny and preserve it," forcing its inhabitants to end the war and bring peace to America and Vietnam.[23]

Given the strangeness of the event, authorities were on alert. The protesters took nearly an hour to reach the Pentagon, and when they did, they were met with several thousand US marshals, military police, and federal troops, including soldiers from the 82nd Airborne Division, who formed a human barricade around the building and defended themselves with tear gas and rifle butts. Ropes were set up to demarcate where protesters could and could not go, and those who crossed those boundaries were subject to arrest. Though most protesters sat peacefully outside, singing "America, the Beautiful" or placing flowers in the barrels of the soldiers' M15 rifles, another group found an unguarded entrance and tried to enter the building, where they were bruised and bloodied for their efforts. After authorities announced at 7:00 P.M. that the protesters' permit had expired, roughly 7,000 of the original 50,000 marchers chose to stay the night. After several dozen arrests, authorities permitted some of the protesters' informal camps to remain, though as temperatures dropped, many others chose to leave. The next morning those who had spent the night outdoors, sharing food and smoking joints, marched to the White House to wake Lyndon Johnson with chants. After a day of rallies in Washington and Virginia, a total of 681 protesters had been arrested and 100 were treated for injuries.

For many, the protest didn't appear to have been a success. The Pentagon obviously didn't levitate, and the war in Vietnam continued apace. But national newspapers were quick to note that this protest differed significantly from the marches and rallies that had come before. The *New York Times* reported that the "surging, disorderly crowd" was primarily made up of brightly dressed young people under thirty, many of whom smoked joints as they crossed the Potomac River. These protesters were vastly different from the "conservatively dressed, middle-aged men and women" who predominated in previous antiwar marches.[24]

For the Peace Eye activists, the event was a revelation. In his 1970 manifesto *Do It! Scenarios of the Revolution,* Rubin proudly declared that "a new man was born smoking pot while besieging the Pentagon." The roughly 200 "lumpen middle-class youth of Amerika" who had sat huddled together in the cold, passing joints and sandwiches and waiting for the Pentagon's walls to fall, were at the forefront of a new revolution, Rubin argued, one that would effectively combine politics and activism with experimentation with drug use. Despite his own arrest for urinating on a wall, Rubin knew that his event had more fully merged the psychedelic revolution with the antiwar movement and made radical rebellion more forceful and, for some, more appealing. For him and others joining his fight, the night at the Pentagon revealed that "a society which suppresses adventure makes the only adventure the suppression of that society."[25]

Two months later, on New Year's Eve, Rubin and Hoffman formed the Youth International Party (better known as the Yippies). A leaderless, "nonorganization, nonpolitical party," the Yippies were, in Rubin's words, the "first national psychedelic political movement" in American history. For Rubin, a Yippie was a new breed of activist, "a stoned politico, a hybrid mixture of the New Left and hippie coming out of something different," and marijuana was a crucial ingredient in the group's cause.[26] Indeed, the Yippies were so supportive of legalization that Rubin and Hoffman emblazoned a marijuana leaf on the flag of their newly formed group.

Rubin and Hoffman saw the Democratic National Convention, to be held in Chicago in August 1968, as the site for the Yippies' official debut. They planned elaborate street theater tactics for the event, including the nomination of "Pigasus," a 145-pound hog, for president and a threat to dose Chicago's public water supply with LSD. Several months before the convention, Rubin and Hoffman hosted a press conference at which they listed the Yippies' demands. The first was, naturally, an immediate end to the war, but the rest showed the activists' interest in creating a nation that not only was more tolerant and just, but also overtly accepting of marijuana use. Their second demand was freedom for the incarcerated Black Panther Huey Newton, as well as for "all other black people," and the third—coming well before calls for the disarmament of the police, the abolition of money, and the end to all forms of censorship—was for the "legalization of marijuana and all other psychedelic drugs" and the "freeing of all prisoners currently imprisoned on narcotics charges."[27] Months before they arrived in Chicago, this announcement made clear that Hoffman and Rubin's goals of an end to the Vietnam War, nationwide racial justice, and the legalization of marijuana were all sides of the same countercultural coin.

By the time thousands of Yippie activists arrived at the DNC, however, the convention was already a debacle. Democrats were divided between the antiwar candidate, Senator Eugene McCarthy, and Lyndon Johnson's vice president, Hubert Humphrey. Johnson had pulled out of the race in March, and Robert F. Kennedy, a party favorite, had been assassinated in Los Angeles that June. Despite McCarthy's strong showings in several primaries, the party ultimately chose Humphrey as its nominee, and the nomination of a man who supported the Vietnam War and had not participated in a single primary led to widespread rumors that the race had been fixed by Johnson and Chicago mayor Richard J. Daley.

Knowing that thousands of antiwar protesters were coming to the city to disrupt the convention, Mayor Daley promised to maintain law and order. In the months leading up to the event, he ensured that his security troops were specifically trained in crowd control and riot techniques. Just days into the convention, the Yippies' elaborate street theater techniques couldn't stop the violent clashes that unfolded between the relatively peaceful, if provocative, pot-smoking protesters and the uniformed, armor-clad police. By the night of August 28, police were beating and teargassing protesters, who were armed with little more than bottles and stones, while news organizations broadcast the riots on national television. Watching the footage, viewers across the country could make up their own minds: either the pot-smoking protesters were innocent young people standing up for what they believed, or they were dangerous drug users too high to realize the damage they were causing. Republican candidate Richard Nixon would ultimately win the 1968 election, in part by playing up the danger of drug-using protesters and preying on Americans' fears of marijuana use.

The protests in Chicago didn't stop the war in Vietnam, but they did help Rubin and Hoffman merge their psychedelic revolution more fully with the antiwar movement, promoting legalization by tying it to the national movement for peace. By 1968, marijuana activism had evolved from small groups of young people carrying signs and asserting that marijuana was "fun" into one of the most visible aspects of opposition to the Vietnam War. Led by a new breed of activist who understood marijuana's political potential, pot smoking became not only a symbol of opposition to the war but also a unifying force. As when it brought together Puerto Ricans and hippies in Tompkins Square Park, marijuana created a unified front out of the diverse factions of the counterculture, and support for legalization generated support for other aims too, including civil rights and peace in Vietnam.

Pot smoking also made more young protesters aware of the negative impact of the country's marijuana laws. Rates of marijuana arrests rose throughout the 1960s, more than doubling between 1965 and 1967— primarily because so many young people were publicly smoking pot at antiwar protests. In 1965, 18,815 people were arrested for marijuana, but by 1967 the number had risen to 61,843, accounting for 51 percent of all national drug arrests.[28] As President Johnson continued to declare that the war in Vietnam was necessary and schools and "social guidance" films continued to argue that marijuana led directly to heroin addiction, a growing number of marijuana smokers began to doubt the country's official stance on the drug. This growing skepticism led many to believe that the nation's burgeoning battle over marijuana was nothing less than a war on the country's rebellious youth. As Paul Krassner, one of the original Yippies, put it, "In the process of cross-fertilization at antiwar demonstrations, we had come to share an awareness that there was a linear connection between putting kids in prison for smoking pot in this country and burning them to death with napalm on the other side of the planet."[29]

Compared to rising civil unrest, the draft, the assassinations of Martin Luther King Jr. and Bobby Kennedy, the tumultuous election, and the ongoing battle for African American civil rights, marijuana was hardly the country's most pressing concern in 1968—even though Richard Nixon, when he took office the following year, would do everything in his power to convince the country otherwise. Still, the marijuana activism that emerged in the late 1960s was stronger and more vibrant than ever. Far more than inspiring people to play with their consciousness, marijuana activism taught people to question authority, whether they were proto-hippies reading *Marijuana Puff-In* in 1964 or Yippies protesting Humphrey's nomination in 1968. And as more people protested the war, this capacity for engaging other social concerns became one of marijuana activism's greatest strengths, bringing more people into the legalization fold. As Dana Beal said in an interview in 2015, "You can't separate the early marijuana legalization movement from the antiwar movement, from civil rights, from the hippies and the Yippies or from anything else. By '68 pot was everywhere, and that's exactly where we needed it to be."[30]

2

IT'S NORML TO SMOKE POT

R. KEITH STROUP was born two days after Christmas in 1943, on the outskirts of tiny Dix, Illinois. He and his brother Larry, older by one year, were raised by their parents, Russell and Vera, on a 160-acre farm, with both sets of grandparents less than a dozen miles away. Russell was a farmer turned building contractor and a pillar of conservative Republican values in the area, while Vera, a deeply religious Southern Baptist, disavowed earthly pleasures like smoking, drinking, and dancing. For Vera and the rest of the town's population of 120, life in Dix revolved around the church, and young Keith (whose last name rhymes with "cop") had perfect attendance at the Dix Christian Assembly, attending tent revivals every summer to hear traveling evangelicals preach.

Despite their rural lifestyle, Stroup's parents weren't without connections. As the most influential Republican in Dix, Stroup's father was on good terms with Everett Dirksen, the conservative Illinois senator who served as minority leader in the US Congress in the 1960s. One summer while he was still in grade school, Stroup's family took the train to visit Washington, where Dirksen ensured that they enjoyed VIP status on tours of the White House and Capitol Hill. The experience seared the city in the young boy's mind. "My father taught me early on that Washington is the seat of real power in this country," Stroup remembered, "and that those with serious ambitions should look to the nation's capital. It was a message that resonated with me." In 1965, after finishing his undergraduate degree at the University of Illinois, Stroup abandoned the conservative Midwest and drove across the country to "make Washington my home." Though he hadn't yet been accepted to any law schools, Stroup was nothing if not ambitious: by fall, he had enrolled at Georgetown Law School and was working part-time in Dirksen's office on Capitol Hill.[1]

Meanwhile, Blair Newman was already there. Born in Washington in 1947, Newman was the son of Dorothy Mahon Newman, a Québécoise who had moved to the United States in the early 1940s to work at the Canadian embassy. By the 1960s, Dorothy had become a successful real estate agent, specializing in selling properties to foreign governments for embassies and chanceries, and she would raise Blair and his brother Ross in an urban environment of wealth and prestige.[2] But Newman rejected his mother's cosmopolitan lifestyle, and by the late 1960s he had grown a beard, dropped out of college, and entered the city's underground. As he ran "Washington's only hip record store" and hosted "head shows" on WHFS-FM, the area's first progressive rock radio station, Newman discussed starting some kind of marijuana legalization lobby with his friends as early as 1968. But the idea never took off, and that year Newman abandoned Washington for what he saw as the real center of the nation's thriving counterculture: San Francisco.[3]

Stroup and Newman were opposites in every sense—one a law student who wore a suit and tie, an outsider who came to Washington from the rural Midwest; the other a Washington native and college dropout with long hair and a beard who fled that city to join the hippies on the West Coast—but they shared a mutual interest in turning marijuana activism into a career. By 1970, both men had formed organizations that effectively transformed the battle for legalization by professionalizing and financing the fight far better than LEMAR had done. In California, Newman formed Amorphia, a counterculture-oriented "cannabis collective" that saw legalization as a vehicle for wider social change and that funded its plans through the sale of hemp-based rolling papers. Meanwhile, in Washington, Stroup formed the National Organization for the Reform of Marijuana Laws (NORML), a significantly more straitlaced organization that sought to protect marijuana smokers' rights by lobbying legislators and educating the public on the need for drug law reform.

Given their mutual interests, it wasn't long before Stroup and New-man became rivals. Though their end goal was the same—to decriminalize and ultimately legalize marijuana across America—the two men didn't agree on how best to approach the fight. Influenced by the thriving counterculture of California, Newman wanted to use marijuana to speed the social and cultural changes he advocated—achieving civil rights, international peace, and environmental protection. For him, legalization was not only about marijuana: it was inherently connected to the larger social revolution that the counterculture had worked on for years. Given the popularity of Amorphia's rolling paper sales, Newman also knew that legalization could make marijuana extremely lucrative. A savvy businessman, Newman promised that all profits from his papers would be rolled back into funding the social actions he desired, making marijuana a financial vehicle for larger social change.

Stroup's buttoned-up East Coast approach was more professional, if less lucrative. Focusing specifically on marijuana rather than cultural revolution, Stroup saw legalization as less about the actual use of the drug and more about an adult's right to privacy and freedom from government intrusion. NORML's aim was libertarian at heart: Stroup advocated the right to make personal choices, no matter the potential harm associated with drug use, and he defended marijuana users as consumers who deserved the same marketplace protections as those who bought dangerous products like flammable clothing or Chevy Corvairs. Unlike Amorphia, which was run like a cooperative, NORML was also a traditional lobbying group, with offices in downtown Washington, DC, and a membership model that depended on soliciting donations. Though they agreed on the basic principle that legalization was a natural extension of personal freedom and civil rights, for Newman the battle belonged to the counterculture, while Stroup used NORML to cater to the needs of a growing, and smoking, middle class.

By the time Stroup and Newman founded their organizations, they were hardly the only people turning marijuana activism into a career. In the wake of LEMAR, and amid growing marijuana use, many pro-legalization groups formed in the late 1960s and early 1970s, with a cornucopia of clever names. There was BLOSSOM (Basic Liberation Of Smokers and Sympathizers Of Marijuana) in Washington state; CAMP

(Committee Against Marijuana Prohibition) in Atlanta; CALM (Citizens Association to Legalize Marijuana) at Colorado State University; POT (Proposition Of Today) in California; MELO (Marijuana Education for Legalization in Oregon); STASH (STudent Association for the Study of Hallucinogens) at Beloit College in Wisconsin; COME (Committee On Marijuana Education); and SLAM (Society for the Legalization and Acceptance of Marijuana).[4] Most of these organizations lived and died quickly as activists moved on to other things or, in the case of college students, graduated. Only Amorphia and NORML were powerful and professional enough to succeed in bringing the legalization debate to Capitol Hill and monetizing the battle for marijuana smokers' rights. By 1971, straddling the nation from the East and West Coasts, they were the country's largest pro-marijuana groups.

With their personality differences, however, and their differing visions of how legalization efforts could achieve their goals, Stroup and Newman continually butted heads, and it would prove impossible for them to overcome those differences. Both men recognized that they could make a career out of marijuana activism with an organization run in the same fashion as a paraphernalia company (Newman) or a lobbying firm (Stroup)—in short, by taking marijuana activism pro. But neither man would modify his view on the purpose of legalization. Newman continued to see legalization as a means to extend the reach of a radical counterculture, even though the counterculture had peaked in the 1960s and was losing steam as the war in Vietnam ended and activists aged, often into the suburban middle class. Stroup's view of legalization—as a means to defend marijuana smokers—remained unchanged as smokers became a legitimate voting bloc, one with increasing power and potential for political influence. This battle between Stroup's attempt to normalize marijuana use and Newman's effort to keep it within the radical fold defined the debate over the professionalization of marijuana activism in the early 1970s. By 1972, when the federal government weighed in, only one group—and one viewpoint—was able to survive.

•

Marijuana wasn't on Keith Stroup's mind when he first went to Washington. In the spring of 1965, less than a year after Lowell Eggemeier

launched the nation's first legalization protest, Stroup was far more concerned with starting law school at Georgetown and working for Senator
Dirksen. He hadn't even yet tried the drug.

Marijuana and the city's growing counterculture would soon find
him, however. That winter he smoked pot for the first time while on a
ski trip with friends, and two years later, he and his wife, Kelly Flook—
a farm girl who had left her family's Maryland dairy ranch in much the
same way Stroup had abandoned Dix—witnessed firsthand the city's
overwhelming response to the Vietnam War. Living in an apartment
in downtown Washington, they opened their doors to the flood of
young people arriving for antiwar rallies, and Stroup saw how marijuana inspired their growing radicalism. He had no fear of being drafted
himself—his student deferment while he was in law school exempted
him from military service—but the protesters left an indelible mark. "I
found [the scene] so inspiring at the time," Stroup remembered, "the
long-haired protesters burning their draft cards and smoking a joint. . . .
Marijuana had become synonymous with opposition to the war."[5]

Once he graduated from Georgetown in 1968, however, Stroup's deferment expired, and he was desperate to avoid the draft, Stroup considered relocating to Canada, and he spoke with a psychiatrist in Baltimore
who was willing to tell officials that Stroup was gay, which would make
him ineligible to serve in the armed forces. But Flook disliked lying
about Stroup's sexuality, and neither wanted to leave Washington. Instead, after seeing a notice on the law school bulletin board, Stroup
applied to join Ralph Nader's newly formed National Commission on
Product Safety, hoping that the commission's two-year mandate and his
contribution of "critical skills" would keep him from being sent to war.

Ralph Nader was a unique figure in the late 1960s, and his commission, the first of its kind, was unique as well. Established in 1968, the
National Commission on Product Safety was tasked by Congress with
identifying broad categories of potentially hazardous goods and eval-
uating methods for securing consumer safety. Such a mandate would
be seen as unremarkable today, but it was considered revolutionary at
the time, when a dearth of product information had led to thousands
of annual deaths from consumers' use of everything from sports cars to
flammable polyester clothing. "Passing the burden to the consumer is
one of the oldest tricks of the marketplace," Nader argued, adding that,

"in reality, the consumer has almost never [been] offered a meaningful choice." Allowing private companies to regulate themselves wasn't good enough, he said; only stricter government regulations could protect consumers' rights.[6]

Nader had risen to prominence three years earlier with the publication of his first book, *Unsafe at Any Speed*. In it, Nader argued that the American auto industry was producing cars that, like the Chevy Corvair, were flashy and appealing but also patently unsafe. Manufacturers, along with the "automobile accident industry" (a coalition of medical, legal, insurance, repair, and funeral professionals), had a vested interest, he insisted, in producing unsafe goods because crumpled cars and injured bodies led to higher profits and better business. The result of people driving the Corvair, Nader argued, was that "billions of dollars" constantly flowed into the lucrative field of "post-accident response."

Nader believed that consumers deserved certain rights, but he also knew they weren't going to be easy to get. Because "the roots of the unsafe vehicle problem are so entrenched," Nader wrote, "the situation can be improved only by the forging of new instruments of citizen action." That meant picketing, marching, writing letters to elected officials, and taking the consumer rights revolution into activists' own hands. For Nader, it also meant elaborate and well-staged presentations of his findings to government officials. Using photos that graphically showed the danger of driving cars like the Corvair, with bloodied bodies strewn across the street, and stacking his panels with experts sympathetic to his cause, Nader was able to show how dangerous such products were for the average American. For him, "our society's obligation to protect the 'body rights' of its citizens with vigorous resolve and ample resources requires the precise, authoritative articulation and front-rank support which is being devoted to civil rights," he wrote. Nader considered the battles for consumer rights and for civil rights the same fight and argued that the former required the same levels of financial and tactical resolve as the latter—an approach that would deeply influence Stroup.[7]

With his countercapitalist ideals and demands that the government protect individual rights, Nader appealed immensely to the counterculture. He became an unlikely representative of hippie values in Washington, and dozens of young activists, many armed with law degrees, flocked to the city, eager to join his team. Nader also became a natural

ally and mentor to Stroup when he joined the commission shortly after graduation. "Nader was the individual who first piqued my interest
in starting a marijuana legalization lobby," Stroup remembered. "He
was an inspiring consumer advocate" whose "skillful use of the media
and . . . willingness, even eagerness, to take on major corporations" left
a mark. Stroup began toying with the idea of a Nader-like organization
that would advocate for marijuana smokers' rights, taking the position
that those who purchased an illegal drug deserved the same protections
as those who bought Chevy Corvairs or flammable clothes.[8]

Consumer advocacy was only one part of the equation, however.
The most important shift that occurred during Stroup's tenure with the
National Commission on Product Safety was his transformation into
a regular marijuana smoker. There Stroup befriended Larry Schott, a
fellow Midwesterner and heavy smoker who was serving as the commission's chief investigator. As two of only a handful of staff members
who weren't from the moneyed eastern elite, Schott and Stroup bonded
immediately and began visiting each other regularly, getting high and
going to see the Beatles' *Yellow Submarine*. The rest of Nader's staff was
experimenting with the drug as well. While Nader was a straight ar-
row, Stroup, Schott, and the other commission members were not, and
smoking together on the weekends "created a bond among us," Stroup
remembered. "We were fellow stoners daring to travel to new places in
our minds. We felt as if we were pushing the levels of our consciousness,
and experiencing new realities."[9]

Stroup's years as a researcher at the commission would influence
the rest of his career, but the organization itself had a short life span:
it folded in 1970 after delivering its final report. By that point Stroup
was twenty-nine and no longer eligible for the draft, but with a wife
and young daughter to support, he knew he needed to find a new job.
He worked briefly as a lobbyist for the American Pharmaceutical Association, but he "had no passion for the subject" and quickly decided to
do something else.[10] In the evenings and on weekends, he and Schott
continued to meet, smoking pot and discussing the possibility of forming a new organization, one that would function as a union to research
and understand, and ultimately protect and defend, marijuana smokers'
rights. Stroup envisioned an organization that would be different from
groups like LEMAR—one as professional and serious in its approach

as Nader was on the commission. More suits and ties than blue jeans and burned-up draft cards, their organization would be a respectable group working to change local and national laws by appealing to smokers like themselves—the growing contingent of otherwise law-abiding middle-class marijuana users who believed that smoking a joint was little different from relaxing with a cocktail.

The young lawyers' timing couldn't have been better: by 1970 marijuana was migrating away from college campuses and into the suburban middle class. Stroup was one of the first activists to understand that the nation's population of smokers was growing to the point of becoming a legitimate voting constituency, one with a habit so legally fraught that they would soon want their own defenders on Capitol Hill. Several years later, while testifying before Congress, Stroup defended America's marijuana users by declaring, "Most of us who smoke marijuana are neither radical nor criminal. We are simply otherwise law-abiding citizens who happen to enjoy marijuana. We span all socioeconomic and age subgroups, and to continue to confuse us with criminals is indefensible."[11] Stroup and Schott named their nascent group the National Organization for the Repeal of Marijuana Laws, or NORML for short. "I liked the directness of the name," Stroup said. "It sent a clear message about the goal of the organization. And I appreciated the double entendre. We wanted to make the point that it was normal to smoke marijuana."[12]

NORML argued that marijuana smokers were consumers, not deviants, and deserved the same rights to protection and safety as any other group—including access to the drug without pollutants or contaminants, a competitive marketplace free from monopolies and conglomerates, and especially freedom from harassment by the police. Most importantly, Stroup wanted to change national laws. Unlike other budding marijuana rights groups, he understood that his organization could have more influence if he never publicly condoned drug use itself. "We do not advocate the use of marijuana," Stroup told a reporter, "but we know of no medical, legal or moral justification for sending those to jail who do use it."[13]

It took months to get everything together. Stroup knocked on numerous doors looking for financial and legal aid, and his wife Kelly invested the first $5,000, but support did not come immediately. Stroup called on a half-dozen foundations before he found his first influential backer: retired attorney general Ramsey Clark. Clark had served in the Johnson administration, and his civil rights activism, including protecting marchers at Selma and supervising the draft of the Voting Rights Act of 1965, had made him a hero in Stroup's eyes. "I idolized Ramsey Clark," Stroup said. "He was a compassionate criminal justice expert who valued personal freedom and opposed wasting law enforcement resources on victimless crimes."[14] Clark also supported legalization. In his 1970 book *Crime in America,* Clark argued that the long sentences handed down to young people for simple possession "embitter thousands—including those opposed to marijuana—who see them for what they are, punishment without reason or compassion."[15]

Though he was unwilling to join NORML's board of directors for fear of jeopardizing his civil rights work, Clark gave the organization his blessing. He also made a valuable suggestion: that Stroup change the name to the National Organization for the *Reform* (rather than the Repeal) of Marijuana Laws, which Clark thought would be more palatable to elected officials. Others had made this suggestion to Stroup before, but he had refused to change the organization's name. When the suggestion came from Clark, however, Stroup made the change.

Clark also helped NORML in other ways: for instance, he wrote on the organization's behalf to Hugh Hefner, the founder of *Playboy* magazine whose Playboy Foundation gave grants to nonprofits interested in researching human sexuality and challenging authority. With Clark's recommendation, Hefner and his staff agreed to support NORML. Though the Playboy Foundation declined to give NORML the full $20,000 Stroup had requested, it did give the organization $5,000, along with verbal assurances that more money would be forthcoming. Along with the money from his wife, Playboy's grant allowed Stroup to feel financially confident enough to leave the American Pharmaceutical Association and begin working on NORML full-time, from the basement of his Dupont Circle home.

On March 2, 1971, after six months of planning and negotiations, NORML was officially incorporated as a lobbying organization in Washington, DC. Compared to organizations like LEMAR, which had sought the wholesale repeal of laws that criminalized the drug, NORML's initial goals were modest: to compile a list of all existing marijuana laws; to publish pertinent information relating to those laws; to report the results of marijuana research; and to educate legislators and the public on the benefits of reforming the nation's marijuana laws. But the group's ultimate aims were far more profound. Stroup and Schott wanted to develop model legislation that would legalize, or at least decriminalize, marijuana at both the state and federal levels, thus normalizing the drug's regulation and sale. Stroup also hoped that, as more people came out of the cannabis closet, NORML could be as legislatively influential as Nader's commission in challenging the status quo and leading a movement for national change.

•

When he founded NORML, Stroup was certain he was breaking new ground, but he soon learned that in fact there were other people working on marijuana reform, in Washington and elsewhere across the country—he just hadn't met them yet. Key among them was Blair Newman, the young counterculture activist and businessman with an eye for untapped openings in the market who sought to use his skills to transform the country's marijuana legalization campaign.

By 1969, Newman had built up a successful business selling rolling papers, made exclusively of hemp, because he had realized it was a lucrative time to enter the market: the marijuana boom had given rise to more smokers than ever, and many of them regularly used rolling papers to consume their drug of choice. Newman had also done his research. After spending a year studying the international cigarette-paper market, he found a company in Spain that could produce hemp paper and secured $16,000 in start-up funds; he then launched his business. He called his papers Acapulco Gold, after a popular marijuana strain from Mexico. Using the proceeds from sales to finance advocacy for the changes he wanted to see enacted on a national scale, Newman hoped to transform his company from a simple paraphernalia purveyor into a major proponent for legalization. "Tax statistics show that last year heads used over 150 million packs of paper, spending at least $20 million to roll weed," Newman wrote in the *Ann Arbor Sun*. "For each 10% share of that market, Acapulco Gold papers will generate well over half a million dollars non-profit toward legalization."[16]

To achieve these goals, Newman formed Amorphia: The Cannabis Collective in 1969. As he envisioned it, Amorphia would sell hemp-based rolling papers for fifty cents a pack (three times the cost of other, nonhemp papers on the market), and proceeds from those sales would fund a pro-legalization program that would eventually include a media campaign, a news service, a speakers' bureau, court tests of marijuana laws, and expert witnesses to appear before state legislatures considering changes to their marijuana laws. It was an ambitious plan, but one that would use money that smokers were already spending (on rolling papers made by other companies) to fund a new and wide-ranging legalization campaign that, Newman hoped, could transform laws while also promoting his radical, countercultural approach.

Newman was also looking to the future. He presciently recognized that corporate interest in the marijuana market would develop when companies realized its profit potential—an outcome that Amorphia sought to guard against by advocating for everyone's right to grow free, legal marijuana in their homes and backyards. Once marijuana was fully legalized across the country (which Newman expected to happen by 1980 at the latest), Newman promised that Amorphia would then market cannabis to those unable or unwilling to grow their own, lending the names Acapulco Gold and Panama Red (trademarked by Newman in 1969) to legal, sustainable, affordable weed. This would keep marijuana firmly in the hands of the people and the market in the hands of counterculture nonprofits like Amorphia. When the time came, Newman believed, Amorphia could then expand by using "all the proceeds [from marijuana sales] to serve as an economic foundation for social action, alternative culture, experimental communities, research, education, etc. All the Co-op's non-profits would be given to the social causes chosen by the members—ecology, peace, poverty, racism, sexism or whatever," he wrote.[17] For Newman, the legalization and sale of marijuana was "not an end," as he told *Rolling Stone* in 1970, "but a means to an end that is both revolutionary and capitalistic, but mostly ambitious."[18]

Newman was uniquely positioned to act on his plans. Besides several thousand dollars in start-up funds, Amorphia had acquired a built-in network of supporters when it absorbed LEMAR's California outposts and brought on Mike Aldrich as the group's codirector. As LEMAR's most prominent leader after Allen Ginsberg stepped into an advisory role in 1967, Aldrich also brought with him the mailing list of the newsletter he had been editing for two years, the *Marijuana Review,* which was the most visible and popular marijuana publication at the time. By 1969, with Aldrich in California, the *Review* was proudly announcing Amorphia's birth. In its October–December issue, Aldrich asked readers, "Are you ready for . . . Amorphia!" He promised that the "California Consolidated Cannabis Corporation" would work on legalization by "wrest[ing] commercialization from the hands of the tobacco troglodytes." The article also declared that Amorphia—"controlled by 300 far-out heads" (an exaggeration, since the group was run solely by Newman and Aldrich at the time)—would sell "stock" in its organization and "use the money to set up a legalization lobby and to finance communes." By combining the worlds of business and the counterculture, Amorphia hoped to achieve success in ways no legalization group had imagined before.[19]

Amorphia did achieve success, but it came too quickly for the group to handle. The company ran into serious supply issues when Newman realized that it took four months for the Spanish company to produce and ship the hemp papers to California; within a year, Amorphia was receiving three times as many orders as they could fill with the papers they had in stock. Newman kept Amorphia's costs low—members of the expanding staff were paid $125 a week ("one-third the salary in other legalization groups," he noted), and rent for their San Francisco headquarters was $150 a month—but without the necessary supplies, the company was foundering financially just as its mission took off. "If we could fill all the orders," Newman said, "Acapulco Gold's [*sic*] would already make over $10,000 a month for legalization." With Amorphia's finances dwindling, Newman's plans for a speakers' bureau, lobbying group, and communes were all sidelined.[20]

Amorphia may have been struggling, but the demand for Newman's papers showed that support for legalization was growing, especially because Amorphia made supporting changing marijuana laws easy to do. Purchasing Acapulco Gold papers made every smoker a potential legalization activist, and every activist a potential customer. But the ease of joining Amorphia's ranks made Stroup, who was still struggling to get NORML the same level of recognition and financial support, extremely nervous. From his base in Washington, Stroup watched as Amorphia began dominating the legalization conversation in the United States. "I was seriously concerned that [Amorphia] might have the West Coast cachet that would catch a wave of public support, that they might raise millions of dollars from selling their rolling papers, and that NORML might be lost in the wake," he later said. "I felt threatened that Amorphia could become the dominant marijuana smokers' lobby, and that NORML might fade into oblivion before we had a chance to achieve anything substantive."[21]

Stroup needn't have worried. In September 1971, when Stroup and Newman met for the first time at a conference in Denver, Colorado, the two men discussed a potential merger. Still dogged by the four-month lag between ordering papers from Spain and their receipt, Newman felt that Amorphia needed to align with similar groups rather than compete against them for the same supporters and the same goals. Stroup, who wanted NORML to absorb some of Amorphia's popularity and support, agreed that unification would be beneficial. "To demonstrate goodwill, and to overcome distrust between the two groups, I invited Amorphia to send [Newman] to live and work in D.C.," Stroup remembered, "so we could begin to develop cooperative projects and see if we wanted to move in that direction."[22] A month later, Newman left Amorphia's San Francisco headquarters in the hands of Aldrich and moved east to DC, where he lived and worked in Stroup's basement apartment. Though the two groups remained separate entities, Newman was their common ground. In Washington, he served as codirector of Amorphia while taking on the new role of deputy director of NORML, working directly under Stroup.

For the short time the organizations were allied, it was a period of "heady solidarity among the hip generation," wrote the underground journalist Michael Chance in 1978. The union seemed natural and, for many, compelling. "By using local head shops, campus malls, rock concerts, smoke-ins and other new-world hot spots as recruiting centers, and by receiving free ink from alternative presses, it was not long before Amorphia/NORML was an established functioning lobby for dope law reform, complete with mailing lists, a newsletter, offices on both coasts and tenured personnel," Chance wrote. Once Amorphia's customer base was combined with NORML's Washington location to increase support for legalization among hip youth and middle-class smokers nationwide, the two groups had the power that neither had been able to muster on its own.[23]

But the partnership between Stroup and Newman didn't last long. Two months after moving in with Stroup, Newman and Stroup's wife took MDA, a powerful psychoactive amphetamine known for enhancing sex, and spent the night together while Stroup was visiting the Playboy Foundation in Chicago to solicit funds. When Stroup returned home, they admitted the affair. Stroup flew into a rage, kicking Newman out of his house and refusing to ever speak to him again. Stroup moved out of the house too, initiating a divorce and shifting his residence to NORML's new offices near Georgetown, in a row house whose bedroom he painted a violent shade of red to match his angry state of mind. Separated from his family, Stroup could now live and breathe his work with NORML, energized by a new sense of bitter betrayal. By contrast, the affair devastated Newman, who abandoned Washington for the second time and then found, upon returning to California, that his betrayal had made him unwelcome at Amorphia too. Aldrich and the rest of Amorphia's staff were furious that Newman had fractured their relationship with NORML, since the affiliation, however brief, had given Amorphia a moment of reprieve from its ongoing struggles with paper supplies.[24]

Even Newman and Flook's affair, however, couldn't prevent NORML and Amorphia from fully merging in 1972, in a move that was increasingly necessary for both groups. Amorphia's supply issues had cut deeply into its budget, and with its staff already going weeks without pay, the group faced the possibility of closing. Meanwhile, Stroup struggled to gain respect. An October 1971 Associated Press article had dubbed NORML "Washington's feeblest lobby" and argued that, despite its 1,400 dues-paying members and "a prestigious advisory board" (which finally included Ramsey Clark, who had joined the organization earlier that year), NORML's legislative results were "zero. So far."[25] With little money and little respect, the groups had found success only when they were briefly aligned. A new merger, which subsumed Amorphia under NORML's name and made Stroup director of the combined organizations, offered hope for better results.

Newman, who had no place in this new union, was furious that Amorphia was moving on without him. In the spring of 1972, before the merger was complete, he fought back by writing a lengthy article called "The Prospects and Potentials of Legalized Marijuana: Playboy Corporation vs. the People," which was published in underground newspapers nationwide. In it, Newman warned that people had to choose what kind of legalization effort they wanted to support. On the one side was Amorphia, a cannabis collective that wanted to recycle the counterculture's resources back into itself (even if, at the moment, it was too cash-strapped to do so), and on the other side was NORML, which Newman thought was little more than a corporate shill. Newman warned readers, incorrectly, that NORML was a "wholly owned subsidiary of Playboy" and argued that Hugh Hefner had used the group as a prop to build a new empire that would profit off the activists' work. "Playboy is moving to grab the legalize marijuana movement lock, stock and barrel, and thus be in position to take a major share of the multi-billion dollar legal marijuana market" when the drug was legalized, Newman warned. "What's needed is an alternative system, so people can choose to direct their resources toward social change instead of the status quo."[26]

Stroup vehemently disagreed with Newman—he hardly believed that NORML was upholding the status quo—but by that point NORML had gained too much strength to be derailed by one angry article. As NORML's dues-paying members combined with Amorphia's customer base, Stroup saw that the number of people involved in the legalization movement was growing. More importantly, NORML, with its suited lobbyists and Washington base, appealed to the growing population of comfortably middle-class smokers who were older than the radical counterculture activists who made up much of Amorphia's supporters and staff. As more people began experimenting with the drug, Stroup's description of smokers as a legitimate voting constituency, not radical drug users or counterculture activists, became increasingly influential on Capitol Hill and beyond, and NORML's promise to normalize marijuana use became more popular than Newman's attempt to use legalization to revolutionize society from the ground up. Realizing that he had lost his campaign, Newman resigned from the legalization movement and got involved instead in the burgeoning computer industry. Developing an early version of the Internet was a more fitting way, Newman felt, to put the counterculture ideals that so appealed to him into action. The sense of connectivity and personal enlightenment he had once found in drugs now seemed more readily available online.

After their successful absorption of Amorphia, it also became clear to Stroup and NORML's growing staff that they had brought their argument to Washington at precisely the right time. An influential federal commission, staffed with Republican leaders handpicked by President Nixon, was about to release a report that, for the first time in American history, called for the national decriminalization of marijuana. Pointing to the growing use of the drug, as well as the negative effects of stigmatizing and incarcerating its users, the commission gave weight and legitimacy to the arguments that Stroup and NORML had been making for years. Though NORML started as the city's "feeblest" lobby, when Washington insiders began supporting its claims, it was NORML—and not LEMAR or Amorphia—that emerged as the most powerful marijuana rights advocacy group, one that was poised to dominate legalization discussions for years to come.

3

MARIJUANA: A SIGNAL OF MISUNDERSTANDING

IN OCTOBER 1967, slightly more than a year before he would be elected president for the first time, Richard Nixon published "What Has Happened to America?" in that month's edition of *Reader's Digest*. It was a damning article, full of anger at the riots that had rocked twenty cities across the country that summer and set the United States, in Nixon's opinion, "blazing in an inferno of urban anarchy."

The article was also about something else that Nixon considered far more dangerous than the "snipers, looters and arsonists" he blamed for the unrest. In recent years, the civil rights movement, which Nixon purported to support, had spawned a threatening new outgrowth that he felt bastardized the movement's original goals. "Our teachers, preachers and politicians have gone too far in advocating the idea that each individual should determine what laws are good and what laws are bad, and that he should obey the law he likes and disobey the law he dislikes," Nixon wrote. This dangerous new trend of overpermissiveness was pervading all aspects of society, Nixon argued, and was symptomatic of a far more insidious disease: the decline of personal responsibility and respect for the rule of law. This could most obviously be seen "in the public attitude toward the police, in mounting traffic in illegal drugs, in the volume of teenage arrests, in campus disorders and the growth of white-collar crime"—in short, in the pervasive and destructive actions of the counterculture, whose emphasis on political protest, alongside the young participants' overt marijuana use, had led to a "national deterioration of respect for authority, the law and civil order." As the most visible symbol of the counterculture, marijuana was emblematic of young people flouting the nation's drug laws, Nixon argued, and its use threatened the country's moral foundations.[1]

Of all the people elected to the Oval Office, no president despised marijuana more than Richard Nixon. Tapes of his secretly recorded White House conversations revealed his intense hatred for the drug, as did his statements to the press. In private, Nixon linked "homosexuality, dope, [and] immorality in general," and he drew a line between marijuana and the "radical demonstrators" who were often outside the Oval Office.[2] In public, Nixon was no less dismissive of the drug, though he was somewhat more diplomatic. "You know, you don't turn to drugs unless you can't find satisfaction in another way in your own life," he said during an interview on NBC's *Today Show*. For him, the fundamental cause of drug use was psychological: young people's drug use stemmed from "a sense of insecurity that comes from the old values being torn away," which could be healed if marijuana were replaced with the belief that "this is a good time to be alive" and that "this is the best country in the world in which to live."[3]

If Nixon played an armchair psychologist in the press, he was a master manipulator in Congress, using his time in the White House to lobby extensively to make marijuana illegal. By 1968, when he was first elected, marijuana remained in legal limbo at the federal level. In 1970, working with like-minded colleagues, including his attorney general, John N. Mitchell, Nixon helped pass one of the most sweeping drug laws in American history. The Comprehensive Drug Abuse Prevention and Control Act included a provision, entitled the Controlled Substances Act (CSA), that regulated the manufacture, possession, distribution, and use of nearly every licit and illicit drug available in the United States.

Though the act was specifically tailored to control drugs used for medical purposes, Nixon used the CSA to transform the federal laws surrounding marijuana. The act created five schedules for drugs, ranking them from Schedule V for the least addictive drugs, ones that had little potential for abuse and were widely accepted as medically useful (such as antidiarrheals and cough suppressants), to Schedule I for the most addictive—those drugs deemed to have a high potential for abuse and no currently accepted medical use. Though placement was temporary pending further congressional review, Nixon and Mitchell lobbied aggressively to have marijuana placed in Schedule I, thus effectively outlawing marijuana nationwide, deeming it as dangerous and addictive as heroin and LSD, and imposing punishments for its use and distribution that were equally as severe.

Nevertheless, even as Americans elected a man who despised marijuana to the highest office in the land, Nixon couldn't stop the drug from going mainstream. The antiwar movement had brought millions of marijuana smokers out of the cannabis closet, and the drug now seemed to be merely a harmless habit of millions of otherwise law-abiding college students and the suburban professional elite. By the early 1970s, 24 million people reported having tried the drug at least once, and 12 million said they were regular users. Marijuana became so commonplace that a joint graced the cover of an issue of *Life* magazine with photo essays that showed marijuana being used by doctors, lawyers, and socialites, as well as articles denouncing the negative effects of enforcing marijuana laws on the young. The face of marijuana use, no longer the sole terrain of jazz musicians and bead-wearing hippies, had changed, and national comfort with the drug was increasing.

•

All you could see was an open mouth, lips parted, ready to take a toke, and three fingers gently holding the joint. The skin was white, the nails were trimmed and clean, and the face was hairless, making the image seem androgynous. "MARIJUANA," the bold headline read. "At least 12 million Americans have now tried it. Are penalties too severe? Should it be legalized?"

Inside *Life* magazine's October 31, 1969, issue, most of the ten pages devoted to marijuana specifically questioned whether laws against the drug were just. "Marijuana, until recently a conspicuous liturgy of the rebellious young, is spreading into the middle class and fast becoming an institution," an opening editorial declared. "In New York a group of middle-aged professional people begin an evening with a marijuana 'cocktail party.' In Detroit, some lawyers and executives get together in the small hours for wine-and-pot. In Beverly Hills, at a stately black-tie dinner, the matronly hostess beckons the butler who brings a silver tray with a single after-dinner joint to be passed around." As marijuana became increasingly "respectable," the magazine suggested, "the whole question of legalization will have to be faced."

It wasn't hard to see where *Life*'s editors stood on the matter. In photo essays, guest articles, and reports, the magazine portrayed marijuana use as a middle-class, respectable, and homogeneously white phenomenon. Portraits of well-dressed adults smoking outdoors at a garden party in New Orleans appeared alongside a picture of "middle-aged business and professional people" sharing a joint around a table in suburban Boston, a candelabra and chandelier visible behind them. These images of wealth and ease showed how mainstream and mild marijuana had become, even as the editors pointed out the "disproportionate severity of laws that define mere possession of marijuana as a felony." These laws, which predominantly targeted the young, led to "travesties" like the case of Frank LaVarre, "a 20-year-old college student sentenced to 20 years for possession."

A track star at the University of Virginia, LaVarre, a "well-rounded, fine young man," was pictured wearing his prep school military uniform and setting records with his 4:35 mile. After getting caught trying to transport six and a half pounds of marijuana on a bus to Atlanta, he was sentenced to twenty years in prison in Virginia—the same penalty, the magazine noted, given for first-degree murder. Now the runner, who had once spent so much time outside, was "pallid as your belly from having been outdoors for only three days since last February." LaVarre's struggles were indicative of the growing resistance to America's harsh marijuana laws among the young. "If [the older generation is] going to lock up people like Frank LaVarre," an anonymous UVA "honor student" told *Life*, "they're going to have a violent revolution on their hands."

The section concluded with a guest editorial from James L. Goddard, the pioneering doctor who served as commissioner of the Food and Drug Administration (FDA) from 1966 to 1968 and whose belief in strong standards of evidence for drugs' efficacy and harm had transformed the agency into a scientific powerhouse during his tenure. "Man has used marijuana both socially and medicinally for several thousands of years,"

Goddard wrote, but "today there is little scientific knowledge of its dangers or merits." Though he didn't go so far as to recommend legalization, Goddard argued that the country's current laws governing marijuana were "unenforceable, excessively severe, scientifically incorrect and revealing of our ignorance of human behavior." Goddard recommended intensive testing of the drug instead, to see if it had any harmful long-term effects. If so, the laws against it were justified. But if not, the doctor concluded, "we will be embarrassed by harsh laws that made innocent people suffer." Decriminalization was the implicit choice.[4]

Nixon, clearly, did not agree. Even as *Life* was publishing articles that featured a growing number of respectable marijuana users, the president spent his first year in office working on a new drug law that would, he argued, protect the nation's youth. In July 1969, he sent a preliminary message to Congress on the "Control of Narcotics and Dangerous Drugs," which explained his intention to use his presidency to target all forms of illegal drug use. "Within the last decade, the abuse of drugs has grown from essentially a local police problem into a serious national threat to the personal health and safety of millions of Americans," he wrote. Though his message primarily focused on the need to suppress international trafficking routes and support the rehabilitation needs of the country's growing number of heroin addicts, Nixon wrote at length about the effects of marijuana on the young. "Several million American college students have at least experimented with marijuana, hashish, LSD, amphetamines, or barbiturates," he wrote. "It is doubtful that an American parent can send a son or daughter to college today without exposing the young man or woman to drug abuse." Furthermore, he claimed, "parents must also be concerned about the availability and use of such drugs in our high schools and junior high schools."

To deal with this alarming situation, Nixon proposed a ten-point plan that included efforts to suppress international trafficking by working with drug-producing nations abroad. More importantly, Nixon advocated dramatic changes to the nation's domestic drug laws and, more specifically, the nation's marijuana laws. All of the nation's current drug laws were "inadequate and outdated," the president wrote, and he demanded a new and "comprehensive legislative proposal" that would serve as a "revised and modern plan for control."

It was the "constitutional deficiencies" in the Marijuana Tax Act of 1937 that disturbed Nixon most. For the past thirty years, states had determined their own marijuana laws, and while some, like Texas and Virginia, had strict laws that punished marijuana possession as a felony, others were more lenient toward the drug. Meanwhile, the federal government had no specific marijuana legislation on the books. Looking to close these loopholes, Nixon placed Attorney General John Mitchell—a politician who also openly denounced marijuana—in charge of crafting the new law and tasked him with creating a federal statute that would "allow quicker control of dangerous drugs before their use and misuse reach epidemic proportions." This measure, which would result in marijuana's Schedule I placement the following year, was one that Nixon hoped Congress would "act favorably and swiftly" to approve in order to eradicate "this rising sickness in our land."[5]

Nixon and Mitchell were of a single mind when it came to marijuana: both men agreed that the drug was dangerous, and they saw new, harsher marijuana laws as an opportunity to crack down on the counterculture, which actively opposed Nixon's administration. In private conversations, Nixon was particularly vociferous in his condemnation of the drug, seeing in its use threats both to the country and to his presidency. In May 1971, Nixon told his chief of staff, H. R. "Bob" Haldeman, and counsel John Ehrlichman that "homosexuality, dope, [and] immorality in general" were "the enemies of strong societies. That's why the Communists and the left-wingers are pushing the stuff, they're trying to destroy us. . . . An awful lot of nations have been destroyed by drugs." The "radical demonstrators" who were often outside the White House protesting the Vietnam War were "all on drugs, virtually all." When it came to respectable adults who supported lenient marijuana laws, Nixon was no less inflammatory. Furious at the growing pro-legalization movement, the president lamented, "Every one of the bastards that are out for legalizing marijuana is Jewish. What the Christ is the matter with them? I suppose it's because so many of them are psychiatrists, you know. . . . By God we are going to hit the marijuana thing, and I want to hit it right square in the puss."[6]

As attorney general, John Mitchell was the ideal candidate to help Nixon achieve his goal. A personal friend of Nixon's and director of his 1968 presidential campaign, Mitchell was a hardline conservative who condemned the civil rights movement, desegregation, and the growing national opposition to the Vietnam War. Naturally, he denounced marijuana as well. When asked about marijuana by *Newsweek* in September 1970, Mitchell replied, "Why should we use it when it has no redeeming value? The desire of someone to get high and out of this world by puffing on marijuana has no redeeming value."[7] Making marijuana illegal under federal law would allow authorities to arrest smokers even in states where drug laws weren't as strict, Mitchell reasoned, letting officers crack down on casual smokers who represented a threat to Nixon's "law-and-order" approach.

Mitchell crafted the Comprehensive Drug Abuse Prevention and Control Act of 1970 to accomplish several things: it required the pharmaceutical industry to maintain tighter controls over certain drugs, and it increased funding for law enforcement, treatment, and rehabilitation. But the act is best known for Title II, known as the Controlled Substances Act, which outlined the five-level scheduling system that rated licit and illicit drugs on their medical use and potential for abuse. Much of the scheduling didn't come as a surprise: aspirin was placed in Schedule V, and antidepressants and sleep aids were placed in Schedule IV. But some scheduling was surprising: despite their high potential for abuse, cocaine and morphine, because they were prescribed, if rarely, by doctors, were placed in Schedule II. Meanwhile, the drugs most closely associated with the counterculture, including LSD, heroin, and peyote, were placed in Schedule I. If not already outlawed before, the act declared that the possession, use, and trafficking of Schedule I drugs were now federal offenses.

Nixon lobbied aggressively to have marijuana categorized as a Schedule I drug. Continuing to argue that marijuana adversely affected the young, Nixon and Mitchell claimed that marijuana had no accepted medical value, and that it did little more than lead people to abuse harder drugs, as well as make them oppositional and violent. Many members of Congress admitted that they didn't know enough about marijuana to permanently categorize it in Schedule I, but Nixon and Mitchell convinced a sufficient number of representatives—many of whom were also distrustful of the counterculture—to temporarily place marijuana there, pending further congressional review. This review was written into the law itself: Part F of Title II of the Controlled Substances Act established the National Commission on Marijuana and Drug Abuse, a thirteen-member committee with a $1 million budget and the task of conducting a two-year survey that would finally explore the scope and depth of the nation's marijuana use.

The commission carried out the most wide-ranging and exhaustive study of marijuana in American history. Its tasks included finding out who was regularly using the drug and why; examining the efficacy of existing marijuana laws; determining the drug's physical and psychological effects and the connection, if any, between marijuana and aggressive behavior and crime; detailing the relationship between marijuana and the use of other drugs; and recommending effective methods for international control. Twenty-eight research assistants and sixteen "youth consultants" (hired to give the middle-aged commission a young person's perspective on national drug use and possible solutions) would assist the thirteen committee members, nine of whom were appointed by Nixon himself, with two others appointed by each house of Congress. The commission was required to present its findings by 1972 in a comprehensive report, which Nixon hoped would finally cement marijuana's reputation as a dangerous drug.

To serve as the commission's chairman, Nixon appointed Raymond P. Shafer, a fellow Republican and former governor of Pennsylvania whose previous career as a prosecutor and state senator had made him a leader among the moderate right and a major player in national politics. Shafer was a surprising choice. He had supported Nelson Rockefeller over Nixon for the Republican nomination in 1968, and he and Nixon had long had a rocky relationship. Nixon knew that Shafer eventually hoped to be appointed to a federal judgeship, however, and believed that he could use his own power to satisfy Shafer's ambitions to control the outcome of his findings. "I have very strong feelings" about marijuana, Nixon told Shafer in a private meeting before the committee convened. "I want a goddamn strong statement" against the drug, he continued, "one that just tears the ass out of" legalization supporters.[8]

The president's views were known to Shafer but, surprisingly, didn't influence his work. The Shafer Commission, as it would be known, was scientifically rigorous in its approach. Members spent time in six

metropolitan areas and visited thirty-six countries in order to understand marijuana use. They conducted numerous research projects, interviewed dozens of doctors, law enforcement officials, and scientists,
and even heard testimony from Allen Ginsberg, who, speaking before
the commission in San Francisco and wearing a hat and tie, emphasized that marijuana was a "creative tool for artists, and no one should
be put in jail for using it."[9] The members also met a surprising number of people who believed that marijuana should not be illegal. "We
would talk to government officials and they would give us the official
line: marijuana use is very serious, we are very concerned about it, we
want to work with your government to stamp it out," a commission
member recalled. "Then, that night, we'd go out drinking and they'd
tell us the truth: they thought marijuana was harmless, but the Nixon
administration wanted a hard line and they feared economic reprisals
if they didn't go along."[10]

The Shafer Commission didn't fall into line. Its explosive 1,184-page
report, which was released in March 1972, came out conclusively in
support of decriminalization by arguing that the widespread views of
marijuana's harm were almost uniformly wrong. After conducting over
fifty studies and numerous hearings, the commission found that not
only was marijuana widely used—24 million Americans had tried the
drug at least once, and 12 million considered themselves regular users—but that anti-marijuana laws did more harm than good, and the
drug caused none of the violent effects that Nixon hoped to correlate
with its use.[11] Instead, the report found that marijuana users were in no
way "physically, biochemically, or mentally" different from non-users,
and that claims regarding the country's "marijuana problem" were exaggerated, polarizing, and frequently wrong. Harsh anti-marijuana laws
and restrictions on pot-related medical research were not solutions, the
commission concluded, and in fact only resulted in antagonizing young
voters and generating public distrust of the police.

The commissioners also found that the nation's laws against marijuana were out of proportion to marijuana's potential—and relatively
minimal—harm. The report declared that anti-marijuana laws were "too
harsh a tool to apply to personal possession even in the effort to discourage use. It implies an overwhelming indictment of the behavior, which

we believe is not appropriate. The actual and potential use of the drug is not great enough to justify intrusion by the criminal law into private behavior, a step which our society only takes with the greatest reluctance."

The biggest danger of marijuana, the report found, was in distracting Americans from the real drug problems plaguing the country. Heroin was a serious and deadly issue, and there had been a national crisis in its abuse since 1967. Even more dangerous was "the compulsive use" of alcohol, which, despite its legality, the report declared, was by far "the most destructive drug-use pattern in this nation." Although it did not advocate full legalization, the Shafer Commission's conclusion was clear: the country should decriminalize marijuana by ending criminal penalties for those caught with small amounts for personal use. The drug's "relative potential for harm to the vast majority of individual users and its actual impact on society does not justify a social policy designed to seek out and firmly punish those who use it."[12]

Nixon was furious with the report's findings, and he punished Shafer by not nominating him for the federal judgeship Shafer wanted. But Nixon was also shrewd when talking to the press after the report's release. "I oppose the legalization of marijuana and that includes sale, possession, and use," he said two days after the report was published. "I do not believe you can have effective criminal justice based on a philosophy that something is half-legal and half-illegal." But Nixon never addressed what the Shafer Commission actually recommended, which was the decriminalization, not legalization, of the drug. It was a tactical move: by focusing on legalization—something even the Shafer Commission denounced—Nixon could criticize the report's overall findings, while affirming himself as a stalwart supporter of traditional law and order and a warrior in the country's ongoing battle against drugs. By ignoring the report's findings and conclusions, Nixon ensured that marijuana remained a Schedule I drug.[13]

But others were not so sure. After the report's release, Shafer vocally advocated for decriminalization in the press, and newspaper editorials across the country wondered at Nixon's inability to consider the findings. Columnists like Clayton Fritchey, a Nixon opponent, were convinced that the president had simply ignored the truth. "Can 24 million Americans be wrong?" Fritchey asked. "Prison, of course, is not the

answer, for the law the President wants strictly enforced is as pernicious and impractical as the old Volstead Act." Fritchey compared the
nation's relationship with marijuana to Prohibition, arguing that "the
government found that it could not enforce Prohibition without putting
most of Americans in jail, so in the end it gave up." If the findings of the
Shafer Commission were true, Fritchey concluded, eventually it would
do the same with marijuana, "but not before years of political agony."[14]
Others, including editors of the *Sarasota Herald-Tribune*, were even
more direct. In a cartoon published on March 30, 1973, Nixon is pictured leaning over his Oval Office desk, shouting at a man holding the
commission's final report in his hands. "Don't confuse me with facts!"
the president yells.[15]

The release of the Shafer Commission's report and Nixon's dismissive response to it were emblematic of marijuana's strange situation in
the early 1970s. Even as comfort with the drug increased, federal law
equated marijuana with heroin and arrest rates skyrocketed nationwide
as an expanding drug war targeted drug use, and especially marijuana
use, as "public enemy number one." Indeed, during the very period the
commission worked on its report, marijuana arrest rates jumped from
188,682 in 1970 to 292,179 in 1972. By 1973, they had spiked again, rising to 420,700.[16] For the hundreds of thousands of Americans incarcerated for marijuana, the Shafer Commission proved what they had long
known: that arrests for marijuana did little more than generate distrust
toward authorities and increase support for decriminalization. But for
Nixon, the Shafer Commission's report was simply another example of
the pernicious decline of personal responsibility and decreasing respect
for the rule of law that he had been denouncing for years.

For a growing number of people who were in a position to change
state and local drug laws, however, the report was a clarion call. For
them, the Shafer Commission had made it clear that marijuana smokers were being unfairly targeted by law enforcement officials and that
prohibition violated civil rights. Beyond smoking marijuana, the report declared, marijuana users were law-abiding citizens whose drug
use posed no social harm. To incarcerate hundreds of thousands of
pot smokers every year for using a drug that was less problematic than
alcohol made little sense, and it made marijuana activists out of an

increasing number of people, from university students worried about their friends to conservative Republicans disobeying the president's commands. Soon a growing number of state legislators and local activists would take the Shafer Commission's findings into their own hands. By 1972, when Nixon took office for his second term, support for decriminalization was growing across the country and laws were about to change, whether the president approved or not.

4

"YOU WON'T HAVE TO BE PARANOID ANYMORE!"

IN 1972, WHEN Democrats took control of the Oregon House of Representatives for the first time in twenty years, thirty-one-year-old Stephen Kafoury was a member of that freshman class, one of the youngest and most revolutionary in the state's history. During his two terms in the state house and senate, "we passed a whole lot of groundbreaking legislation," Kafoury remembered. Along with future senator Earl Blumenauer and future Portland mayor Vera Katz, Kafoury was one of twenty-nine freshmen, making up nearly half of the sixty-member house, who were able to push legislation that protected "women's rights, land use, open records bills," Kafoury said. "We established Oregon [as] the environmental state that it is. It was a very exciting time."[1]

Kafoury went on to have a remarkable career in Oregon politics. A Peace Corps veteran, Kafoury spent nearly a decade in state government and then twelve years on the Portland school board before launching a law practice, where he still works today to protect Oregon's environment from corporate control. But perhaps nothing was more extraordinary than Kafoury's unlikely partnership, in 1973, with a sixty-year-old Republican pig farmer named Stafford Hansell to produce the country's first statewide marijuana decriminalization bill and launch a revolution that would eventually extend to eleven other states.

Kafoury was elected in the fall of 1972 in a wave of Democratic victories that, despite Nixon's landslide reelection, brought Democrats back to power in the US Senate and in state legislatures across the country. Many of these victories were the result of the Twenty-Sixth Amendment, which lowered the voting age to eighteen in 1971, and Kafoury took these electoral victories as a sign that, although the "law-and-order" president had been given another term, there was still growing support for new ideas and for finding peace between the generations, who had been warring for years over Vietnam, racial justice, and women's rights.

Kafoury believed that peace was possible in the battle over marijuana too, at least in Oregon. He had spent the year before his election canvassing his hometown of Portland, going from house to house trying to garner votes. Dozens of times his knock on the door, as an unexpected visitor, had sent residents inside the house scrambling, only to reveal themselves when they opened the door reeking of marijuana smoke. Nixon's war on marijuana users had made people scared: too many young people, Kafoury said, feared that every knock might come from the police, that every visitor was an undercover narc. But the recently released Shafer Commission report demonstrated that even some government officials were no longer convinced of the drug's absolute harm. After hearing dozens of people rush to hide evidence of their marijuana use as he waited outside their doors, Kafoury began making his young constituents a promise. "If I get elected, I'll do something about this," he told them. "You won't have to be paranoid anymore!"[2]

Kafoury was part of a cohort of young, activist state legislators across the nation who helped transform the politics of marijuana in the 1970s. In the wake of widespread protests against racism and the Vietnam War, young people, aware of the value of political activism, were taking the next step and shifting their work to state capitals, where they could continue to incite change. Bolstered by the Shafer Commission's claims, between 1973 and 1978 a new generation of activists ran for office, collected signatures, submitted ballot initiatives, and challenged laws in court in order to put decriminalization laws in place in a dozen states. Even though the Controlled Substances Act had outlawed the drug on the federal level, this wave of state-based decriminalization represented the first time marijuana gained widespread legal sanction in the United States.

Young people like Stephen Kafoury were responsible for the bulk of the introduction and approval of decriminalization laws, but by the mid-1970s they weren't alone. Other, increasingly surprising figures were joining the decriminalization movement, including Stafford Hansell, the sexagenarian pig farmer from rural Oregon, and conservative columnists James J. Kirkpatrick and William F. Buckley Jr., as well as respected organizations like the National Education Association (NEA) and the American Bar Association (ABA). Decriminalization gained this widespread support because marijuana's growing use among the white middle class made the drug seem less alien and far more relatable, and also because the Shafer Commission's findings provided federally supported evidence of the need for a new approach.

The decriminalization floodgates truly opened, however, when Richard Nixon resigned from the presidency in August 1974. With the most virulently anti-marijuana politician since Harry Anslinger out of the White House, state legislatures no longer feared reprisals from Washington if they altered their marijuana laws, and bills that had been discussed since 1972, when the Shafer Commission first released its report, could finally be passed. Even Congress held a hearing in 1975 to discuss whether marijuana should be decriminalized at the federal level, showcasing the government's shifting priorities on the drug.

By 1978, with decriminalization laws passed in a dozen states and Washington far more sympathetic to the drug's users, over one-third of the country's population lived in states where the penalty for personal possession of small amounts of marijuana was the equivalent of a traffic fine. It was a remarkable, and remarkably rapid, shift. Fourteen years after the first pro-legalization demonstration, the promise that Stephen Kafoury made to his constituents had come true for millions of Americans across the country. For good or for ill, marijuana was out in the open, and smokers in a dozen states didn't have to be paranoid anymore.

•

In Oregon, Kafoury wasted no time after taking office in tackling the marijuana issue. Along with Senator Bill Stevenson, Kafoury was asked to cochair the newly formed Joint Committee on Alcohol and Drugs in February 1973, Oregon's first attempt to look specifically at intoxicant use in the state. The committee was tasked with "some big agenda items," Kafoury remembered, including decreasing the drinking age from twenty-one to eighteen and declaring that drug addiction was an illness, not a crime. Most importantly, the committee was asked to examine the Shafer Commission's recommendations and test their potential for implementation in Oregon. "We are urging the committee to carefully study the proposals for removals of penalties for use of marijuana," Speaker of the House John Eymann told the *Eugene Register-Guard*. "I trust this committee will aim its legislation at the roots and not just the symptoms of drug and alcohol abuse in Oregon."[3] Kafoury hoped to do the same thing. "We all knew the war on drugs wasn't working, and that locking people up for marijuana was nonsense," Kafoury said. "The committee gave us a chance to talk about that."[4]

The committee had four months to craft a bill that would hold Kafoury to the promise he had made to his constituents. For a state that had previously considered marijuana possession a felony, Kafoury's bill brought the drug out into the open and combined the most lenient recommendations of the Shafer Commission with Amorphia's calls for backyard cultivation. If approved, Kafoury's bill, known as HB 2003, would have removed all criminal penalties for the possession of up to eight ounces of marijuana and permitted the personal cultivation of up to two plants. By mid-June, with the bill in hand, Kafoury was in Salem defending it to the state legislature, where it gained a significant level of support, particularly from officials who were already sympathetic to the cause. Republican governor Tom McCall had defended decriminalization before the Shafer Commission the previous year, and Pat Horton, the Lane County district attorney, was no longer prosecuting marijuana cases. Decriminalization was already being implemented de facto, Kafoury argued. Now he wanted it enacted into law.

But Kafoury's impassioned arguments for decriminalization were nothing compared to the performance of Stafford Hansell, who strolled into the chamber and immediately rolled up his sleeves. "There is no element of conflict of interests here," he said. "I am not a dope addict. I haven't smoked a cigarette for twenty-five years, nor had a drink of intoxicating beverage for twenty-four." But the sixty-year-old pig farmer supported decriminalization, he said, because he knew that marijuana was no better, and certainly no worse, than the wide variety of substances that were already legal. He then brought out a series of props—a cup of coffee, a pack of cigarettes, bottles of wine, beer, and whiskey, and amphetamines, aspirin, and sleeping pills—and placed them all alongside a small joint. After he explained the health hazards and penalties (or lack thereof) for each, he told his audience that he supported decriminalization because "Prohibition was not the answer to our alcohol problem in 1919, nor is it the answer to the marijuana problem in 1973." When Hansell was finished, to Kafoury's surprise, the entire chamber rose in applause.[5]

Hansell's speech was remarkable not only for its bluntness, but for who he was. One of the largest pig ranchers in the United States, Hansell was the epitome of the Western farmer, tall and strong with a square jaw and a gritty demeanor. He was first elected to represent Oregon's conservative Umatilla County in 1965, and his emphasis on protecting land use rights and preserving Oregon's rural heritage would keep him there for another eighteen years. By 1973, he was also the changing face of grassroots support for decriminalization of marijuana. "If we wish, truly, to teach young people about drugs, we must stop telling lies about marijuana and we must get rid of the laws that support those lies," Hansell told the *Eugene Register-Guard*. "To me, the most serious cost of our present system is the loss of credibility that my generation has with the youth of the country."[6]

Despite Hansell's rousing performance, HB 2003 was too broad for most of Oregon's house members to support, and it was soundly defeated when it came up for vote. But Hansell's speech kept decriminalization in the news, and Kafoury seized the opportunity. Two days later, the Joint Committee on Alcohol and Drugs introduced a new and far more moderate bill in which home cultivation remained outlawed and criminal penalties were eliminated only for possession of up to an ounce of the drug, which would instead be punishable by a $100 civil fine. The revised bill passed easily, and by the summer of 1973, Kafoury and Hansell had made Oregon the first state to turn the Shafer Commission's recommendations into law. For activists across the country, especially Keith Stroup of NORML, it was a groundbreaking shift.

NORML had played no role in the bill's creation, but Stroup closely watched the proceedings from Washington and rushed to Eugene when the bill was passed. "My god, man," he told Kafoury after the bill was sent to the governor to sign, "this is the first state to stop locking people up. This is the biggest thing that has ever happened to marijuana reform."[7] Stroup was surprised by, and a bit jealous of, the events in Oregon. In the two years since NORML had launched, Stroup had been testifying in numerous state legislatures and serving as a pro-decriminalization witness in states like Massachusetts, Maine, Maryland, Rhode Island, Montana, Hawaii, and Connecticut, all of which had discussed changing marijuana laws in late 1972 and 1973. Although "there were interesting individual stories in each state campaign," Stroup remembered, "the end result was the same: our side lost."[8]

But Oregon had never crossed Stroup's radar. The rural but liberal state was home to less than 1 percent of the country's population, but suddenly, through the work of two state legislators who weren't even affiliated with his organization, Oregon had managed to do what no other state had done: decriminalize marijuana for its 2 million inhabitants. Even though he wasn't responsible for its passage, Stroup saw Oregon's new law as a collective victory for the movement as a whole, and a harbinger of things to come. "We felt that once we had our first state, others would quickly follow," Stroup said. "Science was on our side, the Shafer Commission report was on our side, and we were riding a wave of public support that seemed to suggest we were on the verge of a major breakthrough."[9]

That breakthrough would not come quickly, however, and not without serious effort on Stroup's part. Numerous states debated decriminalization bills throughout the rest of 1973 and into 1974, but none seemed willing to follow Oregon's lead. If he wanted more states to decriminalize, Stroup realized, he would have to prove that what happened in Oregon wasn't an aberration, and that the effects of decriminalization were both overwhelmingly positive and repeatable in other states. A survey would be useful, he reasoned, one that would ask Oregon residents about their drug use habits to learn whether they had changed in the wake of the bill. But with NORML's limited budget, Stroup wouldn't be able to conduct such a survey alone.

Luckily, NORML was beginning to attract some wealthy new sup-porters. Stroup's organization had recently begun working with the Drug Abuse Council (DAC), a progressive think tank founded by the Ford Foundation in 1971. The groups already had much in common: both were located in the heart of Washington, and both functioned as refuges for liberals during the Nixon years. Prior to coming to DAC, its president, Dr. Thomas Bryant, a boisterous forty-year-old with de-grees from Emory University in medicine and law, had been dedicated to Lyndon Johnson's War on Poverty, serving as the health affairs direc-tor in the Office of Economic Opportunity until 1969. In 1971, when the War on Poverty gave way to Nixon's war on drugs, Bryant moved on to DAC, where he was charged with finding moderate responses to drug abuse issues, including researching policies that could contain the use of heroin in urban slums and examining the marijuana issues being debated in the states.[10]

When he returned to DC from Oregon, Stroup approached Bryant and asked if DAC would be willing to sponsor a survey of the state's drug use habits in the wake of decriminalization. The think tank was open to the request, and Bryant and DAC's head writer, Bob Carr, offered $10,000 to a Portland-based public opinion firm to survey over 800 Oregon adults. By the fall of 1974, they had their results, which were stunningly, and overwhelming, positive. "The results were about as good as we could have hoped for," Stroup remembered. They showed that "elected officials had nothing to fear from supporting decriminalization laws" and were full of "new data to disarm our political opponents."[11]

Based on 802 interviews with adults over the age of eighteen, DAC's survey, released publicly with the headline "New Marijuana Law Works in Oregon," found that, in the year since marijuana had been decrimi-nalized, there had been no significant increase in marijuana use in the state and a majority of citizens supported the new approach. The survey also found that only 9 percent of the respondents were regular marijuana users and that 40 percent of those surveyed had actually decreased their marijuana consumption since the bill was passed (though the survey neglected to explain why). Although 32 percent of respondents favored the existing law, over one-quarter of respondents said that it hadn't gone far enough: 15 percent argued that possession of small amounts should be completely legal, and 11 percent preferred that the state legalize both possession and sale.

When the report was released nationwide, Stroup and DAC officials refined their talking points, noting that, rather than increasing marijuana use, decriminalization actually decreased usage rates. In an interview with the Associated Press, Carr argued that other states considering changing their marijuana laws had nothing to fear. "The importance of this survey is that many people have predicted that reducing the penalties will increase the usage of marijuana," Carr said. His survey had found, however, that the opposite was true: it was legal deterrents, like increased arrests, that "have been ineffective in reducing the amount people smoke."[12]

The Shafer Commission report and the findings of the Oregon survey pushed even more individuals and organizations to lend their support to the decriminalization cause, and soon NORML and DAC had increasingly high-profile support from powerful and influential national groups. By 1974, the National Education Association, the National Council of Churches, the Central Conference of American Rabbis, and Consumers Union (CU) had all thrown their support behind decriminalization. The CU had even released the 632-page *Consumers Union Report on Licit and Illicit Drugs*, which called for marijuana's immediate decriminalization and eventual legalization. "Marijuana is here to stay," the report concluded. "No conceivable law enforcement program can curb its availability."[13] But it was the American Bar Association, the organization that set moral and ethical codes for lawyers and law schools, whose backing seemed the most persuasive. Reporting on the dramatic growth in support for decriminalization, *Time* magazine asked its readers in September 1973, "With the ABA behind decriminalization of pot, can the rest of the nation be far behind?"[14]

Some of the country's most famous conservatives were also throwing their weight behind the idea. In a 1972 editorial in the *Washington Star-News*, the syndicated columnist James J. Kilpatrick supported decriminalization as an extension of the basic tenets of ideological conservatism. "The conservative philosophy holds, if I understand it correctly, that within certain limitations, a free people should be just that: free," he wrote. Decriminalization aligned with Kilpatrick's views because, "as a general proposition, conservatives hold that no human conduct should be prohibited by law unless that conduct causes positive harm to the innocent bystander or to society as a whole." For him, marijuana use simply didn't fit that bill.[15]

Even the nation's most famous conservative, William F. Buckley Jr., echoed these sentiments when he published an editorial in the same paper two years later, defending decriminalization as a validation of individual freedom as well as a protective measure for the parents of pot-smoking teens. Supporting decriminalization may "appear to capitulate to the counterculture," he wrote, but most parents "did not desire *their* 18-year-old boys and girls to be sent to jail for smoking pot." Buckley recognized that voters would support decriminalization if, as had happened with the thousands of parents of incarcerated kids, the enforcement of marijuana laws affected their own lives. He also predicted that if marijuana arrest rates continued at their current pace, changing drug laws would soon gain predictable and overwhelming support. Buckley even admitted to trying the drug himself, though he was quick to note that "I was on my boat, outside the 3-mile limit, so I wasn't breaking any law."[16]

Nevertheless, despite positive press coverage and several state legislatures debating new bills, nothing much happened in the wake of the Oregon survey. No state was willing to follow Oregon's lead and alter its marijuana laws—that is, not until August 9, 1974, when Richard Nixon resigned from the presidency after announcing his departure in a dramatic television address from the Oval Office the night before. After two years of intense and bitter debate over the Watergate scandal, Nixon finally submitted to public pressure and became the first (and so far only) president to resign from the White House.[17] His departure had enormous consequences for the country as a whole, including the marijuana decriminalization movement. In the wake of the president's resignation, long-stalled decriminalization bills began to move, gaining new strength not only from state legislators but from the federal government.

With Nixon's departure, his vice president, Gerald Ford, a moderate former congressman from Michigan, became president, and a very different view of marijuana took hold in Washington. Ford was too distracted by a series of other issues, including the tumultuous end of the Vietnam War, a struggling economy, and the fallout from pardoning his predecessor, to dedicate much time to prosecuting marijuana cases. Ford also replaced some hardline marijuana opponents on his cabinet with people who were far more sympathetic to the counterculture. To replace John Mitchell as attorney general, Ford nominated Edward H. Levi, a law professor and scholar and the former president of the University of Chicago from 1968 to 1975. The son and grandson of rabbis, Levi had famously refused to call the Chicago police to evict students who had occupied university buildings in the 1960s, arguing that their actions constituted freedom of speech; clearly, he wouldn't continue Mitchell's legacy of persecuting marijuana users. Even Ford's wife Betty was open, and even blasé, about marijuana use. She told reporters that she "assumed" her children—Michael, Jack, Steven, and Susan, all of whom were under age twenty-four when their father assumed the presidency—had smoked pot, and that, if she were their age, she would "be smoking a joint herself."[18]

The Ford administration's softer view of marijuana was also shaped by a second federal report, one that followed the Shafer Commission's lead by emphasizing marijuana's ubiquity and general lack of harm. A year after Ford took the Oval Office, his Domestic Council Drug Abuse Task Force—a committee consisting of White House officials and the director of the National Institute on Drug Abuse, Dr. Robert DuPont—released a white paper that outlined the administration's assessment of the country's drug abuse problem and presented its recommendations for "improving the Federal government's overall program to reduce drug abuse." Four years after Nixon declared that drug abuse was "America's public enemy number one," the task force's prognosis was bleak. Although "drug abuse is one of the most serious and most tragic problems this country faces," the report declared, it acknowledged that there was little hope that the government could completely eliminate the scourge. Instead, the report came to the conclusion "that the optimism about 'winning the war on drugs' expressed so eloquently and confidently only a few years ago was premature. . . . We should stop raising expectations of the total elimination of drug abuse from our society." Even the "total elimination of illicit drug traffic" was, in the view of the task force, "impossible."[19]

Following this new line of thought, the paper advocated that more attention be given to addictive narcotics like heroin, which the task force unanimously concluded posed the "greater risk," and less to drugs whose use didn't result in "serious social consequences such as crime, hospital emergency room admissions, or death." These drugs included cocaine, some solvents, inhalants, hallucinogens, and, most notably, marijuana.

Following the recommendations of the Shafer Commission, the paper then argued that the federal government should deemphasize simple possession and use of marijuana in its law enforcement efforts and eliminate the requirement that "non-compulsive" marijuana users enter treatment systems. Though the report warned that "rates of marijuana use have been rising steadily over recent years," and that the use of "more potent" marijuana derivations could cause "serious physical and social effects on the user," it concluded that marijuana was the "least serious" drug problem facing the nation, in terms of its "dependence liability" and the severity of personal and social consequences of its use.[20] The report didn't support outright decriminalization, but its findings represented such a dramatic shift from the priorities of the Nixon administration that Stroup could hardly be blamed for telling *Time* magazine that he fully believed that "marijuana may be legal nationwide by 1976."[21]

With Nixon out of the White House, Congress also began exploring decriminalization on a federal level. In May 1975, the Senate Judiciary Committee held hearings on a proposal to amend the 1970 Controlled Substances Act by decriminalizing the possession of "not more than one ounce of marijuana within a private dwelling or other residence for [personal] use, or for the use of others." Senator Birch Bayh of Indiana, who chaired the committee, asserted that he hoped his committee could "still the hysteria, and that we can pursue the truth, wherever it leads us. And if we make some people angry, that is the price we pay and the responsibility we have."[22]

The hearing clearly favored changing the law. The committee heard from an exclusively pro-decriminalization panel of witnesses that included law professors, district attorneys, and Keith Stroup. "In a free society," Stroup argued, "the individual is permitted, though discouraged, to take certain risks as long as they do not endanger others. Skydiving, drinking alcohol, smoking cigarettes and overeating are but some of the high-risk activities people engage in every day. Yet they remain free from arrest." Stroup promoted marijuana users like himself as law-abiding citizens whose habit was no more harmful than drinking alcohol or smoking cigarettes, and he told the committee that he resented the idea that, "although I am an adult citizen with a value system much like yours, I am subject to arrest simply because I choose to smoke marijuana." Smoking pot, Stroup asserted, was no different than skydiving: risky and potentially a bad idea, but not something that should be outlawed or banned from public use.[23]

In addition to witness testimony, the committee received many personal letters from citizens whose lives and families had been touched by anti-marijuana laws. Senator Bayh submitted for the record a letter from Robert P. Woodman of Willoughby, Ohio, who wrote to the senator the night his son Jimmy was arrested for a marijuana transaction in 1975:

> I wrote my feelings as a father of a 20-year-old son who has fallen victim to an imperfect system of justice. . . . This incredible punishment visited upon my son is wholly irrational and disproportionate to the imprudent, foolish, and victimless act of a 20-year-old boy. (Jimmy sold an ounce of reefer to an undercover narc.) While the court has called my son a criminal and has sentenced him to from one-to-five years in prison, he has the consolation of knowing that his parents, seven brothers and sisters, relatives, friends, and understanding neighbors in no way consider him to be a criminal. Immature and foolish? Yes! Criminal? No!

Woodman summed up the hearing's theme when he stated that "my most intense feeling is one of righteous anger with a system which allows punishment which inflicts real harm and injury on Jimmy who has harmed no one and who lacks the capacity to do so."[24] Supporters of decriminalization like Woodman, Bayh, and Stroup argued that marijuana use was simply too minor an infraction to warrant the massive expenditures in time, police work, and money, and their negative impact on the future of America's youth.

Although nothing came of Bayh's effort to amend the Controlled Substances Act on a federal level, several states were poised to agree. Five states took steps toward loosening marijuana laws in 1975. After a Senate hearing, a federal white paper, and positive results from Oregon all supported changing marijuana laws, Maine, Colorado, California, and Ohio decriminalized possession of up to an ounce of pot that year, making the penalty for marijuana possession the equivalent of a civil fine for 35 million people. Just one year after Nixon left office, over 16 percent of the country no longer faced criminal prosecution for possessing a limited amount of marijuana. And for the first time since Lowell Eggemeier launched his protest in San Francisco in 1964, arrests for marijuana fell, dropping from 445,000 across the country in 1974 to 416,100 in 1975.[25]

In Alaska, something even more remarkable happened. In October 1972, Irwin Ravin, a thirty-two-year-old lawyer and father of two young sons, tested the state's privacy laws by intentionally allowing himself to be pulled over by the Anchorage police for a broken taillight, knowing that he had marijuana in his pocket. When he refused to sign his ticket, police searched him and his vehicle and found the drug. With his law partner, Robert Wagstaff, and financial support from NORML, Ravin appealed his conviction all the way to the state's supreme court, where, in October 1974, his case was heard. Defending Ravin in *Ravin vs. State,* Wagstaff argued that the burden of proof lay with the Alaskan government to show that there was "compelling public interest" in prohibiting his client's use of marijuana.

The court ultimately found that there was not. After seven months of deliberation, the court determined in May 1975 that Alaska residents had a constitutional right to privacy, which included an adult's ability to use, possess, and cultivate a small amount of marijuana in the home. For Ravin, the issue was a matter of conscience. "It wasn't about pot. It was the right to privacy," he later told the *Homer News.* "That's an important distinction to make. It was the philosophy of freedom from government intrusion into personal life." It was also a remarkable shift. While other states were decriminalizing the possession of small amounts of the drug, *Ravin vs. State* represented the first—and to this point only—time any court found that marijuana rights were protected by state constitution, including the right to personal cultivation. As Clem Tillion, a Republican state senator who supported the case, remembered, the case was about making sure the government "stayed out of your hair." And the person responsible for making that change was Ravin, a young lawyer originally from New Jersey who was drawn to Alaska for its freedom and independence. He "was a funny-looking hippie," Tillion remembered, "but by God he did good work."[26]

After 1975, the drumbeat for decriminalization was steady, and it spread to surprising places, including the conservative Midwest and the Deep South. During the next three years, decriminalization laws passed in Minnesota (1976), South Dakota (1977), Mississippi (1977), New York (1977), North Carolina (1977), and Nebraska (1978). Not all of the laws, however, were quite what reformers like Keith Stroup had in mind. Mississippi, for example, charged a $250 fine for a first-time marijuana possession offense, and North Carolina's law enacted a $100 fine and up to six months in jail for second offenses. Not all the new laws lasted very long either. South Dakota's decriminalization measure, passed in the spring of 1976, created the lowest fine in the country: $20 for simple possession. But after the November election, when a new class of more conservative legislators was put into office, they changed the bill before it went into effect in 1977. Raising the fine from $20 to $100, the new bill also tagged on a possible thirty days in jail if the amount of marijuana was deemed sufficiently dangerous.[27]

Although activists may have considered some of the new laws imperfect, they nonetheless signaled that states across the country—from the western frontier (Oregon and Alaska) to the Midwest (Minnesota and Nebraska), to the South (Mississippi and North Carolina), to the East Coast (Maine and New York)—had decriminalized the possession of marijuana. In just five years, nearly 70 million people—31 percent of the American population—were no longer necessarily subject to arrest or incarceration for possessing small amounts of the drug. And nearly all of the measures were initiated and supported by young activists like Stephen Kafoury and Irwin Ravin, who argued that marijuana use was a matter of freedom and personal privacy. Endorsed by an unlikely cohort of supporters, including Oregon pig farmers, senators, and legal groups, decriminalization was also being defended as a matter of judicial and financial restraint. People like Stafford Hansell argued that the enforcement of anti-marijuana laws simply wasn't worth the drain on the resources of state and local police or the loss of support of young voters.

As in Oregon, NORML could not take full credit for any of these bills, but the group's leaders and prominent allies lobbied in support of their passage. Stroup and Larry Schott helped pay for sympathetic experts, including members of the Shafer Commission, to testify at decriminalization hearings, and they repeatedly traveled to these states— as well as to thirty-four others that considered decriminalization by 1977—to testify in support of the initiatives, defending decriminalization on the basis of everything from an adult's right to privacy to the new laws' benefits for local taxpayers. "Decriminalization means that the public funds from the American taxpayer spent on enforcing marijuana laws can be diverted to controlling more serious crime," Schott told an audience in Florida in 1977. "But in the greater sense, it means the government stops messing around with people's lives for smoking a joint in their living room."[28]

For Stroup, the nationwide trend toward decriminalization had brought NORML to the threshold of something important and new. Although it had been founded with the assumption that the battle for decriminalization would be fought at the federal level, NORML quickly adapted to a new state-by-state strategy and actively supported every move toward reform. Stroup and Schott were constantly talking to the press about the benefits of decriminalization, positioning themselves as experts on both the drug and the new laws. By 1975, in response to growing demand for his expertise, Stroup moved NORML into a larger office and hired a secretary to handle media and speaking requests. The "behind-the-scenes maneuvering and political horse trading in each state was breathtaking," Stroup said, but the thrill of being the face and voice of the movement was even better. It was intoxicating and empowering for NORML to suddenly have "gained a new respectability" by constantly being at the forefront of the new laws, Stroup said. "Decriminalization was no longer a fringe issue, and anyone in the media wanting to write about the progressive movement, or any legislator interested in pursuing a similar policy in their state, started by contacting NORML."[29]

With a growing number of states changing their laws and an increasingly powerful lobbying group in Washington, the decriminalization movement was nearing its political peak in 1975. Legal support would soon birth wide-ranging cultural support as well, as decriminalization expedited the growth of a thriving new marijuana subculture, complete with "head shops" that sold drug paraphernalia and a growing number of magazines, movies, and music that glorified marijuana use and united the country's pot-smoking constituency.

But another phenomenon was lurking behind the growing support for decriminalization, and pro-marijuana activists like Stroup and Schott were too busy to acknowledge it. As advocates subscribed to magazines like *High Times* and celebrated the right of an adult to "smoke a joint in their living room," the rise of head shops brought its own set of complications. New decriminalization laws didn't set age restrictions for the purchase of paraphernalia or drug-related goods, and store owners rarely checked customers' IDs. By the end of the 1970s, reports of young children easily purchasing drug paraphernalia were filling the national news, and surveys found that rates of adolescent marijuana use were starting to spike. With head shop owners and paraphernalia manufacturers celebrating their industry's newfound success rather than working to protect kids from drug use, the nation's new drug laws were destined to fail. With an anti-decriminalization counterrevolution forming, by the time pro-marijuana activists recognized the need to regulate their own industry, it was already too late.

5

"I'M LIKE A BOTTLE MAKER
DURING PROHIBITION"

DECRIMINALIZATION COINCIDED WITH a period of intense economic instability in America. The middle years of the 1970s witnessed a series of economic shocks: the stock market tumbled between 1973 and 1974, declining by over 40 percent in eighteen months; an oil embargo in 1973 created endless gas lines; and high levels of unemployment compounded by high rates of inflation caused the term "stagflation" to enter the national lexicon. The marijuana accessories marketplace birthed in decriminalization's wake was one of the few growth areas in this otherwise bleak economic landscape. In a legal marketplace that sold goods for use in the still-illegal act of smoking pot, the small boutique head shops and vibrant mail-order system that developed in decriminalized states (as well as in those where the drug remained illegal) catered to customers' blossoming desire for pot paraphernalia—the papers, pipes, bongs, clips, grinders, toys, books, cans, games, screens, incense, and scales that helped smokers get high and accompanied marijuana's evolving use.

By the mid-1970s, smokers also had a surprising amount of money to spend. In 1976, when seven states had decriminalized possession, paraphernalia vendors were pulling in over $120 million a year, with $50 million in sales of rolling papers alone. By 1977, that number had more than doubled, with paraphernalia sales generating $250 million a year. This market served to help smokers consume the nearly $4 billion in underground marijuana they purchased annually. And while sales of pipes, bongs, and rolling papers were small compared to the market for other intoxicants like tobacco (in 1976, Joseph F. Cullman, chairman of Philip Morris, said that sales of cigarettes had earned his company $265.67 million that year alone, and production volume had increased by 7.5 percent), as the drug moved off college campuses and into the middle class it was clear that marijuana users had the financial resources to sustain a multimillion-dollar market in new marijuana-related products.[1]

Smokers had a variety of new places where they could spend their money. Besides drug paraphernalia, the small head shops that had opened in cities and towns across the country also sold products to accompany the drug's evolving use, from incense to beaded curtains and clothes, while a slate of new magazines, like *Head, Stone Age,* and, most notably, *High Times,* advertised paraphernalia and tied the burgeoning marijuana scene to articles on politics, music, and art. In a radical departure from the days of *Reefer Madness,* pot smoking also began to dominate pop culture and was referenced in a growing number of songs and movies. Songwriters wrote love letters to marijuana's effects (Black Sabbath's 1971 "Sweet Leaf," Rick James's 1978 "Mary Jane") or made campy humor out of being high (Cheech and Chong's *Up in Smoke,* released in 1978, first brought stoner humor to the big screen).

The new pot-themed magazines had another purpose as well. Unlike the hand-illustrated, mimeographed copies of the *Marijuana Review,* magazines like *High Times* were glossy, legitimate publications, with color centerfolds, celebrity interviews, and national distribution. *High Times,* which quickly became the nation's leading dope magazine, served as a bulletin board for the nation's marijuana activists, running announcements and reviews of decriminalization campaigns, publishing a monthly drug price market report, and offering readers a breakdown of drug laws in every state. When the magazine's founder joined with NORML to promote decriminalization, pro-marijuana activists had a powerful new place to find all their movement-based news.

The decriminalization movement of the mid-1970s helped spark not only a legitimate drug culture but, by 1976, growing federal support. That year, when Jimmy Carter ran for president based partially on a platform of support for state-based decriminalization laws, he earned the support of Keith Stroup and NORML. After Carter won the presidency,

Stroup became a regular White House presence, advising Carter's drug policy expert Dr. Peter Bourne on marijuana and even drafting one of the president's most important drug statements, advocating for a change in federal marijuana laws. By 1978, NORML's pro-marijuana lobbyists were so comfortable at the White House that they could often be found playing softball with Carter's staffers on the South Lawn.

For many in the grassroots marijuana movement, the 1970s were an idyllic time, the moment when their movement peaked and coalesced. As support for decriminalization spread across the country, paraphernalia companies reaped previously unimaginable profits, and smokers were being treated, as Stroup once envisioned, like regular consumers, offered everything from drug paraphernalia to movies and toys that served to increase their enjoyment of the drug. National decriminalization movements were under way, organized with the help of a new wave of marijuana magazines that helped to give grassroots activists a voice.

But the movement's peak also brought with it the movement's downfall. Much of the new paraphernalia for sale deliberately riffed on children's toys, as smokers were offered everything from pot-themed Frisbees and board games to Christmas stockings. Even more troubling, children were quickly becoming the targets of paraphernalia marketing themselves. By 1978, newspapers were reporting that kids had easy access to head shops and were able to purchase pipes, papers, and bongs with no questions asked. The paraphernalia market that sprang up in the wake of decriminalization developed too quickly for government oversight and, with its interest in quick profits and giving the growing smoking population what it desired, it also chose not to regulate itself. In doing so, it set itself up for its own demise when a new generation of marijuana activists—parents angry at the rising rate of adolescent pot use—emerged in the wake of the paraphernalia boom. Once they made their power felt, it would be decades before decriminalization was spoken of positively in Washington again.

•

A man who "never met a drug he didn't like," Thomas King Forçade was born Kenneth Gary Goodson in Phoenix, Arizona, in September 1945. By the time he was in his twenties, Forçade dressed in all black, constantly wore a flat-brimmed hat, and sported a Fu Manchu mustache that dipped down to his chin. He also had a mercurial personality, a penchant for recreational nitrous oxide use, and a belief that he was under investigation by the CIA. A licensed pilot and large-scale marijuana smuggler, Forçade repeatedly told his friends that there were only two kinds of dealers—"those who need forklifts and those who don't"—and he made it clear that he was proudly one of the former. When he founded *High Times* magazine in the summer of 1974, he gave the marijuana community its voice.[2]

High Times was Forçade's brainchild, but it wasn't his first publication. The son of a politically conservative engineer and former Air Force officer who died when Forçade was ten, Forçade had shown an interest in both marijuana and publishing for years. He began smuggling pot over the Mexican border while still in high school, graduated from the University of Utah with a degree in business administration, and served a brief stint in the Air Force until he was kicked out for his increasingly erratic behavior. By 1968, Forçade was back in Phoenix, publishing a magazine called *Orpheus* out of "a roving 1946 Chevrolet school bus" parked in the desert outside his hometown.[3] Tie-dye colorful, *Orpheus* was a classic counterculture magazine, with art and articles on the country's burgeoning drug culture, including material from the Underground Press Syndicate, a loose coalition of underground publications that freely shared material written specifically for alternative publications like Forçade's. *Orpheus* set the precedent for what *High Times* would become: a place where poetry, manifestos, and film reviews sat comfortably next to articles about international smuggling and drug use.

A year after founding *Orpheus,* Forçade abandoned both the magazine and Arizona. In 1969, he officially changed his name (both to save his family embarrassment and as a play on the word "façade") and moved to New York to work for the Underground Press Syndicate full-time. In New York, Forçade joined the Yippies, continued to smuggle marijuana, and, in the summer of 1974, put out the first issue of *High Times*. Published with $12,000 generated from donations and a lucrative drug deal, the magazine was supposed to be, in the words of one of the magazine's first writers, Dean Latimer, "a joke, a lark, a one-shot spitball into the eye of Spiro Agnew's Silent Majority," its premise being "to be *Playboy*'s sexual materialism lampooned on terms of dope materialism." With a cover price of one dollar, the first issue of the country's first marijuana magazine featured articles on hemp paper, market quotations of national drug prices, an interview with a "lady dealer," and a piece called "Marijuana: Wonder Drug." Most uniquely, it featured a color centerfold, just like *Playboy,* but rather than featuring a nubile young woman, the photograph was of ripe marijuana. For Latimer, this first issue was all about satire and shock value. "Those white folks out there in Darkest America, they didn't know hardly *any* of this dope stuff then," Latimer said. He and Forçade thought "it would be fun to teach them about it."[4]

But *High Times* quickly developed a life of its own. The initial run of 25,000 copies sold out within a week, and subsequent printings sold out quickly as well. Within a year, *High Times* was selling 400,000 copies a month, its reputation so strong that *New York Times* writers were publishing in it under pseudonyms. Subsequent issues featured work from Truman Capote, William S. Burroughs, Hunter S. Thompson, and Allen Ginsberg. As the magazine evolved, it continued to cover America's drug culture, but it also included articles on politics, interviews with artists and musicians, and even short stories. Within three years, circulation had grown into the millions through pass-along readership, and the magazine's office had moved from a small basement on West Eleventh Street to a large space on East Twenty-Seventh Street capable of housing a staff that had ballooned to over 100 people. No longer a "one-shot spitball into the eye of the Silent Majority," *High Times* had evolved into one of the most prominent mouthpieces of the counterculture, and Forçade continually wanted to make it better. In a statement published in November 1976, he declared that he wanted *High Times* to feature "the best, the most accurate, the most interesting and entertaining, the most wide-ranging, creative, wildest, courageous coverage of dope anywhere. If you see any serious competition, let us know."[5]

And indeed, there was competition. By the late 1970s, a growing number of marijuana-themed magazines had come on the market, trying to match the success of *High Times.* Magazines like *Stone Age, Head, Rush, Stoned, Home Grown,* and *Flash* were published across the country, though mostly in places like San Francisco and New York, and featured a format similar to *High Times.* In *Stone Age*'s sixty-page debut, released in the winter of 1978, there were full-color photos and articles on smuggling and music, book reviews, an interview with Norman

Mailer, and a recipe for peyote salad. Like many of the new magazines of the era, *Stone Age* was about "the art and science of getting high-end high," and it offered its readers articles and ads that epitomized the "evolving dope lifestyle."[6]

All of these magazines came into existence because of the booming paraphernalia industry that advertised in their pages. Readers of *High Times* saw ads for everything from pipes and bongs to a board game called "You're the Dealer!" and the BuzzBee, a Frisbee with a tiny filter for smoking between passes. *Stone Age* featured ads for "Mr. Slick's Combo Cane-Pipe with Stash Cap," a walking cane that looked, "to the undiscerning eye," like an ordinary cane but revealed, upon closer inspection, "six different smoking pipes, complete with instructions and a lifetime unconditional guarantee."[7] The wide variety of drug paraphernalia advertised was being crafted and sold by everyone from high-level importers of foreign goods to amateur woodsmiths whittling pipes in their garage. "A remarkable new marketplace is emerging in America because the marijuana subculture of the 1960s has established itself as the center of the new leisure market of the 1970s," boasted an editorial in the June 1976 issue of *Dealer, High Times's* sister magazine. "A revolution in retailing on all fronts . . . will continue as paraphernalia retailers try to capture the imagination of the dope consumer."[8]

Some of the head shops that sprouted across the country to reach this consumer stood alone, and some were situated within record shops or other stores that sold counterculture-oriented goods, but all of them were a paradox: they sold legal products, including pipes, rolling papers, clips, scales, and canisters, that were used in the illegal process of smoking and selling marijuana. Many of these shops had a strong counterculture mission and were run by "activist entrepreneurs" who wanted to imbue conventional capitalistic enterprises with a sense of marijuana activism; they believed that the booming paraphernalia industry was a way to bring the fight for marijuana rights to strip malls and storefronts across the United States. Head shops inherently helped the decriminalization cause: they often served as a gathering place for local "heads," and the money they spent on advertising helped support a growing number of magazines that brought arguments in favor of decriminalization to readers across the country. And the lucrative mail-order system that developed to serve paraphernalia consumers who didn't live near a hip retailer further reinforced the decriminalization effort.[9]

With the growth in retail outlets, the number of marijuana entrepreneurs soared; they created products that catered to smokers' every whim and often profited mightily in response. "I'm like a bottle maker during Prohibition," twenty-nine-year-old Burt Rubin, creator of E-Z Wider rolling papers, told the *New York Times Magazine* in March 1976. "I make something legal to hold something that's illegal. When it's legalized, I'll make even more money than I do now." By 1977, Don Levin, the twenty-eight-year-old proprietor of Adam's Apple Distributing Company, was selling $10 million worth of goods annually. He told *Rolling Stone* magazine that his products included everything from grinders and rolling trays to a Christmas stocking containing "a pipe, *Everything You Always Wanted to Know About Marijuana,* a rolling machine, some papers, a clip, incense, some screens, and, to give it the Christmas effect, we threw some Zots [a candy] on the bottom. So, you know, if somebody's parents should see it, they'll say, 'Oh, it's a candy-filled stocking.'"[10]

NORML also benefited from the paraphernalia and pot magazine boom, in that the growing paraphernalia market became even more closely tied to the decriminalization cause. Stroup and Forçade met for the first time in Miami Beach at the 1972 Republican National Convention, where both men had gone to protest President Nixon's renomination. Given their mutual interests, they quickly became friends. Forçade appreciated NORML's political efforts to decriminalize marijuana, and Stroup appreciated Forçade's creativity and entrepreneurial spirit. To help promote NORML's work, Forçade agreed to publish a free ad for the group in *High Times* every month. Soon these ads were bringing NORML $1,000 a week in donations—almost as much as the single ad Hugh Hefner promised Stroup that *Playboy* would run twice a year. Forçade made his own donations to NORML as well: once, when NORML was facing a particularly difficult month, he dropped off a briefcase containing $10,000, suggesting that it came from an anonymous alliance of marijuana dealers known only as "The Confederation."[11]

By 1975, it was clear that the paraphernalia marketplace was catering to a small but mighty contingent of consumers with an interest in new products and money to spend. But the industry did more than cater to smokers' growing demands: it also helped legitimize the decriminalization movement by giving it both an economic foundation and a unified voice. During a period when the economy was suffering and the national unemployment rate had spiked, a growing paraphernalia market offered new opportunities for young people to find jobs, earn a paycheck, and pay their taxes; in short, to help grow the American economy. Though it seems ironic that a market catering to an illegal activity was one of the few bright spots in the American economy in the 1970s, it was the legitimate paraphernalia marketplace that grew in the wake of decriminalization that brought marijuana to strip malls and storefronts across America, giving activists the economic stability and power necessary to fight for their cause.

•

Still, nothing could prepare people like Stroup and Forçade for the assistance the decriminalization movement would receive when Jimmy Carter ran for president. Though it was hardly the largest issue of his campaign, Carter was the first presidential candidate in American history to openly advocate for state-based marijuana decriminalization, and the only one to do so during the 1976 campaign. In a questionnaire published by the *New Hampshire Times* that February, Carter said he favored "a modified form of marijuana decriminalization along the lines of the Oregon law, which has civil penalties for small amounts of possession. I feel that this legislation should be left up to the individual states themselves." The rest of the Carter family, including his sons Jack, Chip, and Jeff (all of whom publicly admitted to using the drug), backed him up. Even Carter's wife, Rosalynn, said that she felt better knowing that her children had smoked pot, rather than having them "slipping around and doing it and not letting me know." Her assistant press secretary made it clear that the future first lady agreed with her husband, stating that Mrs. Carter "feels marijuana should be decriminalized, but not legalized."[12]

Carter's stance put him ahead of incumbent Gerald Ford in the view of the nation's pot smokers, but in an indication of how lenient Americans had become on marijuana, even Ford declared that he felt possession should not be so harshly punished by federal law. In that same questionnaire, Ford expressed fears that state-based decriminalization could be "interpreted by potential users and by other nations as a signal that the US government no longer opposes marijuana." But Ford also said, pandering to the nation's shifting mood, that he supported "reduced federal penalties for simple possession."[13]

What Ford did not have, however, was a campaign adviser telling him to openly advocate for decriminalization. Carter's position on pot can be credited to one of his closest political aides, Dr. Peter Bourne. A physician and anthropologist, Bourne had spent years working with heroin addicts in Atlanta, and he understood the drug problems the country was facing at the time. Between 1967 and 1976, the United States experienced a severe heroin epidemic, one that killed 1,000 New Yorkers in 1971 alone. Much as the Ford administration's 1975 white paper on drugs recommended, Bourne wanted the federal government to focus its time, energy, and money on the drugs that were killing Americans and not on marijuana, which Bourne considered relatively harmless. Bourne also believed that incarcerating pot smokers did more harm than the actual use of the drug. Arresting marijuana users placed them in a confined space with addicts, dealers, and criminals more dangerous than themselves, Bourne said, introducing them to a darker, more drug-oriented lifestyle. Marijuana didn't immediately lead to heroin addiction, Bourne knew, but incarcerating a pot smoker with a heroin addict might. Though he was unwilling to claim that marijuana was harmless or that smoking anything was a good idea, after years of working with heroin addicts, Bourne strongly supported replacing marijuana's criminal penalties with civil fines.

Born in England, Bourne grew close to Carter during Carter's tenure as governor of Georgia from 1971 to 1975, when Bourne served as head of the state's narcotics treatment program. Bourne appreciated Carter because, like the future president, he was deeply liberal. As an undergraduate at Emory, he had demonstrated against segregated lunch counters and supported the expansion of civil and women's rights. After graduating from Emory's medical school in 1962, Bourne then served as a captain in the army, heading the military's Psychiatric Research Team and spending a year in Vietnam stationed with the Green Berets, where he completed a landmark study on combat stress. He returned to the United States a committed pacifist, and Carter's emphasis on international peace and humanitarianism appealed to him immensely. "I was incredibly impressed with [Carter's] intellect and how he cared for people," Bourne told *People* magazine in 1976. Bourne's wife, Mary King, a committed feminist and civil rights activist, was equally admiring. "I had never heard any public official talk with that compassion or self-disclosure—I became a supporter," she said.[14]

Carter also supported Bourne. As governor, he had funded Bourne's heroin addiction treatment clinic in Atlanta, and he came to rely on the doctor's political advice. Carter was eyeing a vice presidential run in the 1972 election, but after the chaotic Democratic National Convention in Miami, Bourne wrote Carter a nine-page memo, exhorting him to avoid joining Senator George McGovern's campaign and to launch his own presidential campaign in four years instead. Carter agreed to the plan, but only if Bourne would serve as an adviser. Bourne took the future president's offer and began organizing Carter's presidential campaign on the weekends while running his clinic in Atlanta during the week.

In November 1976, Carter eked out a win over Gerald Ford. The following January, Bourne came to the White House, where he was given an office in the West Wing and the title Special Assistant to the President for Drug Abuse.[15] Once there, Bourne became even more outspoken in his belief that decriminalization was the nation's most logical choice. Still troubled by the nation's heroin epidemic, Bourne argued that nationwide decriminalization of marijuana was necessary to keep state and federal resources focused on battling lethal drugs and preventing international trafficking by large-scale smuggling rings. He even argued that decriminalization was necessary because marijuana grew wild across the United States. Because it was produced in-country, marijuana was "very different" from cocaine or heroin, Bourne told the Senate Human Resources Committee during his successful nomination process. "Past experience has shown that there is virtually no way of controlling its use or distribution," he said.[16]

Bourne came to Washington at the precise moment when Keith Stroup needed him most. NORML had experienced a steep decline in membership in the months after Carter won the presidency. With six states already decriminalized and more on their way, many members, feeling that NORML had already achieved its goals, no longer felt compelled to keep paying dues. Others believed that, since Carter had made it to Washington, federal decriminalization would be passed within a year or two—or by 1980 at the latest. With membership dropping, NORML's coffers were running low, and the influence Stroup had spent years generating could be lost to bankruptcy in just a few months. For Stroup, gaining the ear of the White House through Peter Bourne was one way to make up for everything NORML's success had, surprisingly, taken away.

Nevertheless, Stroup and Bourne proved uneasy allies from the beginning. The two men started off on the wrong foot when Stroup invited Bourne to serve as the keynote speaker at NORML's annual convention in December 1976 to discuss what federal drug policy would be like under the Carter administration. Although Bourne supported decriminalization, he was a politician and a professional physician above all else. With no interest in compromising his reputation, Bourne was disturbed when he saw people smoking pot in the back of the room. "I found that a most unacceptable and embarrassing situation," Bourne later told *People*. Supporting decriminalization was one thing, but openly flouting the law was another. When Stroup invited him back the following year, Bourne politely declined.[17]

Still, both Bourne and Stroup sought to foster their relationship. Despite the snafu at the NORML event, Bourne trusted Stroup as an authority on marijuana policy and consulted him on speeches and official statements. Bourne knew that no one understood pot better than Stroup, whose nearly decade-long career lobbying for marijuana rights had made him the undisputed authority in the field. And Stroup, confident in the possibility of new national laws, was reveling in his increasing power. "After all those years on the outside, suddenly it looked like we were going to be insiders," he recalled. "It was like we were all working on the same side for a change. I was in and out of the White House all the time. Peter Bourne had the president's ear whenever he wanted it, and he had been one of our most sympathetic supporters for several years. We didn't expect to legalize grass straight out, but we did believe we had won the first battle."[18]

That first battle was officially won on August 2, 1977, when Stroup inserted a call for federal decriminalization into Carter's first official position paper on drugs. The president's "Drug Abuse Message to Congress," which was drafted by Stroup and then vetted by Bourne, endorsed not only the sort of state-based decriminalization that had already occurred but also an expansion of decriminalization on the federal level, with the complete removal of federal penalties for marijuana possession.[19] Not that the message wasn't also extremely diplomatic. Carter declared that "marijuana continues to be an emotional and controversial issue. After four decades, efforts to discourage its use with stringent laws still have not been successful. More than 45 million Americans have tried marijuana and an estimated 11 million are regular users." With hundreds of thousands of arrests taking place for a drug that millions of people continued to use, Carter continued, there had to be some middle ground.

Then, in a line penned by Stroup that would come to embody Carter's drug policies, Carter made his most famous statement in favor of decriminalization. "Penalties against possession of a drug should not be more damaging to an individual than the use of the drug itself," the president wrote, "and where they are, they should be changed." Carter then advocated a simple solution to achieve this goal: "Legislation amending Federal law to eliminate all Federal criminal penalties for the possession of up to one ounce of marijuana."[20]

For activists in the pro-marijuana movement, Carter's statement was a coup. After years of federal harassment during the Nixon administration, the White House was publicly endorsing decriminalization. Stroup and others could hardly believe their good luck and sought to build on the growing momentum. In the wake of Carter's statement, *High Times* ran an increasing number of notifications of nationwide events. For the thousands of people who listened to speakers, smoked free pot, and rallied for decriminalization in San Francisco, New York, and even historically conservative areas like Cedar Rapids, Iowa, the massive smoke-ins organized by NORML were equal parts party and political protest. "'We'd like to teach the world to toke in perfect harmony' seems to be the theme of these momentous gatherings," the magazine reported, "as local chapters of NORML, along with independent Johnny Marijuana-seeds, donate truckloads of golden weed from sea to shining sea."[21]

Most importantly, activists continued to tie their fight for marijuana to the ongoing battle for civil rights. In 1977, the "White House Smoke-In" was held across the street from the president's mansion in

Lafayette Park, where 6,000 activists, many dressed in Revolutionary War costume, publicly smoked pot and proclaimed that doing so was an act of rebellion as authentic and important as any in American history. *High Times,* which chronicled the event, declared that the activists "follow[ed] in the steps of those great Americans who threw tea into Boston Harbor, fermented corn whiskey in their bathtubs and produced homegrown dope instead of guns during the Vietnam War."[22]

By April 1979, almost two years after Carter threw his support behind federal decriminalization, the fight for marijuana civil rights was only growing stronger. That month Shay Addams, the founder of the Coalition for the Abolition of Marijuana Prohibition (CAMP), argued in *High Times* that outright legalization was nothing less than "the civil rights fight of the '80s":

> Like sitting-in to denounce racist laws or burning the American flag to protest US military intervention in Vietnam, smoking a joint at a reefer rally constitutes a legitimate form of symbolic protest, an act of civil disobedience equally protected by the First Amendment.
>
> Just as blacks had a right to break an unconstitutional law ordering them to sit in the back of Birmingham, Alabama, buses in 1953, pot smokers not only have a constitutional right to break the marijuana laws in protest but have a responsibility—yes, a duty— as patriotic Americans to smoke as much marijuana as we can get our hands on, to go more than just "one toke over the line" this spring as the movement to legalize marijuana marches on to ultimate victory.[23]

For the more financially minded, federal support for decriminalization was also nothing less than a golden economic opportunity, especially if Addams's predictions came true and decriminalization led inexorably to outright legalization. A December 1977 ad in *High Times* declared: "Carter Proposes Decriminalization! Paraphernalia Industry BOOM Expected!" Money Tree Press in Miami told *High Times* readers that "now that Jimmy has opened the federal doors, the US paraphernalia business will soon EXPLODE to more than three times its present level." The ad was nothing if not hopeful: it proclaimed that "the beautiful and useful accouterments of high society will multiply like mushrooms after a rainfall!" It also offered a money-back guarantee for a book that promised to tell readers how they could begin their own marketing campaigns and sell paraphernalia to national distributors "from coast to coast." "Don't delay," it concluded. "Think about your future today."[24]

•

By the late 1970s, with Carter and Bourne in the White House, millions of dollars flowing into the paraphernalia industry, and activists rallying across the United States, the "ultimate victory" that Addams envisioned seemed imminently possible. But what none of these pro-marijuana activists realized was that reports of children purchasing paraphernalia in strip malls and head shops across the country were starting to make national news. "Like babes in Toyland," the *New York Times* reported in 1978, "three boys from 11 to 14 and a 13-year-old girl went on a buying spree recently in 'head shops' around the metropolitan area. They came back with $300 worth of drug-culture paraphernalia that included . . . a baby bottle fitted with both a nipple and a hashish pipe and a felt-tipped pen that allows a surreptitious snort of cocaine in the classroom." Addiction expert Dr. Mitchell Rosenthal of the Phoenix House drug rehabilitation agency in New York told the paper that "little kids and adolescents" were able to purchase such items, warning that the availability of these products produced a "casual" attitude toward drug use—which paraphernalia manufacturers seemed not to mind.[25]

By the fall of 1979, youth access to marijuana paraphernalia had grown so widespread that a national group of pediatricians released a paper denouncing the phenomenon at their annual conference in San Francisco. Dr. Robert Petersen of the National Institute on Drug Abuse warned that "comic books that tell kids how to hide marijuana [and] pot-smoking paraphernalia that look like space guns" set a dangerous precedent. Though paraphernalia manufacturers argued that these products were intended only for adults, Petersen warned that they increased adolescent interest in drug use by making it seem toy-oriented and fun. "There is unanimity of informed professional opinion concerning marijuana use by children," Petersen said, warning that adolescent exposure to the drug could limit classroom learning and harm the development of social skills.

Petersen also feared that his warnings might have come too late. Pediatricians and drug use researchers were already seeing an alarming shift: 16 percent of twelve- to seventeen-year-olds had reported in a national survey that they had used marijuana in the previous month, and recent studies in Maine and Maryland had shown that one in six high school students smoked pot almost daily. "Five years ago marijuana use was primarily among young adults. Now use by youngsters under 18—many under 15—has markedly increased, stimulated by an industry that is promoting its use," Petersen said. He had no desire to "revitalize the old style 'reefer madness' campaign"; nevertheless, he warned, decriminalization and a growing paraphernalia marketplace were having some surprising, and negative, effects. Marijuana was dangerous for America's young, and Petersen warned researchers, doctors, and parents that that they should be on the lookout for suspicious toys that might encourage adolescent drug use.[26]

Meanwhile, across the country in Atlanta, Petersen's warnings had already been taken to heart. Parents in that city, led by two mothers who were deeply concerned about adolescent marijuana use, were forming into "parent peer groups" in hopes of keeping their kids away from pot. Angry at the "drug culture" they saw forming around cannabis, with its magazines, toys, and shops, these parents formed the leading edge of a new wave of grassroots activism that would turn the concept of "marijuana rights" on its head. Rather than promoting the right of an adult to access the drug of his or her choice without fear of arrest, parent activists promoted something new: the right of a child to grow up drug-free. The president and a booming paraphernalia market had it wrong, these parents argued. They were too focused on what marijuana meant for adults, and they ignored the drug's dangerous, potentially lethal effects on kids.

Despite Carter's support for federal decriminalization, pro-marijuana activists' celebrations may have come too soon. In the president's home state, the "parent movement"—the most powerful coalition of antidrug activists to form since Prohibition—was about to be born.

6

ATLANTA, 1976

THE PARTY TOOK place in 1976, during the summer of the nation's bicentennial, in the backyard of a large brick house that sat on a winding road in a wooded neighborhood just east of Emory University, in the northeast corner of Atlanta. Druid Hills was a quiet, well-to-do area where the children of professionals and academics walked to school in the morning and mothers, who rarely worked outside of the home, met them at the end of the day. Even as divorce rates skyrocketed across the country, few homes here had yet been touched by marital separation, and the neighbors who formed this tight-knit community celebrated together on holidays and special occasions. The unrest that had rocked the nation the decade before seemed far removed from Druid Hills, and as distant from these tidy, stately homes as the city's crumbling, crime-ridden downtown. It was not where a revolution was supposed to take place.

But it was here in Druid Hills that a mother of three discovered that she couldn't shield her eldest daughter, then only turning thirteen, from the thriving marijuana culture, which, to her surprise, had stretched beyond college campuses and urban cores and into her own child's backyard birthday party. That night, away from the swinging lanterns and floating balloons that lit the treetops sheltering their yard, her daughter spent the evening with her preteen friends huddled in the dark, sharing bottles of malt liquor and freshly rolled joints, leaving hamburgers uneaten on the porch.

The mother, Marsha Manatt Schuchard, known by her nickname Keith, watched later as the friends of her daughter Ashley, bleary-eyed and mumbling, stumbled through her house. One young guest struggled to make a telephone call, and another pushed past her on the way to the bathroom, unwilling or unable to say hello. As the backyard filled with unfamiliar faces and cars full of older teens cruised by, Schuchard stood at the kitchen window and stared out into her yard, asking herself, *Were these children impossibly rude? Or were they stoned?* Upstairs, as he watched lighters flicker in the bushes, her husband, Ron, wondered the same thing.

After the guests had left and their daughter was asleep, the Schuchards (pronounced SHOE-hard) walked outside, flashlights in hand. There they found evidence that confirmed their fears: empty bottles of malt liquor and wine, homemade roach clips, and other detritus of joints that their own child and her adolescent friends had smoked hours before. Schuchard and her husband "felt baffled and slightly sick," she recalled. How had adolescent drug use come to peaceful Druid Hills? And how long had it been going on under their noses?[1]

As they cleaned up the mess before going to bed, Schuchard's mind raced. Equal parts researcher and activist, the woman who would launch America's marijuana counterrevolution promised herself two things: first, that she would learn as much about marijuana as she could so that she'd know exactly what kinds of damage her daughter had done to herself; and second, that she would work with other parents in her community so that, together, they could halt this terrifying trend. It wasn't only her daughter who was drinking and smoking pot, Schuchard reasoned, so she needed to work with other parents if she wanted to ensure that her daughter got clean.

Schuchard went to work the next day. Guest list in hand, she approached the other parents and told them what she had found. The parents' reactions, she remembered, ran the gamut from "shock, confusion, indignation, concern, denial, and from a handful, hostility," but a few of them, she found, were eager to talk. These parents had also noticed a change in their children's behavior and were feeling worried and helpless about the possibility of drug use. For those she could convince to come, Schuchard and her husband hosted a meeting to talk about their concerns. No one knew exactly what was going on, she said, but it was

clear that marijuana was becoming a problem. Drugs and paraphernalia were in the hands of kids—*their* kids—and social pressures had
normalized marijuana and made it seem cool. It was practically legal
in six states, Schuchard worried, and no one was discussing the drug's
potential impact on kids. Instead, there were multimillion-dollar marijuana marketing campaigns and an entire "drug culture" promoted in
head shops, movies, and magazines. Parents were beginning to realize
that their children inhabited what she called an "alien world"—a highly
organized subculture that revolved around marijuana and that, prior to
that summer, they simply hadn't recognized before.

Schuchard discussed with the Druid Hills parents the need to retake control by enforcing uniform rules to help keep their children,
and their neighborhood, safe. Together, Schuchard said, "parent peer
groups" could learn about the dangers of marijuana, control their children's environment, and keep the growing "drug culture" out of their
homes and schools. There was strength in numbers, Schuchard continued. Children couldn't sneak around if every parent in the neighborhood was alerted to what was going on.[2]

Schuchard was a surprising figure to lead the marijuana counterrevolution. A liberal Democrat long supportive of civil rights, she understood that decriminalization was being defended on the argument that
adults had a right to use a drug that, many said, was less harmful than
alcohol without the threat of arrest or prison. But what kind of message was that sending to children? she wondered. And if the booming
market following in decriminalization's wake continued as it was going,
unregulated and unrestrained, how could any parent protect their children from drug abuse? After examining government reports and the
effects of decriminalization in her own community, Schuchard decided
that adults didn't have a *right* to smoke pot, or a *right* to stay out of jail
for its use. Marijuana was still illegal, after all, and its effects on children
were still unknown. If her own daughter was going to be a guinea pig in
a dangerous national experiment, Schuchard decided, she would have
to fight back.

In just a few years, legions of concerned parents would join
Schuchard's "parent movement," as it became known. Built on the idea
that parents had every right to question marijuana's long-term effects
on children's bodies, and therefore to be skeptical of state and federal

decriminalization, the movement encouraged parents across the country to learn as much as they could about the drug and to launch lobbying campaigns to convince legislators to pass anti-paraphernalia laws. Within a few years, the group Schuchard founded in her living room would give birth to a national movement that perfectly aligned with the growing social conservatism of the incoming Reagan era, bringing a strict antidrug voice to arguments about children's safety and the dangers of federal overreach. For the tens of thousands of parents across the country who were struggling with adolescent marijuana use and were hungry for solutions, Schuchard's parent movement seemed like the perfect answer, one that would allow them to increase control over their families while combating a drug culture they saw as encroaching on their everyday lives.

With their effective arguments and ability to tap into people's fears and concerns, parent activists turned grassroots marijuana activism on its head. After years of pro-decriminalization campaigns that emphasized an adult's right to access marijuana without the threat of arrest, parent activists argued that children had an equally important right: the right to grow up drug-free, away from the influence of a powerful drug culture that made marijuana seem fun and cool. By the late 1970s, this argument took on increased urgency as rates of adolescent marijuana use spiked nationwide, even as decriminalization laws continued to be passed. Parents were also able to take up the mantle of grassroots activism because pro-pot activists had become complacent, abandoning membership in NORML and feeling too certain that national decriminalization was only a few years away. Though they seemed unlikely figures to lead a revolution, it was suburban parents, many of them middle-class and well into middle age, who were poised to lead the fight over marijuana rights. "*We* were the real counterculture," Schuchard would later declare. In just a few years, thousands of parents across the country would agree.[3]

•

Atlanta was changing, and Keith Schuchard could feel it. *Time* magazine had reported that "pot-smoking hippies were a key target" of the city's police force in 1968, and "virtually all of Georgia drug law enforcement

resources were directed against pot." But by 1973, after decriminalization in Oregon had generated national headlines and the Georgia state
legislature had reduced first-time possession of an ounce or less from
a felony to a misdemeanor, "only 20% of the state's antidrug campaign
[was] aimed at marijuana."[4] Three years later, as the city prepared to celebrate the Bicentennial, even the state's former governor Jimmy Carter
was launching his presidential campaign by promoting states' right to
decriminalize the drug.

Still, Schuchard didn't expect marijuana to follow her home. First
there was her daughter's change in behavior. Over the previous few
months, Ashley had been transformed from a happy, sunny girl into
someone who was morose and withdrawn. It might have been puberty,
Schuchard thought, and the onset of the teenage years. But then came
the birthday party and the harrowing discovery of her thirteen-year-
old's drug use. At that point, Schuchard knew that her daughter's transformation wasn't due to a hormonal shift—marijuana was turning her
daughter into someone she hardly knew.[5] The next morning brought a
choice. Schuchard could have punished her daughter—grounded her,
forced her to find new friends—and that would have been the end of
that. But it was what she chose to do instead that transformed Schuchard
into one of the most powerful grassroots antidrug activists of the twentieth century, the woman who launched a revolution of angry parents
who would transform the drug war for decades to come.

Schuchard was an activist both in nature and in practice. A strongly
liberal Democrat with ties to the party (her cousin, Charles Manatt,
served as the chairman of the Democratic National Committee from
1981 to 1985), Keith and her husband, Ron, worked for the US Agency
for International Development's "Teachers for East Africa" program
in the early 1960s, prior to completing their PhDs in British literature
at the University of Texas at Austin. From 1962 to 1965, they lived in
Uganda and Kenya (they were in Kenya when Ashley was born) and
helped open and run several high schools as the countries transitioned
to independence. When they returned to America and settled in Atlanta so that Ron could begin work at Emory, both were active in supporting civil rights; they volunteered at voter registration drives and
championed school desegregation. Schuchard, who turned thirty-six

the year she discovered her daughter was drinking and using drugs, saw antidrug activism as a natural extension of her moral duty to "do something" to help those who were oppressed.[6]

It was in forming her first parent group that Schuchard's activism took on its most powerful sheen. Meeting with neighborhood parents, Schuchard discussed the need to retake control: to pool their resources, share information, and collectively enforce new community and family rules. Like the second-wave feminists who gathered in the late 1960s to discuss the problems affecting their lives, Schuchard emphasized "consciousness-raising"—collectively sharing problems and solutions— as a means to understand how their children were being affected by the drug culture. She also emphasized the need to create a community that was both supportive and safe, one that would provide the necessary resources for parents to achieve their goals. By meeting regularly and sharing what they learned, Schuchard explained, "parent peer groups" would "shape and control their children's immediate environment" (by collectively banning access to magazines like *High Times* and implementing a zero-tolerance policy toward drug use) and "develop an 'extended family' with uniform rules and expectations." By forming a united front—which their children would derisively call the "Nosy Parents Association"—Schuchard hoped her grassroots efforts at "parent power" could "outmaneuver 'peer power'" and ultimately overcome "dope power."[7]

Schuchard, a scholar by trade, then learned as much as she could about marijuana. Searching through the available government reports, Schuchard learned that most federal agencies considered marijuana smoking to be harmless and argued that enforcing marijuana laws was less of a priority than targeting drugs like speed and heroin. As far as scientific research was concerned, the few reports that studied marijuana's health effects were useless: they made no distinction between how the drug affected children and how it affected adults. Instead, the overwhelming majority of the available information argued that the federal government should focus on the treatment and rehabilitation of heroin users and promoted the belief that decriminalization would help marijuana smokers by keeping them away from dangerous criminals in jails.[8]

Meanwhile, a survey from the University of Michigan found that, at the same time the government was supporting decriminalization, rates of adolescent marijuana use were rising, even among the very young. In 1976, 56 percent of the nation's high school seniors reported that they had tried marijuana: 27 percent had used it in the past month, 26 percent smoked weekly, and 6 percent smoked daily. Younger children were also using the drug: one out of twenty-five twelve- to thirteen-year-olds used marijuana monthly, as did one out of seven fourteen- to fifteen-year-olds. Eighty percent of high school students and 60 percent of junior high school students also reported that marijuana was "easy to get."[9]

With this many students admitting to smoking, the few negative reports that Schuchard could find about marijuana were especially frightening admonitions against youthful drug use. Dr. Gabriel Nahas, an anesthesiologist at Columbia University who became one of the parent movement's most trusted medical advisers in the 1980s, was one of the few doctors conducting research on adolescent marijuana use, and what he had found terrified Schuchard's group. He warned that pot could stunt children's physical and mental growth. It could complicate puberty, causing boys to grow breasts and rendering young girls infertile, and it could destroy chromosomes, resulting in multiple generations impaired by the drug. The drug also, Nahas warned, made young smokers "amotivational"—lethargic, less likely to pay attention in school, and more prone to rebelling against their parents.[10] That was precisely what Schuchard had seen in her own daughter, and she wanted to prevent other children from going through the same thing.

Unsatisfied after poring over medical journals and pediatric reviews, Schuchard decided to demand action from the federal government. On March 17, 1977, she wrote what she called her "mad mom letter" to Dr. Robert DuPont, the head of the National Institute on Drug Abuse (NIDA). She hoped that DuPont, as a drug researcher himself, might understand and aid her mission. Describing herself as "a lifelong liberal Democrat" worried about the nation's "short-sighted and unnecessary capitulation to an increasingly aggressive and commercialized 'popular drug culture,'" Schuchard explained that she belonged to a group of parents who were concerned about the growing rate of marijuana use among the young. Noting that she could not find any federal acknowledgment of the "serious behavioral changes" and "deterioration of values" that she saw accompanying adolescent drug use, Schuchard expressed doubts about the country's, and the government's, current relationship with marijuana. The heart of the drug problem, Schuchard argued, "was not heroin addiction, which affected a small, marginalized population, but pot smoking, which touched so many families."[11]

DuPont was leery at first; in many ways, he embodied the decriminalization-supporting federal approach that so angered Schuchard's parent group. Appointed to lead NIDA in 1973, DuPont was a graduate of Harvard and Emory's medical school (where he attended classes with the leader of the Drug Abuse Council and NORML supporter Thomas Bryant) and a psychiatrist who prioritized treatment over incarceration. He had years of experience treating heroin addicts, starting when he worked in Washington's Department of Corrections in the late 1960s as the city struggled with race riots and high rates of drug abuse. Over 45 percent of the city's inmates tested positive for heroin; by using methadone, a synthetic opioid that mimicked heroin's physical effects without the sense of euphoria, DuPont was able to wean many of them off the drug, greatly reducing rates of recidivism along the way. Marijuana's effects paled in comparison to the danger and destruction of opiate abuse, DuPont said, and he had little real interest in or concern about the drug.[12]

Heroin remained his primary focus when DuPont transitioned to leading NIDA, with widespread methadone treatment as his ultimate goal. Meanwhile, marijuana decriminalization seemed, for DuPont and many of his staff, like the simplest, most logical way to keep pot smokers out of prison and away from harder drugs. At a press conference in February 1976, DuPont told reporters that "there is no question that alcohol and tobacco are causing us far more health problems than marijuana does. Personally, my view is that we do not have to threaten young people with imprisonment to discourage use of marijuana." Most interestingly, DuPont seemed relatively unconcerned about adolescent use of the drug. When asked what "ammunition" DuPont could give "to a parent of a teenaged child to discourage him from consuming marijuana," DuPont replied, "I think it's important for the parent not to get so terribly uptight about whether the child does or does not use any particular drug once or twice, or even a number of times, recreationally. This is certainly the approach I have [with] my children."[13]

DuPont was slow to respond to Schuchard's letter. It seemed emotional and overwrought, coming from the very epitome of the "uptight" parent he had warned about the year before. But as leader of NIDA, he was required to respond to letters from the public, and he was moved enough by her predicament to have an assistant arrange a phone call. DuPont even went to Atlanta in early June 1977 to visit with Schuchard's parent group. Listening to the stories and struggles of the parents and young people there, DuPont became convinced that he was wrong about marijuana, and that these parents and children were right. In an interview in 2000, DuPont recalled that Schuchard "made a very simple point that I still think is very profound. She said, 'When we're talking about marijuana, let's distinguish between marijuana use for kids and marijuana use for adults.' . . . I had never heard that distinction before, so that was really very striking. She also made very clear that support for decriminalization was seen as being pro-pot, and that had a very negative influence. It had a negative influence in her life, and a negative influence in people's families' lives across the country, and I was personally responsible for that."[14]

DuPont returned to Washington a new man. Nine months later, in March 1978, DuPont left his post at NIDA to found the Institute of Behavior and Health (IBH), a consulting firm located in Rockville, Maryland, that was a forerunner for what would become a thriving new antidrug industry in America in the 1980s. IBH produced drug tests that could be used in schools and workplaces, "encouraged" changes in federal and state drug laws, and promoted strategies that reduced demand for illegal drugs. Before he left NIDA, DuPont held a press conference at which he admitted that he had been wrong about marijuana. "I made a mistake. Decriminalization is a bad idea," he told the press. "Marijuana is not non-addictive. In many ways, it's the worst of all the illegal drugs."[15]

The transformation of Robert DuPont, a former decriminalization proponent who became one of the parent movement's most vocal supporters, was Schuchard's first major victory. DuPont was also instrumental in introducing Schuchard's ideas to the rest of the country. Prior to leaving his post at NIDA, DuPont commissioned Schuchard to write a guidebook about her experience forming the first parent group. *Parents, Peers, and Pot,* Schuchard's eighty-page booklet published under her maiden name Marsha Manatt, was both a guide to forming a parent group and a denunciation of the nation's commercialized drug culture. Although scientists at NIDA distrusted her claims, criticizing her sometimes hyperbolic prose, and it earned Schuchard "a minimal amount—almost enough to cover baby-sitting expenses," the book was an enormous success: after its release in 1979, the institute received requests for over 1 million copies, making *Parents, Peers, and Pot* one of the most popular publications in NIDA's history.[16] In a matter of years, *Parents, Peers, and Pot* had helped spread Schuchard's parent group model across the country, with "Nosy Parents Associations" forming in almost every state by 1983.

Another way DuPont supported Schuchard was by introducing her to Thomas "Buddy" Gleaton, an associate health professor at Georgia State University. Gleaton was a longtime antidrug activist who had hosted a conference for drug prevention specialists every year since 1974. Given the pro-marijuana climate of the time, these tended to be dull affairs. So Gleaton was deeply impressed when, on DuPont's recommendation, Schuchard came into his office in May 1978 and spoke for over five hours about her research, her fears about marijuana's impact on young bodies and minds, and the parent groups she had already helped to form. She also described her profound disappointment that, besides DuPont, very few federal officials seemed to care about her findings. If Gleaton allowed her to speak at his conference, she said, she would tell parents to "trust your gut instincts. You have every right to worry about the use of any psychoactive drugs, especially illegal drugs, by your child." It was exactly what Gleaton wanted to hear.

Gleaton invited Schuchard to be the keynote speaker at his upcoming conference, and later that month, on May 25, she gave her first public antidrug address. Schuchard presented "The Family Versus the Drug Culture" before a crowd of 150 professors, parents, and officials like DuPont. She opened her speech by arguing that she "really [had] no business being here. I am not a professional drug expert. I am a literary historian by profession, and a parent by an act—or several acts—of God. But, during the past two years, I have become a kind of do-it-yourself drug abuse professional, because I learned that I would have to—if, as a parent, I wanted to understand or deal with the distressing growth of adolescent drug and drinking problems." She went on to present her indictment of the adolescent drug lifestyle:

> The youngster who is quietly stoned during school does not learn math or grammar or biology, or how to cope with boredom, pressure, and discipline. He will not have much going for him when he leaves the protective nest—home and high school—as an eighteen-year-old. The real world out there is tough, and it does not make excuses for the supposed young adult who befuddled his adolescence with marijuana or any other drugs, for the youngster who messed up or opted out of his apprenticeship to adulthood.[17]

After outlining the debilitating physical effects of marijuana use on youth ("the skinny body, the slack muscle development, the scraggly beard, the listless stride, the slouching posture, and the flatness of facial expression"), Schuchard called all parents to come together to help stop childhood drug abuse. "Regardless of their sophistication about drugs or their political liberalism or conservatism," Schuchard argued, all parents shared the same "sickening feeling" when they realized that their child was using drugs. Schuchard used the speech to promote her idea of active and engaged "parental peer pressure." For troubled parents who were worried about their kids, a parent peer group could make a positive change, she said—perhaps the most important change in a child's life.

Journalists were also at the conference, and within a week articles published by the Associated Press had spread Schuchard's message from Miami to Albany, New York, outlining her history as a "do-it-yourself drug abuse professional" and quoting praise for the parent movement from DuPont. "You folks here are in the vanguard of a radical shift in drug education—the energy and power [is] coming from the community, the families," DuPont told parent activists in attendance after Schuchard's speech. DuPont also argued that the movement should steer clear of the federal bureaucracy he had just departed, since it would only hinder their efforts. "You're not under those constraints on a local level," he told parent activists, "and that's good." DuPont argued that government officials should show restraint as well, not only because their actions had done more harm than good, but because the subject of drug abuse involved "complicated questions of personal values as well as medical matters" that, as he had recently learned, were better left to families than bureaucrats.[18]

Several of the articles on the conference also featured Gleaton's office telephone number, and for weeks afterward his phone kept ringing with requests from parents across the country for more information about marijuana. At first Gleaton was overwhelmed, but he and Schuchard quickly realized that the calls presented an opportunity. A month after the conference, Schuchard and Gleaton created a new organization they called PRIDE (Parents' Resource Institute for Drug Education), which was housed in Gleaton's office at Georgia State. The purpose of PRIDE, as Schuchard outlined in the organization's first newsletter in June 1979, was "to educate parents about the current trends in drug and drinking behavior among children and adolescents," in order to help them "organize into effective groups to counteract these negative influences." "We believe a child's parents are his best bulwark against drug involvement," she wrote. "We also believe that the universal instinct of parents to protect their young is society's best bulwark against the expansion of the commercialized drug culture."[19]

For PRIDE's library, Schuchard and Gleaton collected the few reports they could find on marijuana's negative effects, as well as books, articles, audiotapes, and movies, and made these resources available for rent or purchase. For $5, PRIDE sold packets of Schuchard's anti-marijuana research and an early guide on forming a parent group. Each spring in Atlanta, Gleaton continued to host an annual drug prevention conference, now renamed the PRIDE Southeast Drug Conference, where hundreds of concerned parents, doctors, teachers, and drug abuse professionals from across the country began gathering to discuss the issue of adolescent drug abuse. By 1980, the conference had expanded from one day to three and featured workshops, films, and a banquet, alongside presentations by Gabriel Nahas and Robert DuPont and speeches from sympathetic Georgia legislators, including Senator Sam Nunn and Representative Billy Lee Evans. Just two years after Schuchard first approached Gleaton in his office, her new parent-centered approach to marijuana had inspired hundreds of parent groups to form across the country and hundreds more people to come to Atlanta each year to protest the effects of decriminalization on kids.

•

What was even more remarkable was that Schuchard and Gleaton weren't the only activists rallying parents against pot in Atlanta. Sue Rusche, a friend and neighbor of the Schuchards, was also concerned about adolescent drug use, though she hadn't joined Schuchard's initial parent group and wasn't a member of PRIDE. Instead, when Rusche realized that the drug culture had invaded Druid Hills, she was less interested in educating parents about the dangers of marijuana and more committed to influencing state and federal politicians to pass increasingly powerful antidrug legislation, especially laws that would target the booming paraphernalia market.

Rusche (pronounced ROO-she) first became aware of Atlanta's paraphernalia problem in the fall of 1977, when she went into a store to purchase a *Star Wars* record for her two young sons. There she was shocked by the open display of pipes, bongs, and other paraphernalia available for purchase. With their bright colors and shiny forms, the items looked like toys, and they seemed specifically designed to appeal to kids. Frisbees that doubled as hash pipes, fake soda cans that unscrewed to hide drugs, and joint-rolling instruction manuals printed for *Tots Who Toke* infuriated Rusche, who quickly dragged her children out of the store. Already "reeling from the shock of drug use by neighborhood children as young as 12 and 13," which Rusche had learned about from Schuchard, Rusche was horrified by the toys, gadgets, and magazines that seemed like little more than "teaching tools that broadcast messages in sharp contrast to the teachings of most families."[20]

Like Schuchard, Rusche was an atypical Southerner, an avowed liberal who was not naive about marijuana use. Born in Ohio in 1938, she had studied art in New York City before moving with her husband, Harry, an English professor, to Atlanta in 1962. While Harry joined Emory's English Department and befriended Ron Schuchard, Rusche dreamed of working with Martin Luther King Jr. Trained in advertising, Rusche assisted the civil rights movement by working briefly for the Southern Regional Council's voter education project before opening her own graphic design studio and designing corporate logos and brands. A social drinker who had tried marijuana a few times, Rusche was primarily a heavy cigarette smoker with a longtime addiction to nicotine. By 1977, when she had left her company to raise her sons full-time, what bothered Rusche most about the drug culture was how slick it had become—how captivating its graphics were and how "damn *good*" it was at selling drug-related products to kids.[21]

Unlike Schuchard, however, Rusche didn't believe that education alone was the answer. After her trip to the record store, Rusche formed her own activist group, in November 1977, which she called DeKalb (County) Families in Action (FIA). At its core, FIA was dedicated to securing the passage of anti-paraphernalia legislation, which Rusche believed was the most effective way to battle the drug culture spreading across the United States. Marijuana was frightening, and parents had to learn its dangers—something that parent groups and PRIDE could certainly help with—but they also needed to take action, Rusche argued, against the market forces that had encouraged adolescent marijuana use in the first place. "Paraphernalia was a graphic illustration that there are people in the world intent on promoting illicit drugs to kids in order to increase profits by expanding the market of drug users," she wrote in her 1979 guidebook *How to Form a Families in Action Group in Your Community*. Shops stocked with pipes and bongs were "the most visible symbol of a culture that is saturated with 'use drugs' messages."

But there was a bright side to paraphernalia as well, Rusche reasoned. Paraphernalia presented an opportunity, she wrote, "a third force between parent and child." Because head shops and toy-shaped paraphernalia were so blatant in their appeals to kids, they forced even skeptical parents to push "through their own fear and guilt and compel them into action."[22] For the next two years, Rusche purchased as many pipes, bongs, toys, and magazines as she could and took them on a tour of PTA meetings, churches, and community groups. There, in front of audiences of concerned parents, she would display the numerous products that enticed children into drug use. Her "bong shows" made her a local legend and proved to many that she wasn't exaggerating the problem. When parents saw BuzzBee Frisbees and *Tots Who Toke,* they could no longer deny the issue, she said. And in that sense, "the head shops and the paraphernalia were a gift," she said. "They helped parents struggling with children with drugs to come out of the closet."[23]

Rusche's energy and drive led her to become an effective lobbyist. Within a year, she began courting individuals, including legal scholars, ministers, pediatricians, and teachers, to join FIA's board of directors. Serving as FIA's executive director, she was able to gain entry into Georgia's General Assembly by convincing Lawrence "Bud" Stumbaugh, a Democratic state senator, to serve as FIA's president. Through the effectiveness of Rusche's "bong shows," and with an ally in the Georgia senate, FIA was able to pressure state legislators to propose laws banning products that many of those legislators hadn't known existed. Rusche even alerted the Atlanta-based Coca-Cola Company that paraphernalia companies were using its products as "stash cans" to hide marijuana supplies. Coca-Cola, ever protective of its product, would later win a lawsuit against a California manufacturer that was buying Coca-Cola off the shelf and converting the cans into places to hide pot. That company and several of its distributors were forced to destroy thousands of dollars' worth of trademark-infringing goods.[24]

By April 1978, less than a year after FIA had formed, it secured its first victory. That month Georgia governor George Busbee signed two anti-paraphernalia bills into law, both of which were initially proposed by Stumbaugh. The first bill made it illegal to sell drug paraphernalia to "an unmarried person less than 18 years old." The second bill made it illegal to sell any drug-related literature, including periodicals like *High Times,* to minors. "The intent of the two laws is to keep children out of *any* store that chooses to sell drug paraphernalia or drug literature," Rusche said, and to force merchants who sold ordinary merchandise "to choose whether or not adding a line of drug paraphernalia is worth giving up their teenage customers."[25]

But Atlanta's paraphernalia retailers weren't so easily cowed. Hours after the bills were signed, owners of nine Georgia head shops and one paraphernalia wholesaler brought suit against the state government, contesting the laws' constitutionality, particularly the ban on literature, on First Amendment grounds. Writers at *High Times* were apoplectic at having their magazine censored in this way, especially in the home state of a president who had recently run on decriminalization. After

all, as an editorial in the magazine argued, the paraphernalia industry was a good thing. It provided "employment for hundreds of thousands, contributes millions of dollars in taxes and provides citizens to
whom the 'straight' business world has no appeal with an incentive to
lead useful lives as productive members of our free economy." After the
laws were passed, the magazine even organized a protest and smoke-in,
where hundreds of Atlantans gathered and wore I LOVE MY HEAD SHOP
T-shirts in defense of the drug paraphernalia industry.[26]

A year later, the case that Atlanta's head shops brought against the
Georgia General Assembly went to the US Fifth Circuit Court of Appeals, where Judge Richard Freeman overturned both laws, declaring
them unconstitutionally vague. Meanwhile, growing anti-paraphernalia
agitation had done nothing to stem the industry's growth: by December 1978, paraphernalia sales topped $350 million a year, and subscrip-
tions to *High Times* peaked at 424,000, earning the magazine's owner,
the newly formed Trans-High Corporation, $1.5 million in profits from
ads. Industry representatives also refused to believe that they were in
any way responsible for adolescent drug use. For many, the parents' anger was misplaced. "Getting high is a reality and we just admit to it,"
Victoria Horn, spokeswoman for *High Times,* told the *Washington Post*
that month. "We're not corrupting anybody."[27]

Despite the court's rulings against the laws, Rusche was buoyed
enough by their initial passage to include the text of the bills in *How to
Form a Families in Action Group in Your Community,* alongside an out-
line of a speech that parent activists could use to support similar measures in their own states. Soon, FIA's anti-paraphernalia campaign was
spreading nationwide. "Several other states, counties, cities and towns
have either introduced or enacted laws similar to Georgia's," Rusche
wrote in 1979, and many of these laws would hold up in court. By 1980,
anti-paraphernalia legislation was passed in Colorado, Connecticut,
Delaware, Louisiana, Maryland, and Nebraska, as well as in towns like
Hollywood, Florida; Novi, Michigan; and Oaklawn, Illinois.[28]

Parent activists continued to agitate against paraphernalia distributors because rates of adolescent marijuana use continued to rise. By
1978, with a dozen states having decriminalized marijuana and the paraphernalia industry hitting its peak, 37.1 percent of high school seniors
reported smoking pot in the past month, and 9 percent reported using

the drug every day—a 50 percent increase in just two years. Beyond an increase in daily smoking, students also reported smoking more: the average high school smoker was consuming three and a half joints daily, up from one or two in 1976. Students also reported falling asleep more often in class, forgetting their homework, failing tests, and neglecting school.[29] Terrified by the effects of rising adolescent marijuana use, more parents were turning to groups like PRIDE and FIA to combat the drug culture, which they felt was spiraling out of control. Schuchard, Gleaton, and Rusche, who quickly turned anti-marijuana activism into a full-time career, were only too happy to help.

Spokespeople for *High Times* may have been reluctant to admit that they were "corrupting" anybody, but writers at the magazine were starting to realize that, as far as the national conversation about marijuana was concerned, it was parents like Rusche and Schuchard who seemed more engaged in the debate. After years of marching on Washington, the bulk of the nation's smokers were growing complacent, lulled into the false belief that decriminalization would soon be the law of the land with no effort on their part. The parents' war against paraphernalia made some writers at *High Times* realize that the first shots in a new battle over marijuana were being fired, and that it was time for the nation's smokers to resume their fight. "America is waging war on us," a 1978 editorial warned. A battle between grassroots activists was brewing, with calls on both sides to stand their ground. With head shops increasingly under attack, "we know only that pot smokers must continue to resist, to fight back, to the last," the editorial concluded. "And we must fight this battle ourselves."[30]

Michael Antonoff, the editor of *Accessories Digest* (formerly *Paraphernalia Digest*), also recognized the impact of parent activists and feared for the future of the legalization campaign. In a guest editorial in *High Times* called "Those Mothers Are Trampling Adult Rights," Antonoff denounced the parent activists' "new kind of marijuana McCarthyism" for focusing on paraphernalia manufacturers and distributors—people who, like him, were being punished by "thought police" for selling legal products, even if they were for illegal purposes. "The New Right has in the last two years successfully shifted the public spotlight away from decriminalization to the plea of 'save our children,'" Antonoff wrote. "No one wants children smoking pot, but to scapegoat by stigmatizing legitimate business makes as much sense as banning swizzle sticks to prevent alcoholism."

But it was the parent movement's increasingly powerful activism that concerned Antonoff the most. "Mothers for a straight America carry signs and harass politicians. They circulate petitions. Their guerilla theater occurs in shopping malls," he continued. "They know how to commandeer the attention of the media. They're not in this to win friends. They're resigned to the possibility that another generation may hate them for what they are trying to change." Although Antonoff may have despised their tactics, he couldn't deny that parent activists were effective. In just a few years, they had taken the mantle of grassroots activism from the pro-pot activists who'd held it before. "Mothers for a straight America have become the activists of the '80s while those of us who were the ones doing the marching a decade ago sit on our butts. While Atlanta burns, we roll another one and yawn," he lamented. "Where are the millions of adult consumers? The vast majority don't seem to care that a right they have taken for granted is now being taken away."[31]

Antonoff raised legitimate concerns. After years of seemingly unstoppable success for marijuana supporters, a new force was emerging in Atlanta—one that, only two years after it was first sparked by a backyard birthday party in Druid Hills, had the potential to halt decriminalization in its tracks. By 1978, a growing parent army, led by Schuchard, Gleaton, and Rusche, was seeking to change laws by talking directly to politicians about marijuana, emphasizing children's safety over adult rights. And soon, after a drug scandal enveloped the White House, lawmakers in Washington—including Jimmy Carter—would be willing to agree.

7

THE DOWNFALL OF PETER BOURNE

THE ONLY CONSENSUS regarding the party that prompted Peter Bourne's ouster from the Carter administration is that it happened on December 10, 1977, in a large townhouse on S Street NW, just north of fashionable Dupont Circle in Washington, DC. Over 400 people crowded into the house to celebrate the Christmas season with Keith Stroup and the rest of NORML's staff, including high-profile guests like Christie Hefner and Hunter S. Thompson as well as a wide array of scientists, lawyers, legislators, congressional aides, Yippie activists, hard-core drug smugglers, and reporters from the city's leading newspapers and magazines.

Stroup's parties were known to be cutting-edge, and those who attended were Washington's avant-garde, all of them excited about decriminalization and hopeful for a more open future for marijuana. Waiters passed around silver trays laden with drinks, hors d'oeuvres, and caviar, which were served alongside prerolled joints, and the lavish entertainment included a rock band that played all night and a psychedelic juggler who tossed balls up into flashing strobe lights. But the evening's biggest surprise was the arrival of Peter Bourne, Jimmy Carter's chief drug policy adviser, whose attendance was, for many, a pleasant surprise. After smiling and shaking numerous hands, Bourne was escorted upstairs to a room where a more private party was being held, and that was where the trouble began. As some attendees later said, while Bourne was seated next to Stroup, he took several hits off an offered joint and asked to snort a line of cocaine.

By the winter of 1977, Stroup must have felt that his connection to the Carter administration was unshakable. He was welcome in the White House, and Carter and Bourne had used his draft of a major drug policy announcement declaring Carter's support for federal decriminalization in a message to Congress that past August. After seven years of hard work building NORML from the ground up, the president's chief drug adviser was attending NORML's holiday party and everything finally seemed to be going Stroup's way. With marijuana decriminalized in eleven states and seemingly more to come, Stroup was ready to ring in 1978 with a bang.

When allegations about Bourne's behavior at the Christmas party made national headlines eight months later, however, the men's relationship imploded, and it spelled the end of their respective careers, as well as the end of federal and state support for decriminalization. Bourne's belief that marijuana was relatively harmless had long endeared him to Stroup, but by July 1978, Stroup had grown increasingly suspicious of both Bourne's and Carter's commitment to decriminalizing the drug. Bourne and Stroup had been fighting for months over the Mexican government's use of the herbicide paraquat on its illegal marijuana crops: Bourne believed that Mexico had the right to destroy the crops, while Stroup was horrified at paraquat's potential effect on smokers if surviving plants were harvested and trafficked into the United States. Increasingly angry over Bourne's refusal to end Mexico's use of paraquat and frustrated with the president after months of inaction on federal decriminalization, Stroup leaked news of Bourne's alleged drug use at the NORML party to the press, hoping to push Bourne and Carter to action. But even the leak was filled with confusion: there was little agreement among anonymous witnesses on the details, and Bourne himself refused to admit that he had used cocaine, on that night or at any time before or since.

The downfall of Peter Bourne wasn't entirely Keith Stroup's fault, however. Bourne sealed his own fate that summer when it was discovered that he wrote an illegal prescription for Quaaludes for his attractive young secretary, using a false name. When Bourne's prescription scandal was compounded by allegations of his own illegal drug use, he was swiftly forced to resign. Days later, Carter admonished his staff against any illegal drug use, and his support for federal decriminalization disappeared. By fall, states that had been considering new marijuana laws silently removed those bills from debate.

Ironically, Bourne's resignation spelled the end of Stroup's career as well. Members of NORML's board of directors were furious that Stroup had done something that cost NORML its closest connection to the White House, and rank-and-file members hounded Stroup with angry phone calls and letters, demanding that he leave his position. Though he held on for an awkward additional five months, Stroup finally recognized that his continued presence at NORML's helm was doing the organization more harm than good. In December 1978, eight years after founding the group, NORML's director also resigned.

The year 1978 should have witnessed Keith Stroup's ultimate success—a flood of additional states passing new marijuana laws and the president decriminalizing the drug at the federal level. Instead, the downfall of Peter Bourne and the subsequent downfall of Keith Stroup brought the country's first experiment with decriminalization to a close, thwarting marijuana law reform for decades to come. As parent activists warned of marijuana's negative effects on kids, and paraphernalia shops continued to cater to young customers, few respected leaders were left in Washington to defend marijuana and its users or generate support for additional decriminalization laws in the states. Moreover, an energetic new wave of parent activists traveled to Washington in the aftermath of Bourne's departure to exert their growing influence over his successor, who, with the president now vocally admonishing against drug use, was quick to adopt their perspective on the dangers, rather than the decriminalization, of pot.

•

It was late 1977, only a few months after Carter had advocated federal decriminalization to Congress, and Keith Stroup's relationship with the White House, rather than becoming stronger, was growing tense. At the same time Carter advocated a change in federal marijuana laws, his administration was also supporting the Mexican government's controversial plan to spray paraquat on thousands of acres of illegal marijuana that grew across the country. Mexican antidrug agents had used paraquat on illegal opium fields for years, using helicopters donated by the United States. Mexican officials had recently come to Bourne requesting permission to use the helicopters to spray marijuana fields as well. Neither Bourne nor Carter felt strongly about the initiative, and they told Mexican officials that their government could use the helicopters as they liked, so long as they didn't require the American government to provide the herbicide as well. As Bourne later recalled, "It wasn't a high priority for us."[1]

But it was a high priority for Keith Stroup, who feared for the health and safety of the growing number of pot smokers who got their drug from across the border. Tests done on Mexican marijuana showed that 1 percent of the marijuana available on the East Coast, in the Midwest, and in the Pacific Northwest was contaminated by paraquat, and over 12 percent of the pot available in the Southwest contained traces of the chemical. Stroup was infuriated that Mexican traffickers were continuing to harvest and ship surviving leaves to the United States. Though he didn't know the effects of smoking paraquat-laced marijuana, he feared that the Carter administration was committing a form of "cultural genocide" by allowing the poisoned drug to enter the American supply. Despite NORML's years of working to convince legislators that smokers were a legitimate voting constituency, the federal government seemed to be backtracking on marijuana issues, even as it advocated federal decriminalization. Supporting the Mexican government's plan by permitting it to use paraquat and allowing a poisoned substance to cross the border showed, in Stroup's view, that the Carter administration didn't actually care about marijuana smokers or their health. Bourne, on the other hand, reasoned that "marijuana was illegal. The Mexicans had every right to destroy it."[2]

To Stroup, Bourne's support for the paraquat spraying was tantamount to treason. Despite the close relationship between NORML and the White House, Stroup's growing anger over the paraquat issue and Bourne's reluctance to shift position were beginning to drive the groups apart.[3] Stroup came out forcefully against paraquat spraying, telling reporters about the alleged dangers of the herbicide and blaming the Carter administration for not changing its stance. Then Bourne turned down a speaking engagement at NORML's annual conference in the fall of 1977. He claimed to have declined because of his embarrassment over people smoking pot in the back of the room the previous year, but in truth, he chose not to speak because of the growing tensions between him and Stroup.

Still, Stroup continued to recognize what an asset he had in Bourne. A positive relationship with Carter's chief drug adviser gave Stroup access to the White House, and losing that access would quickly render NORML's mission moot. So, three months later, he put aside his anger long enough to invite Bourne to NORML's annual Christmas party, which was going to be held on December 10, 1977. And Bourne, who recognized the value of good relations with Stroup, having turned to him repeatedly for advice, accepted. "Because we had enjoyed their support in the past, I agreed to go to their party," Bourne told *People* the following year. If he didn't, "Keith was concerned that it would look as if there was a rift between NORML and the administration"—an image that neither Bourne nor Stroup wanted to project.[4]

Given the wave of successful decriminalization measures across the country, this party promised to be NORML's biggest one yet. Stroup had always hosted an annual event, usually in his small house on N Street NW, but this year, buoyed by changing state drug laws and Carter's support for federal decriminalization, he rented a large townhouse downtown and invited over 500 people. As the first wave of partygoers rolled in, Stroup remembered seeing "lots of Capitol Hill staffers and aides who wouldn't normally be seen in such a risky atmosphere but were attracted by NORML's cachet, along with regular supporters of ours who were happy to act as if marijuana were already legalized inside the townhouse."[5] Other attendees included lawyers, state legislators, and other young politicians from around America who had worked with NORML on marijuana law reform, as well as journalists, Yippie activists, major marijuana growers and dealers, and pilots who smuggled the drug in from abroad. Joints and drinks were passed around, and as the night went on, so was cocaine. With such a varied guest list, the party was, as one attendee put it, a coming out of sorts, the place where "the drug culture met the Establishment—[and] everybody came out of the closet at last."[6]

In reality, there were two parties going on. The first was on the main floor of the house, where guests, crammed into every room, were drinking, sharing drugs, and flirting. Upstairs, in a small bedroom packed with a few of NORML's highest-profile supporters, a select group was enjoying a private party of their own. Christie Hefner sat alongside Hunter S. Thompson and Tom Forçade, and together they shared a particularly potent joint with Bill Paley, son of CBS founder William Paley, and Robert Kennedy's son David. Stroup, who arrived fashionably late but entered the house to much fanfare and adulation, went up to the bedroom shortly afterward to relax and enjoy his success. He had just taken a drag from a joint when a wave of excitement spread through the party downstairs: Peter Bourne had arrived, alone, a little after 10:00 P.M.

Bourne hadn't wanted to come, but he also knew that, in Washington, appearances were everything: skipping NORML's Christmas party would have made him look like he was snubbing the group, and that was an image he didn't want to project. Still, he was surprised by the warm welcome he received. Immediately upon entering the party, people crowded around him, shaking his hand and thanking him for his work on decriminalization. For NORML's supporters, Bourne was nothing less than a celebrity—the man who had Carter's ear and who actively advocated for changing federal drug laws. So it was only natural for Bourne to be swept upstairs shortly after he arrived to join the elite party on the second floor.

What happened next has been the subject of speculation for decades, with numerous articles written on the matter and several conflicting eyewitness reports. The only thing known for sure is that Bourne made his way to the party in the upstairs bedroom. Several "unnamed witnesses" later told reporters that Bourne proceeded to take several hits off a joint, and then asked if Stroup could get him some coke. Stroup did, and in a small group that included Stroup, Bourne, and Craig Copetas, a writer for *High Times*, lines of cocaine were laid out on a mirror, and Bourne snorted "cocaine into both nostrils through rolled-up currency in a bedroom with about a dozen other persons," as one anonymous source later told the *Washington Post*. Afterward, Stroup and Bourne descended the staircase to mingle, and shortly after that, Bourne left the party. Still, his brief presence was so important that Mark Heutlinger, NORML's business manager who served as the party's doorman that night, told him before he left, "We really appreciate your coming, Dr. Bourne. You don't know what this means to us."[7]

This is only one version of the story, however. As the events became public months later, the timeline shifted with each retelling, and little consensus could be reached on how many times Bourne snorted or smoked, what kind of paraphernalia was used, or even how many people were in the room. Bourne himself repeatedly denied using any illegal drugs that night and continues to deny using them to this day.[8] Still, Bourne had long expressed openness toward cocaine, which, like marijuana, he considered relatively harmless—"probably the most benign of illicit drugs currently in widespread use," as he wrote in the *Washington Drug Review* in 1974. He argued that "at least as strong a case could probably be made for legalizing it as for legalizing marijuana."[9] In any event, what is beyond doubt is that on December 10, 1977, Peter Bourne was in a room where people were openly using cocaine, and his presence there ultimately ended his career as a White House policy adviser.

Still, the world might never have known about Bourne's presence in the bedroom at NORML's Christmas party if it hadn't been for Keith Stroup. Despite Bourne's attempt at mending their relationship, Stroup's issues with the Carter administration were mounting as 1977 became 1978. "I was seriously angry at Bourne and the Carter administration for their refusal to stop spraying paraquat on marijuana fields in Mexico," Stroup said. "I was disappointed by their failure to provide more support for our various decriminalization proposals pending around the country, and I felt no need to be loyal to Bourne."[10] A month after the party, Stroup continued to talk to the press about the issue of paraquat-laced marijuana, and he wrote a letter to Secretary of State Cyrus Vance and the leader of the Drug Enforcement Administration, Peter Bensinger, complaining about the government's continued support for paraquat use. "A number of recent federal government reports and scientific studies have acknowledged that marijuana is a relatively harmless plant, but now, with the use of herbicides, the United States government may be turning it into the 'killer weed' which it propagandized against in the 1930s, '40s and '50s," Stroup wrote. "How can our government, in good conscience, urge the spraying of marijuana with extremely toxic herbicides without first considering the health consequences of those who smoke it?"[11]

Stroup wasn't alone in fearing for the health of the country's marijuana smokers; several other federal officials were also starting to recognize that paraquat might not be a safe solution for Mexico's and America's problem with marijuana after all. Representative Henry Waxman, a Democrat from California, wrote an impassioned editorial in the *Milwaukee Journal* denouncing the "addle headed policy" of the federal government's support for paraquat and warning of the "sinister harvest's" negative effects. "Now 20% of the marijuana crossing the border from Mexico to the United States is contaminated with paraquat," Waxman wrote. "Health, Education and Welfare Secretary Joseph A. Califano Jr. warned that US marijuana smokers currently face a serious health threat: permanent lung damage from the chemical. Paraquat poisoning may lead to coughing up blood, difficulty in breathing, or other respiratory discomforts."[12] And Daniel Schorr, the nationally syndicated columnist, called paraquat "Carter's cross" to bear, warning that pot smoking, which Schorr felt was relatively harmless, "may have been made hazardous" because of the spray. Schorr compared Bourne's support for paraquat to nothing less than a "Jekyll-Hyde flip": Bourne, who was once "the pot smoker's friend," Schorr warned, had transformed into "Dr. Paraquat, the pot smoker's scourge."[13]

Encouraged by growing public support for eliminating the herbicide's use, in March 1978 Stroup decided to act. If he couldn't get Bourne to stop supporting paraquat, Stroup reasoned, at least he could discredit him. Stroup called Gary Cohn, an aide to the syndicated columnist Jack Anderson, and explained that he had information about a night of illegal drug use and Bourne's subsequent lack of credibility. Anderson's column had long been critical of the "fat cat bureaucrats" who were "boondoggl[ing] public money" for drug prevention efforts, and Cohn kept this information in mind.[14] In later articles, Anderson alluded to drug use by top officials in Carter's administration, but presented the information, given that it was unverified, as rumor.

Then, in July 1978, Bourne condemned himself. Earlier that month, his secretary, Ellen Metsky, a hardworking White House staffer who was often in the office six days a week, had broken up with her boyfriend and was struggling emotionally. Bourne, who described his four-year history of working with Metsky as a "father-daughter" relationship, tried to help Metsky with her problems, but the young woman was distraught. "Why aren't I as tough as I thought I was?" she asked him. "I can't cope. I can't unwind at night."[15] To help Metsky relax, Bourne wrote her a prescription for fifteen Quaaludes, a mild tranquilizer that, though often used to treat insomnia, was also known socially to enhance sex. To protect her privacy, Bourne wrote the prescription under a phony name for her, Sarah Brown. It was "common in normal medical practice," Bourne remembered, to use a pseudonym for patients who wanted to protect their privacy, and Bourne felt comfortable enough using the fake name for Metsky that he signed his own name on the prescription pad.[16]

Because Metsky wasn't feeling well, she sent her roommate, Toby Long, to have the prescription filled at a People's Drugstore in Woodbridge, Virginia. This was where the problems began. The pharmacist asked Long if Sarah Brown was her name, and Long replied that it was not, but it was the name of her roommate, for whom she was picking up the pills. A state pharmacy board inspector present at the time was suspicious of illegal Quaalude prescriptions and called Bourne to verify its legitimacy. Unable to reach Bourne, the inspector then asked Long for more information about her roommate. Long told the truth, telling the inspector that her roommate's name was Ellen Metsky, not Sarah Brown. Despite Bourne's assurance that it was "common in normal medical practice" to use a pseudonym on a prescription, the practice of falsely prescribing commonly abused barbiturates was also illegal, and the pharmacist and inspector contacted the police. Long was arrested on $3,000 bail, and Bourne was notified as to what had occurred.

The rest of the scandal unfolded at whiplash speed. Given the prominent position of the prescribing doctor, news that Bourne was illegally giving sex stimulants to his comely young secretary spread like wildfire through the news. On July 19, the *Washington Post*'s front page screamed, "Carter Aide Signed Fake Quaalude Prescription."[17] The following day Jack Anderson appeared on ABC's *Good Morning America* and announced to the entire nation that Bourne was not just writing phony prescriptions for his secretary: Anderson also had it on good authority (though he didn't mention Stroup's name) that Bourne was using illegal drugs as well.[18] Stroup was contacted by reporters to confirm allegations about NORML's Christmas party, and his response was coy: "I can neither confirm nor deny the story," he said, which Stroup recognized was "an old Washington phrase used by sources who want to drop a dime on an official, but who do not want to be on the record as having said anything incriminating." Still, Stroup knew that "only a fool would have doubted the meaning of my response. I was no longer going to provide a cover for Bourne. If he was unwilling to stop spraying paraquat, or help us decriminalize marijuana across the country, he was on his own."[19]

The pressure on Bourne kept building. After the Quaaludes story broke, White House press secretary Jody Powell disclosed that Bourne had prescribed drugs for at least ten other White House aides, including diet pills for Hamilton Jordan, Carter's overweight chief of staff.[20] Articles about Bourne's "glamorous life" and hedonistic habits soon filled newspapers across the country. Within days, Bourne was being attacked for everything from his salary—$51,000 in 1978, or about $214,000 today—to his "sophisticated style" and political ambition. "Bournes Are Known Social Gadflies" sniffed a headline in the *Washington Star,* and the article quoted a woman who thought Bourne was nothing less than a "snot-nosed social climber." "Every step he made was in anticipation of the next step," said the anonymous Georgian. Another associate confided to the press that they thought Bourne "couldn't say no": "If he were a woman," the source said, "he'd be pregnant every nine months."[21]

Bourne tried to defend himself, to no avail. In an interview with the *Washington Post* the day after the accusations aired, Bourne denied that he had ever used cocaine. "I won't say that I've never used marijuana," he said, "but not since I've been on this job. It's just not my style. I use alcohol."[22] In another interview, with the Associated Press, Bourne said that pot and coke were "everywhere" at the NORML Christmas party, but, "No, no, I was not snorting cocaine."[23] He tried to cool the mounting pressure by agreeing to take a leave of absence and abandon his role as drug adviser, while staying on as a White House staff member. But as articles kept criticizing Bourne for everything from his alleged drug use to putting on European airs, Bourne recognized that he couldn't remove himself from the scandal he had created. Hoping to spare the president some heat, Bourne officially resigned from the White House on July 20, 1978, eight months after the fateful Christmas party with Keith Stroup.

In his friendly but practical resignation letter, Bourne wrote to Carter, "I regret that I must tender you my resignation. You are aware of the difficulty which I face regarding a prescription written in good faith to a troubled person." Bourne apologized for being an "instrument through which others attempt to bring disfavor to you," and concluded with a subtle acknowledgment that he knew America's brief affair with decriminalized marijuana was over: "I fear for the future of the nation far more than I do for the future of your friend, Peter Bourne."[24]

Reaction to Bourne's departure was mixed. Members of Congress described Bourne's departure as everything from a "wise move" to a "deep loss for the administration." Representative Lester L. Wolff, a Democrat from New York and chair of the House Select Committee on Narcotics and Dangerous Drugs, was unsure of the meaning of Bourne's departure. Wolff said that he could not "pass judgment" on Bourne, since he lacked all the background information of the case, but nonetheless he declared that Bourne was "an able individual in the job he had held." Others weren't so sure. Representative Robert Dornan, a Republican from California, said that Bourne's departure was "about the healthiest thing that's happened in the White House in many, many months." And even Stroup was readily talking to the press, admitting that he "did not see [Bourne's departure] with any great sadness." For Stroup, the problem wasn't that Bourne resigned, but that he left the White House over an illegal prescription for a legal drug. Stroup said that Bourne should have been discharged over paraquat, his support for which was nothing less than "atrocious."[25]

Carter simply tried to brush the affair under the rug. In his first prime-time news conference, held the same night Bourne tendered his resignation, the president stayed quiet about the scandal, refusing to address rumors about Bourne's drug use and instead focusing on current events, including the country's battle against a growing inflation rate and Russia's lack of compliance with the Helsinki human rights agreement. In his only concession to the scandal, Carter declared that he "would not want [his] comments inadvertently to affect or to influence" any potential investigations into White House drug use, so he "would have no further comment on this subject." He summed up his feelings on Bourne by calling his departure an "unfortunate occurrence" and noting that Bourne had "never given [him] treatment of any kind."[26]

Four days after Bourne's resignation, Carter released a statement addressing drug use head on. Prior to leaving his position, in an act of retaliation against those in the administration whom Bourne felt had abandoned him, Bourne had told the *New York Times* that he was "leaving behind marijuana and cocaine users in the White House." In response, Carter sent a scolding memo that cracked down hard on the rumors of drug abuse. "I am deeply concerned over recent reports that some members of the White House staff are using drugs," Carter wrote. "I expect every member of the White House staff to obey the law. Whether you agree with the law or whether or not others obey the law is totally irrelevant. You will obey it, or you will seek employment elsewhere. I expect that you will convey my feelings directly and in no uncertain terms to every member of your staff."[27] Already reeling from the loss of Bourne and the negative light being turned on his administration, Carter needed to quash any additional rumors of staff drug use before, or if, they began.

After Bourne's departure, the president also avoided any discussion of decriminalization at either the state or federal level. "Dope? There's really nothing in it for Carter anymore," a former speechwriter for the president told the Pacific News Service. "The only reason Jimmy bothered with the drug question at all was that it was Peter Bourne's specialty. He owed Bourne a lot. But with Bourne gone, and stories floating around that the White House was a dope den, the issue was too hot to walk the wire with. It's not that the White House shifted to a hard line. It's just that nobody there was making any drug policy so the direction was left to the DEA, which has always taken the hard line against grass."[28]

Those involved with decriminalization couldn't stop talking, however, about Bourne's departure, what it meant, and what effects it might have. Nebraska, the last state to decriminalize, had done so in April 1978, three months before Bourne resigned. In the aftermath of the scandal, no other state seriously considered changing its drug laws, and the few states that were considering doing so quietly took those initiatives off the table. Jack Anderson, who continued to write about decriminalization in the aftermath of Bourne's departure, noted in March 1979 that "many states considering the relaxation of marijuana laws will follow the new administration hard line and leave the draconian penalties for pot use on the books." He also predicted that, given the changing nature of marijuana laws, "local police can be expected to crack down on pot smokers."[29] On that point, Anderson was already correct: in 1978, a total of 445,800 people were arrested for marijuana violations, nearly 30,000 more arrests than three years before, and a figure that dwarfed the number of arrests made for the possession of any other drug.[30]

Noting the change in Carter's tone, drug policy experts were increasingly fatalistic, seeing the departure of Carter's chief drug adviser as the death knell for decriminalization. Bob Carr, a pro-decriminalization consultant to the Drug Abuse Council, lamented that "the departure of Peter Bourne marked the beginning of the end of any kind of enlightened drug policy in America. Beyond the White House there was a retreat on all fronts and considerable distrust. The friendly coalition just fell apart. People began to ask each other, 'Can we work together? Can we smoke together?'"[31] Another witness to the NORML Christmas party said that "the drug law reform movement vanished up Peter Bourne's nose."[32]

But others, including the editors at *High Times,* mocked Bourne's dismissal, arguing that, after the paraquat controversy, the "bastard got what was due." Still, the editors, knowing that Bourne had no ability to change laws single-handedly, did not direct their anger exclusively at him. Instead, their anger was directed at the president, who hadn't made good on his campaign promise regarding decriminalization. An editorial in the November 1978 issue declared:

> While Jimmy Earl lets the marijuana smokers of America twist slowly, slowly in the wind, the truth now emerges that his own administration is kept going only by the massive ministrations of the very substances his trigger-happy narcs seek to "control." In all, we view *l'affaire Bourne* more in sorrow than in anger. Oh, it's nice to see that one of the bastards got what was due him. But isn't it getting pretty ridiculous, this whole business about illegal dope? Cut the crap, Mr. Carter—let's legalize dope to save America.[33]

In the end, the person who suffered most from Bourne's resignation was Keith Stroup. Though he played an active role in bringing Bourne down, it quickly became clear that, in doing so, Stroup had destroyed his own career as well. Stories published in newspapers across the country tied Stroup's infamous temper to Bourne's downfall, and after the White House stopped discussing federal decriminalization, NORML supporters turned on Stroup, worried that he had destroyed drug law reform forever. Leaders on NORML's advisory board were just as upset that Stroup had done something so foolish and rash.

After a few more harried days in Washington, Stroup knew he had to get away. In late summer 1978, he took a trip through the Southwest, staying in New Mexico and Las Vegas, smoking and partying with Willie Nelson and friends. But the newspaper stories followed him there, and he knew that eventually he'd have to return to Washington and face the mess he had created. He also knew that, when he returned, his job at NORML would be gone. Stroup recalled in his 2013 memoir:

> I didn't require a fortuneteller to know that I would be a *persona non grata* for the remainder of the Carter administration, and that many friends on Capitol Hill would no longer feel comfortable working with me—and that as long as I was running NORML, the organization would be treated like a leper in political circles. I had created the organization and had spent ten years of my life totally immersed in its work, dedicated to achieving our political goals. And now I had, in one angry moment, totally mishandled this incident, and brought everything tumbling down. The organization might be able to right itself politically and continue as the marijuana smokers' lobby, but my role at NORML was finished.[34]

Stroup stayed on for several more tumultuous months, then officially resigned from his organization on December 2, 1978. His farewell speech at NORML's annual conference in Washington was warmly received. After leaving NORML, Stroup refocused his career and became a lobbyist for farmers' and artists' rights, as well as a personal defense lawyer for those accused of drug crimes. Still, the experience of no longer being connected to the organization he founded was debilitating and depressing. "I felt totally lost," he wrote. "My identity had been wrapped up in NORML for a decade in my role as chief spokesperson for legalizing marijuana in America. Now none of that was possible, and it was a frightening prospect."[35]

Bourne, on the other hand, rebounded surprisingly well. He and his wife, Mary King, who was serving as deputy director of the national volunteer agency ACTION at the time, briefly left Washington in the aftermath of the scandal, but no criminal charges were brought against him, and the couple soon returned to the city, where King continued her job at ACTION and Bourne took a position as the assistant secretary-general of the United Nations, coordinating a water resources project for the UN Development Program.[36] When asked if he felt bitter about losing his job, Bourne told *People* that he actually felt the opposite. Leaving the Carter administration was "very much an opportunity," Bourne said. "I'm fine. I'm relaxed. In many ways, I had not realized how much stress I was under—until I was away from the White House." He also told the reporter that he had received a "stunning" amount of support during this time. "I have been deluged by more than four hundred letters of support from all kinds of people," he said, citing Gloria Steinem and Margaret Mead as two of the biggest names.[37]

In the aftermath of the scandal, Bourne also changed his tune on marijuana. Two months after his resignation, he appeared, surprisingly, in the pages of *High Times,* warning of the dangers that pot posed to kids and condemning the belief that children had the "right" to smoke pot. In an article titled "Kids Shouldn't Get Stoned," Bourne echoed a core message of the burgeoning parent movement: "As we move toward decriminalization the 13-year-old feels that he has as much right to smoke marijuana as the 23-year-old," Bourne warned, "because there is neither a cultural value system nor any laws to say to him that this is something you must resist doing until you achieve a certain age or level of maturity." Bourne concluded by arguing that "adolescence is a time in one's life when a great deal of one's energies need to go into learning skills that will allow one to function happily and productively in an adult world. Spending too much of this phase of one's life stoned . . . can clearly be detrimental to one's long-term welfare."[38] Schuchard and Gleaton couldn't have said it better.

With Carter's former chief drug adviser discussing decriminalization's dangers for adolescents in *High Times* and neither Stroup nor Bourne in positions to affect policy change, discussions of marijuana in Washington began to shift radically. The man who took over Bourne's position, an avuncular liberal named Lee Dogoloff, was easily influenced by parent activists when they came to visit him in the scandal's aftermath, and NORML, which underwent a revolving door of directors after Stroup left, lost the power and influence Stroup had worked for nearly a decade to build. Even *High Times* lost some of its cachet as marijuana smokers across the country became disillusioned by the Carter administration's reversal on decriminalization, and as the magazine's editors began writing about other drugs, dropping their formerly exclusive focus on marijuana. By December 1978, a scandal involving Quaaludes and cocaine had caused the country's brief experiment with decriminalization to come to a standstill. After years of increasing national acceptance of marijuana and its use, the era of parent antidrug activism was about to begin.

8

THE COMING PARENT REVOLUTION

IN THE WAKE of the Peter Bourne scandal and nationwide coverage of the connections between paraphernalia and kids' rising marijuana use, parent activists turned their eyes to the nation's capital in 1978, right when the city was becoming increasingly sympathetic to their cause. Not only did an embarrassed President Carter no longer emphasize federal decriminalization, but Peter Bourne's replacement, Lee Dogoloff, was quickly converted to the parents' platform, while Congress took aim at the paraphernalia marketplace, holding bipartisan hearings on the dangers the industry posed to kids, with several parent activists serving as key witnesses. By November 1980, when Ronald Reagan was elected president in a landslide, many of the politically conservative parent activists felt that the nation had finally elected a leader who could usher their ideas onto the national stage. Reagan's known distrust of marijuana and emphasis on social conservatism and traditional values gave activists hope that Washington would finally listen to their concerns and view parents as experts and allies in the battle against adolescent marijuana use.

Between 1978, when Bourne resigned from the White House, and 1981, when Reagan entered it as president, the parent movement came to Washington riding a wave of growing support. Buoyed by positive media coverage and Keith Schuchard's and Sue Rusche's parent group formation guides, over 300 parent groups had formed in thirty-four states by 1980. And their methods seemed to be working: after peaking in 1978, adolescent marijuana use began to level off, and by 1980 disapproval of the drug was rising among teens nationwide. Keen to secure further gains, movement leaders formed the National Federation of Parents for Drug-Free Youth (NFP) in April 1980; the new national umbrella organization would organize the formation of new parent groups and lobby legislators to make their platform the law of the land.

With the NFP now a presence in the nation's capital, NORML was no longer DC's most active grassroots marijuana lobbying organization. As parent activists celebrated their close relationship with Dogoloff and growing recognition on Capitol Hill, NORML struggled in the wake of Keith Stroup's departure and could offer little to counteract the parent activists' rise.

The influence of the NFP also exposed the political ambitions of the parent movement's leaders, some of whom announced that their new goal was far larger than just keeping kids away from pot. The new organization's name said it all: they were a national federation of parents for *drug*-free, not only marijuana-free, youth. Many of the founding members of the parent movement were liberal Democrats, but now a new breed of activist saw extraordinary potential in aligning with an increasingly conservative and Republican Washington. The NFP chose as its leaders the political conservatives Joyce Nalepka and Bill Barton, who were excited about cooperating with a possible Reagan administration. Both were committed to turning the parent movement's goals into national law, and Nalepka vociferously opposed President Carter or any politician who supported loosening marijuana laws. She realized the political power of the parent movement as a voting bloc, and a growing number of legislators began to recognize this as well. As decriminalization became a dirty word in Washington, politicians began aligning with the parents' platform and meeting their requests.

It was a moment of historic kismet for the parent movement to arrive in Washington just as the Reagan revolution was taking place, and by 1981, with hundreds of local parent groups formed across the country and a national lobbying group in place, activists were primed to take advantage of the city's welcoming environment. Just four years after the first parent group formed in a suburban living room outside Atlanta, the movement's moment in the national spotlight had come.

Lee Dogoloff, Peter Bourne's successor at the Office of Drug Abuse Policy, was genial and easygoing, with a stocky build and thick curly hair. A Baltimore native, he was also a committed liberal with long ties to Washington. Dogoloff's background was in addiction research; he'd gotten his start in the late 1960s, working with Robert DuPont testing inmates' heroin levels in DC's Department of Corrections. Dogoloff had risen in the ranks, moving from local to federal positions, focusing specifically on drug prevention. He worked at Nixon's Special Action Office for Drug Abuse Prevention in 1972, running the office's government services programs, and he continued to work with DuPont at NIDA before returning to the White House in 1975. There he helped write the Ford administration's white paper on drug abuse, which effectively argued for marijuana decriminalization. In 1976, after Carter's election, Dogoloff stayed in the West Wing, working as Peter Bourne's deputy director.

Unlike Bourne, Dogoloff was not a physician. He had studied at the University of Maryland and pursued a master's degree in social work at Howard University, but Dogoloff had never actually treated drug addicts and knew little about how to prevent drug abuse. Instead, Dogoloff's approach to prevention was research based. After cowriting the white paper for Ford, Dogoloff believed that "hard" drugs, such as heroin, were the country's primary concern, and that each drug had to be treated on its own terms. He also believed that the federal government's primary responsibility was the treatment and rehabilitation of hard drug users only, not "soft" users who smoked marijuana. Dogoloff was so committed to this model that even the national controversy that began in 1977 over tainted marijuana from paraquat spraying in Mexico remained a peripheral concern for him. Unlike legislators who were concerned about paraquat's potential effects, in December of that year Dogoloff told the press that the herbicide would pose a threat only if "ingested in large amounts in marijuana-filled brownies"—a statement that shocked and dismayed Keith Stroup.[1]

Nevertheless, Dogoloff's views on the drug were starting to shift when he took over Bourne's position and as rates of adolescent marijuana use continued to climb. Though he was proud that the number of heroin overdoses was falling, statistics showing that, in 1979, 11 percent of high school seniors were smoking pot every day proved that he was failing in his mission to prevent drug abuse. Indeed, by that point Dogoloff felt confused about what, precisely, "drug abuse prevention" meant. As a political idea, he knew that "prevention was something that no one could describe and no one could measure but everyone felt good about." But he questioned what the government's role in prevention should be. His training as a social worker had taught him that "people learn and grow based on relationships, but I didn't know any kids or adults that wanted a personal relationship with their government."[2]

Instead, it seemed that something more fundamental had to change: a realignment of priorities and values on both governmental and personal levels. Dogoloff was hardly a conservative, but he felt that the government needed to step back and reimagine its role in handling sensitive subjects like drug use. Like parent activists who denounced young people thinking they had a "right" to smoke pot, Dogoloff blamed rising rates of drug use on a dangerous overpermissiveness not only in parenting but also in the tacit support of federal officials, like himself, who argued that marijuana wasn't a national concern. In the aftermath of the Vietnam War, he hadn't realized that his position would compound what he saw as the dangerous effects of adolescent rebellion and a lack of parental control. "The war had really emasculated the family," he said, "giving unusual power to adolescents and young adults and blurring the lines between adults and kids. That was a real sea change from what had gone before, and when it eroded the power of the family, well, that seemed to me to be the advent of the epidemic of drug abuse."

Parent activists couldn't have agreed more. Thrilled with Bourne's resignation, Keith Schuchard and Thomas Gleaton moved quickly to influence the man who took his place. Visiting Washington in the wake of Bourne's departure, the two activists held a series of meetings with officials at NIDA and the Department of Health, Education, and Welfare, who reacted to their concept of parent peer groups with derision. When they went to the Office of Drug Abuse Policy and met with Dogoloff, however, they found a much more sympathetic ear. Schuchard and Gleaton, appealing to Dogoloff as a father of three daughters, explained that the federal government's emphasis on heroin, along with Carter's support for decriminalization and the booming paraphernalia industry, had allowed adolescent marijuana use to spiral out of control.

Something had to be done, they said, and with the federal government's help, parent activism could provide the solution.

After listening to Schuchard and Gleaton for several hours, the man who once believed that marijuana was dangerous only if consumed in large doses of paraquat-laced brownies was transformed, and Washington's awakening to the power of parent activism began. Heroin or even alcohol wasn't the heart of the nation's drug problem, Schuchard told him. Instead, marijuana posed the greatest danger to the American family because it was accompanied by a culture preaching that its use was innocent and fun. Marketing campaigns promoted paraphernalia-filled Christmas stockings and Frisbee-shaped pipes, while magazines like *High Times* were on sale at local drugstores and record shops. Parents couldn't push back against a multimillion-dollar industry alone, Schuchard continued. Since few others were denouncing marijuana use, parent activists needed the government's help. That meant ending federal support for decriminalization, passing laws against drug paraphernalia, and aiding the formation of more parent groups. By the end of their meeting, Dogoloff readily agreed. "It all began to make sense to me," he recalled. "What I hadn't realized before was that drug-abuse 'professionals' were supplanting what families should have been doing. Schuchard and Gleaton gave me the answer. If we could support parental involvement at the grass roots level, there was a promise of turning things around. They crystallized my thinking."[3]

Soon Dogoloff was promoting parent activists' claims to Carter and on Capitol Hill. In the wake of positive coverage of parent activism in newspapers across the country, as well as the popularity of Schuchard's guidebook *Parents, Peers, and Pot* and Sue Rusche's *How to Form a Families in Action Group in Your Community*, Dogoloff was thrilled with the energy coming from the hundreds of parent groups that had formed across the country in the vein of PRIDE and FIA. Many of them were in affluent suburban communities, where backlash against the typical signs of excessive adolescent marijuana use—the loss of interest in schoolwork, the changed emotions, and negative attitudes—was particularly strong. Parents there were frightened by this new wave of adolescent drug use: experimentation started younger, and kids were smoking pot that some claimed was nearly ten times as strong as what people smoked in the 1960s. Kids were also smoking before, during, and after school—times when working parents had little control over what their kids were doing, or with whom. Even for parents whose children hadn't yet started using the drug, the wave of national adolescent marijuana use was frightening, and forming a parent peer group—and contacting Lee Dogoloff—seemed like a logical response.

Joyce Nalepka, a mother of two young boys who lived outside of Washington in Silver Spring, Maryland, was representative of this new wave of parent activism. Though her own children weren't using drugs, marijuana use by young adults made her so angry that she formed her own parent group. In December 1977, Nalepka had taken her two young sons and their fourteen-year-old babysitter to a KISS concert at the Capital Centre in Landover, Maryland. The event quickly became a debacle: concert attendees shocked Nalepka with their blatant drug use, and one of her sons "became sick from the fog of marijuana smoke."[4] The Capital Centre was well known for its open drug use: a *Washington Post* article in March 1976 declared that "the arena, home of the Bullets and the Caps, is transformed on the nights when there are rock concerts into a mammoth den where the smell of fresh marijuana fills the air before the first chords of music. . . . Marijuana, hashish and occasionally cocaine are smoked and snorted in the open with the consent of private T-shirted guards who tell concert-goers: 'Yeah, it's OK to smoke dope but try to stay out of the aisles.'"[5]

Nalepka was not amused. She stormed out with the children in tow, and the next day she called the Drug Enforcement Administration to complain. The DEA's response was even more infuriating. Officials told her that drug use at the Capital Centre was a local matter, and that this was 1977, and "some people, including her congressman, thought marijuana penalties ought to be erased." Then she telephoned the White House, trying to reach the first lady. An aide to Rosalynn Carter told her that he didn't understand the fuss.[6]

Clearly, they didn't understand Nalepka either. A tenacious, driven woman, Nalepka was quick to organize a fight. A year later, after hearing about parent activism in the news, she formed the Coalition for Concern About Marijuana Use in Youth, a group that called on President Carter to speak out strongly against marijuana as well as to pass a model law that would ban paraphernalia manufacture and distribution and use the resources of the federal government to block importation of the drug. By October 1979, she had connected with Dogoloff. Already sympathetic to the parent movement's claims after his meeting with Schuchard and Gleaton, Dogoloff took advantage of Nalepka's proximity to Washington and invited her to speak at a Senate hearing the following month on the dangers to kids posed by the paraphernalia industry.

The hearing, held on November 16, 1979, was organized by the Senate Subcommittee on Criminal Justice and was led by Charles Mathias, a Republican from Maryland, and Joseph Biden, Democrat from Delaware. Convened to discuss "whether children are lured into the drug culture by paraphernalia," its witnesses included prominent parent activists and their supporters, including Nalepka, Robert DuPont, and Pat Burch, an activist from Potomac, Maryland, whose husband, Dean, had been chairman of the Federal Communications Commission under Richard Nixon. With no dissenting views or testimony from representatives of the paraphernalia industry, the hearing quickly became a celebration of the power of parent activism. It began with DuPont declaring that parent groups had "the single greatest potential for improvement of the discouraging drug abuse situation in the United States today," and that "the paraphernalia issue has galvanized parents and communities as nothing else." Nalepka was his primary example.

A theatrical witness who used elaborate tactics to prove her point, Nalepka had brought fifty one-ounce jars of dried parsley into the chamber and distributed them to the senators and audience members before her testimony. "Even now, politicians are still talking about relaxing penalties [for the possession of one ounce of marijuana] as a solution to the problem," she said, pointing to the jars before the members of her audience. "One ounce makes forty to sixty joints, the perfect amount for school playground dealers. This is an ounce of parsley, obviously no small amount. . . . It is simple possession, ladies and gentlemen, that keeps the drug pushers in business."

Nalepka then declared that responsibility for marijuana's presence "in every junior and senior high school and even in many elementary schools" fell on every adult in the United States, "from President Carter down to me, the parent [who] didn't take the problem seriously enough soon enough." Furious that any political leader would still promote decriminalization in the face of rising rates of adolescent marijuana use, Nalepka warned of the power of the growing "anti-marijuana lobby" and threatened that she and parent activists like her would "never again vote for a candidate for any office who [supports decriminalization], and we will do everything in our power to remove those now in office who would support this type of legislation." Nalepka then called upon "the members of the House, Senate . . . businessmen in America, the US Chamber of Commerce, and the media to join [her] in a forceful educational effort to pull our country back from the drug culture." She concluded by warning that she would accept nothing less than total commitment to the cause.[7]

Fifteen days before Nalepka's memorable performance, a similar hearing was held before the House Select Committee on Narcotics Abuse and Control to assess "the impact of the advertising and unregulated sale of drug paraphernalia upon drug use, particularly by our youth, and to consider governmental initiatives to exercise effective control over the paraphernalia industry." The hearing, overseen by Democratic representative Lester Wolff, featured testimony from Lee Dogoloff and Sue Rusche. Unlike the hearing in the Senate, however, it also featured dissenting views from Andy Kowl, a journalist who had worked for *High Times* for years. Kowl had taken over publishing the magazine after Tom Forçade, battling depression and drug abuse, committed suicide on November 16, 1978.

Like Nalepka, Rusche argued that drug paraphernalia was particularly harmful to the young. She denounced the fast-growing field that "glamorizes and promotes illicit drugs, an industry that is estimated to take in $3 billion a year, an industry that, in the time-honored tradition of American free enterprise, is developing a new market of illicit drug users—our twelve- to seventeen-year-old children." Worse still, she argued, magazines like *High Times* published information that "distorts or denies medical evidence indicating the harmful effects from drug use." Because magazines like *High Times* were "universally available" to young children, parents and lawmakers had to do everything in their power to prevent more children from falling into the "trap" of drug use.

In response, Kowl maintained that the purpose of paraphernalia and *High Times* was not to appeal to children at all. "No rational adult would think that children should experiment with controlled substances,"

Kowl said, including the staff at his magazine. But banning paraphernalia or condemning publications didn't do anything to stop adolescent drug use, he continued. Instead, "all you do is eliminate thousands of small, tax-paying businesses." Wolff was unconvinced by Kowl's claims, however. In his executive summary of the hearing, Wolff noted that the existence of the paraphernalia industry undoubtedly had negative effects, and the most dangerous of them was that, "through its glamorizing of the drug culture," the industry "acts to undermine parental authority."[8]

The 1979 hearings—whose tenor marked a remarkable shift from the support that decriminalization had received in Congress less than a half-decade before—served as a testament to both the growing strength of the paraphernalia industry and the increasing power of the parent activists' revolt. In 1975, when Senator Birch Bayh had defended decriminalization on the basis that being arrested for marijuana disproportionately harmed otherwise law-abiding young adults, head shops, *High Times,* and adolescent access to paraphernalia weren't much of a concern. But four years later, in the wake of reports documenting rising levels of adolescent marijuana use and the ease with which children could purchase paraphernalia supplies, enabling a young adult to use marijuana without facing criminal penalties seemed less important than protecting the nation's youth from a "drug culture" that parent activists condemned and feared. As the paraphernalia industry boomed, legislators had to react.

But there was another, more self-serving reason why a growing number of politicians began taking parent activists seriously. The 1980 elections loomed, and legislators were recognizing the power of anti-marijuana parent activists as a voting bloc. As Joyce Nalepka threatened at the November 16, 1979, hearing, she represented a growing movement of parents who were willing to campaign against pro-decriminalization candidates and would eagerly vote out legislators with whom they disagreed. As law-abiding and middle-class constituents, parent activists were also a far more natural constituency for legislators to capitulate to than paraphernalia distributors or *High Times* editors, who defended industries that, while legal, still promoted illegal drug use. At the November hearing, Mathias even went so far as to compare Nalepka to a Revolutionary patriot for making the distinction

between adults' and children's drug use, reversing the image adopted by
pro-marijuana forces two years before. "You are like John Paul Jones,"
Mathias said after Nalepka finished testifying. "Not yet begun to fight."

"I guess you are right," Nalepka responded, "and there is nothing
that is going to stop us until this improves."[9]

•

By the spring of 1980, over 300 small, local parent groups had formed
across the United States, pushed by a growing understanding of adolescent marijuana use and widespread coverage of the phenomenon in the
national press. *Newsweek* celebrated FIA in January, describing how the
group had "cracked down" on Atlanta's "drug scene," and a cover story
in the *New York Times Magazine* in February announced a new "parental push against marijuana," offering descriptions of groups formed by
PRIDE and FIA.[10] In the four years since Keith Schuchard first gathered
neighborhood parents in her living room, national news coverage had
inspired the formation of parent groups in thirty-four states, and the
majority of them followed in Schuchard's footsteps: these groups were
small and local, and they focused exclusively on taking care of the children and families within their own communities.

In the wake of supportive congressional hearings, however, leading parent activists began to think bigger. With a blossoming number
of parent groups forming nationwide, activists like Schuchard, Gleaton, and Rusche, alongside Joyce Nalepka, Pat Burch, and Bill Barton
of Naples, Florida, discussed forming a new kind of umbrella group,
one that could oversee their movement's burgeoning membership and
coordinate their members' actions to better influence drug policy on
a national scale. Most importantly, these activists believed that parent
groups could crack down on far more than marijuana. Beyond pot,
leading activists believed that, if parent activists banded together, they
could influence federal and state politicians to pass large-scale legislation that would decrease rates of all adolescent drug use, including the
abuse of alcohol, tobacco, and other legal and illegal drugs.

By April of that year, the National Federation of Parents for Drug-
Free Youth (NFP) was born. The idea came to fruition at a private meet-
ing of parent leaders in Gleaton's living room, held before the annual
PRIDE Southeast Drug Conference in Atlanta convened. The rapid

growth of parent groups nationwide suggested growing political power, Gleaton realized, and leading activists didn't want to waste the energy and enthusiasm of their new recruits. To build this energy into a more cohesive movement, Schuchard discussed the need for a new national organization, one that could "assist in the creation of new parent groups and that could address many issues from the neighborhood, family and legislative level—to do the many things we knew had to be accomplished if we, in fact, were going to achieve our goal of drug-free youth."[11] The NFP was her solution.

Gleaton, Schuchard, and their fellow activists had spent years fighting against decriminalization legislation and pro-pot activists at the state level, but now the parent movement had to turn its attention to national politics, Schuchard said. The purpose of the NFP, she said, was to emphasize "the growth of the parents' movement for drug-free youth from a handful of scattered individuals and groups to an increasingly cohesive, articulate, and powerful national movement."[12] But the NFP wasn't just going to battle against those with whom they disagreed, Gleaton continued. Most important for him was that the NFP concentrate "on positive stands, rather than negative ones." Although the federation would naturally have to "go against" certain politicians and groups that "did not take a firm stand for drug-free youth," it was important for Gleaton that the NFP be a force for good, a group willing and able to collaborate with anyone who wanted to help. Schuchard and Gleaton also believed that the NFP should break from the parent movement's traditional home in Atlanta. To prove that the NFP was indeed a national group, and to better influence national policy, they recommended finding office space in Silver Spring, Maryland, just across the border from Washington, DC.[13]

Gleaton then introduced Bill Barton and recommended him for NFP president. Barton and his, wife, Pat had formed Naples Informed Parents in 1978, shortly after they discovered their teenage daughter's marijuana use and learned about PRIDE. Modeled on Schuchard's original parent group, Naples Informed Parents had educated parents across the region on the dangers of adolescent marijuana use. Working with the local high school principal and the PTA, Barton was responsible for dramatically reducing marijuana use among local youth, and his two years of experience in parent activism had made him an elder statesman in the movement. His prominent leadership among parent groups in Florida made him a natural choice for NFP president. "We are an idea whose time has come," Barton told the parents after he was elected. "We seem to be the only viable solution."[14]

The NFP was then officially introduced at the PRIDE Southeast Drug Conference the following day. Drawing its initial membership from the conference's attendees, a month later the NFP claimed to represent over 420 parent groups in 48 states. With Barton as president; Otto Moulton, an activist from Massachusetts, as vice president; and Mary Jacobsen, from Maryland, as secretary, the NFP featured an advisory board consisting of sixteen parents on ten committees. Sue Rusche was named chair of the Paraphernalia Committee, and Joyce Nalepka was made chair of the Legislative Committee. Jill Gerstenfeld, a lawyer and activist from Maryland, was chair of the Legal Committee, and Dr. Gabriel Nahas, long the source of the parent movement's information on marijuana's medical dangers, was named chairman of the Scientific Committee.

The following month the NFP released its first official press release, which solidified the group's ties to Washington and laid out its leaders' ambitious plans. Written by Bob Kramer, a member of the newly formed organization's board, the memo declared that NFP officers would appear alongside Charles Mathias and Lee Dogoloff at the Dirksen Senate Office Building on May 8 to answer questions on their plans to "mobilize parents throughout the nation." "Growing concern over the increasing drug use among young people has prompted parents from across the nation to join together to combat this drug epidemic," the release continued. In response, parent groups from over forty states had met in Atlanta to form an organization that would "give strength and support to this effort." "The formation of the Federation is a positive, cooperative effort between parents and government," the memo concluded. "The drug epidemic cannot be solved by government alone or parents alone—it must be a team effort."[15]

Things moved rapidly from there. In June, PRIDE's newsletter had outlined the organization's philosophy and official platform, further defining the NFP's role and separating it from preexisting parent groups, like PRIDE and FIA. The purpose of the NFP, the newsletter declared, was "to inform and educate parents, adolescents, children and others about the dangers of marijuana and other mind-altering drugs and to promote, encourage and assist in the formation of local parent groups throughout the country." Bespeaking an unwavering commitment to drug-free youth, the NFP's platform combined much of the work of PRIDE and FIA but expanded it to a national scale as it called for "parents and professionals to cooperate and work together in preventing drug usage by youth," for the president to launch "a nationwide campaign" to combat the problem, and for "government at all levels to pass into law effective bans on the manufacture, distribution, sale and advertisement of drug paraphernalia."[16]

The NFP's formation was, for parent activists and the politicians who supported them, both galvanizing and unifying. At the May press conference, Barton spoke of the group's diversity and power. "The parents in this movement come from a wide variety of backgrounds, political and religious persuasions, and socio-economic groups," Barton said. "Ladies and gentlemen, our potential is awesome. We have within our grasp the opportunity to change the course of a nation. And I believe we will do that. The need is so great we cannot fail."[17] Senator Gordon Humphrey, a conservative Republican from New Hampshire who would go on to chair hearings on the effects of marijuana on youth, agreed. "We can now attack the problem from the grass roots up," he told reporters. "That's the way to do it—not try to deal with it here in Washington."[18]

The formation of the NFP also marked a decisive break from the style of previous parent activism. Although still focused on education and information, the NFP was less interested in teaching parents about the dangers of drug abuse than in organizing and directing parent groups with the aim of changing federal drug policy. The NFP's official resolutions, along with its interest in finding a suitable office space near Washington, highlighted its wider ambitions. Indeed, NFP's national debut—at a press conference on Capitol Hill, where NFP officials stood alongside members of Congress and White House officials— showcased just how far the parent movement had come. In the span of four years, the movement had grown from a few scattered meetings in suburban living rooms into a national lobbying force with growing political clout. Despite originating from within PRIDE, the NFP sought from the beginning to be its own force, working with legislators in Washington to turn the parent movement's platform into a national campaign.

But not everyone agreed that parent groups were either the most successful or the most reasonable solution to the nation's drug problem. Stephen H. Newman, a drug prevention specialist and director of the Charlotte Substance Abuse Prevention Center in North Carolina, wrote in a June 1980 editorial in the *New York Times* that he "would normally welcome" something like the parent movement, but the "direction these groups have taken is worrisome. They have made it clear that they have little patience with the ongoing debate about marijuana's potential to provide physical and psychological damage. For them," Newman argued, "the evidence is in."

Newman then noted that the Carter administration, in response to the embarrassment of the Bourne scandal, was quietly adopting the parent activists' aims. The parents' recent attempts to "influence the Government's approach to the drug problem" were being greeted by federal and state officials, in Newman's words, "with open arms." The hard-line approach of parent groups, which Newman believed put an emphasis on parents spying on their children, thus creating mistrust and suspicion within families, was dangerous, particularly if the federal government endorsed such an approach in an all-out crackdown on marijuana. "There are no simple answers to the problems of drug abuse," Newman warned. "But there are answers." For Newman, declaring war on marijuana was a less viable solution than "attempting to negotiate peace between parents and children, between students and schools, [and] between individuals and their communities."[19]

But even critics of the parent movement couldn't deny that things were changing in the United States. After a rapid and alarming rise in adolescent drug use in the late 1970s, rates of adolescent marijuana use had leveled off by 1980, and there was a sudden and surprising reversal in attitudes toward the drug—one that coincided with the parent movement's rise. Two weeks prior to the May 8 press conference, the University of Michigan had released its annual "Monitoring the Future" survey and reported that, "despite the increasing proportion of youth who became involved with illicit drugs during the 1970's, the majority of American young people today are rather conservative about most kinds of drug use." The survey, which had monitored levels of drug use by high school seniors every year since 1975, noted that adolescent acceptance and use of marijuana peaked in 1979, but that, in the years since, opinions had shifted toward disapproval of even moderate use of the drug. Although a similar number of high school seniors still smoked pot regularly (11 percent continued to claim daily or near-daily use), by 1980 nearly 70 percent of high school seniors reported that they condemned "regular" pot smoking and 34 percent "disapproved of trying the drug once or twice," suggesting that rates of pot smoking would soon fall.[20] Researchers didn't cite specific reasons why adolescent attitudes toward marijuana had hardened, but parent activists were quick to accept credit.

Others saw the growth of parent groups and increased adolescent condemnation of marijuana as evidence of a far more fundamental change. Jeane Westin, a writer and mother from California, observed a change in the country's social climate that predicted the parent movement's acceptance of Ronald Reagan. In her 1981 book *The Coming Parent Revolution: Why Parents Must Toss Out the "Experts" and Start Believing in Themselves Again,* Westin celebrated the moral authority of "New Traditional" parents—including Keith Schuchard and Joyce Nalepka, whom she celebrated by name—who embodied a revitalized sense of social conservatism and confirmed the importance of family values as a grassroots, anti-authoritarian approach to retaking control. In the wake of what Westin saw as the liberal excesses of the 1960s and '70s, her book celebrated families who worked to "hold back the forces that are invading the sanctity of the American home." These forces included adolescent rebellion, violence on television, invasive government regulations, failing public education, and adolescent drug use, especially use of marijuana. In response to these threats, Westin celebrated a parent's "right to snoop" and advocated the formation of parent peer groups. "Children have no 'right' to kill themselves with chemicals," Westin argued. "And parents have every right to fight to stop them."[21]

As an avowed liberal, Schuchard might have disagreed with being called a conservative, but she undoubtedly agreed with much of Westin's platform. Like many parent activists, Westin despised the forces that had dismissed parents' power and authority for years: "Big Daddy" government, "Big Mama" education, and the media's emphasis on "anti-family" values. With the coming parent revolution, however, things were about to change. "Parents are a potent political force," Westin reminded her readers. "Without our support, no legislator could be elected. It is up to us to let our representatives know that we are aware of government's impact on our families, and we want a voice in any policy that affects family unity and stability." By voting to elect legislators who would protect family values and condemn the "excesses of liberalism" that had increased adolescent drug use, "parents in the 1980s can use their political muscle to ensure that family issues win as much legislative care as the environment did in the 1970s," Westin concluded. "That chance is embodied in the New Traditional Family, where ties bind parents and children with a knot no professional can undo."[22]

Writing in 1981, Westin was giving a name to a phenomenon whose force was already being felt in the last days of the Carter administration as the president struggled not only with the aftermath of the Bourne scandal and a surging parent antidrug revolution, but also, and perhaps more famously, with the Iranian hostage crisis, an oil and gasoline shortage, stagflation, and, as Carter put it, the nation's "crisis of confidence."[23] Lee Dogoloff, as Carter's primary adviser on drug policy, sought to convince parent activists that, despite his previous stance, the president now had their best interests in mind. At the PRIDE conference in 1980—the same conference where the NFP was announced— Dogoloff said that activists had "worked on my head" and dramatically influenced how the Carter administration officially addressed the drug. "One of the things that changed is that I have now become absolutely clear about what I say about marijuana for this administration," Dogoloff said. "What we say and what the President says is that we adamantly oppose the use of marijuana, period. Personally, over the past year I have stopped using what I consider the four letter word of the drug vocabulary, 'decriminalization.'"

Dogoloff was also pleased to announce that, because of the activists' influence, Carter had made adolescent drug abuse a "priority" for his administration, and he praised the activists' ability to address an issue that had previously flummoxed White House officials. "You parents have given hope to solving a problem that we in the government had never given up on, but for which we never saw a clear solution," he said. "As individuals, you've been very powerful. Now that you've joined together into a national movement, you're going to be an even stronger voice in this country."[24]

But Dogoloff's declaration that parent activists had given the Carter administration "hope" wasn't enough to earn the president their support. Indeed, by February 1980, with Reagan surging in the polls, Carter's flip-flopping on marijuana had alienated not only many parent activists who, as Nalepka had warned, would never vote for him again, but also his former constituency of pro-marijuana supporters, who were put off by his almost complete reversal on decriminalization. That month *High Times* declared Carter the least likely candidate to win the vote of its "pot lobby" and renounced its support for him, though it didn't go so far as to endorse Reagan. White House speechwriter Walter Shapiro objected that he didn't see abandoning decriminalization as a "sell-out on a vital issue," but he didn't do much to reassure the magazine's readers that the administration might still support decriminalization as it once had. "It's just that you've got to realize," Shapiro continued, "that drugs are not a good issue for Democrats."[25]

Drugs would be a very good issue, however, for Republicans. On November 4, 1980, parent activists overwhelmingly voted for Ronald Reagan, a former actor whose long-held anti-marijuana views were well known. As governor of California, Reagan had supported antidrug programs and, though it was a minor element of his platform, made it known that he was opposed to marijuana use and the counterculture ethos for which it stood. Reagan's successful bid for the White House launched a "Reagan Revolution" that swept Republicans into control of the Senate for the first time since 1954. Candidates from states with strong parent activist groups—including Paula Hawkins of Florida and Mack Mattingly of Georgia—ran explicitly on antidrug platforms and won influential seats, defeating Richard Stone, who openly supported decriminalization, and Herman Talmadge, who spent five weeks in treatment for alcohol abuse.

The election of 1980 effectively drew to a close the days when political hopefuls supported decriminalization and gave speeches written by pro-pot lobbyists. Just four years after Carter campaigned on support for state-based decriminalization and two years after the last state had softened its laws, the country had a vastly different view of what marijuana meant and whose "rights" had to be considered when it came to pot and other drugs. Even as rates of adolescent marijuana use leveled off, the right of children to grow up drug-free soon trumped the right of adults to access the drug of their choice without fear of punishment or incarceration. The pro-marijuana movement, still struggling from the fallout of the Peter Bourne scandal, and lacking leadership with Keith Stroup out of NORML, had nothing to offer in response to the rising wave of parent activism or the incoming Reagan administration, which, in just a few years' time, would emphasize an expanded war on drugs.

Shortly before leaving office, Carter delivered to Congress a final written report on the state of the union, in which he acknowledged his administration's previous mistakes and its shifting stance on adolescent drug use. Packed with bullet points covering topics as diverse as transportation and urban policies to the needs of women and older Americans, the most remarkable aspect of Carter's letter was how it underscored the parent movement's strength. Though Carter did boast that, because of his administration's policies, the population of heroin addicts had been reduced and overdose deaths were down 80 percent, the outgoing president also acknowledged that his previous stance on drug use had been wrong, and that education and social activism were necessary to change the nation's course. In response to the "very serious and disturbing trends of adolescent drug abuse," Carter declared that his administration had "seen and encouraged a national movement of parents." "We need a change in attitude," he wrote, "from an attitude which condones the casual use of drugs to one that condemns the inappropriate and harmful use of drugs." To do that, Carter concluded, "we must look to citizens and parents across the country to help educate the increasing numbers of American youth who are experimenting with drugs."[26]

In his exit interview conducted just weeks after the election, Lee Dogoloff also celebrated the support that the Carter administration had given, if belatedly, to parent activists. "This administration has really taken on the leadership of supporting and getting that grassroots parent movement under way," he said. Crediting the movement for clarifying the administration's previous "inability to clearly communicate the President's view about drug use," Dogoloff praised the nearly 600 parent groups that had formed across the country by 1981, all of which did their work "with virtually no federal funding at all and got a clear message to schools and parents and so forth." Overall, Dogoloff was pleased with the work he had done, and he hoped that the Reagans would continue in the same direction. "I am very optimistic about Mrs. Reagan's interest in the subject" of drug abuse, Dogoloff said. Although he hadn't voted for the incoming administration, because of the Reagans' commitment to antidrug activism and their support for adolescent health, Carter's outgoing drug abuse policy adviser was "convinced that the kinds of things that we've set in motion will go on."[27]

9

"THE MOST POTENT FORCE THERE IS"

BY THE EARLY 1980s, it seemed like the Reagans were the best thing that could have happened to parent activists, and vice versa. During Ronald Reagan's first term, the movement, and especially the NFP, exploded onto the national scene, dominating popular culture and rolling back state decriminalization laws while influencing the federal direction of the drug war. It also experienced some of its greatest triumphs—financially, socially, and politically. With the help of Nancy Reagan, who adopted the cause as her primary platform as first lady, the prevention of adolescent drug abuse became nothing short of a national obsession, with the White House constantly drawing attention to the battle and antidrug messages appearing everywhere from television to comic books to newspapers and magazines.

Both the national media and the White House promoted parent groups as the answer to some of the nation's most intractable problems: this powerful, grassroots, citizen-led initiative would not only lower national rates of drug abuse, they claimed, but it would also accelerate one of Reagan's campaign promises to cut federal spending, saving taxpayers' money as volunteers took over the government's role in prevention. The White House painted parent activists as idealized citizens, effectively tackling the problems the federal government was too large and too inept to handle, while private donations covered the cost and new parents joined the cause in droves. Buoyed by growing national support, by 1983 the number of parent groups had ballooned from 600 to over 3,000 nationwide, and national conferences continued to promote the parent activists' cause, declaring that their battle wasn't over yet.

The parent movement wasn't the only beneficiary of the activists' close relationship with the White House, however: Nancy Reagan needed the parent movement too. After her arrival in Washington, Reagan battled low approval ratings and the suspicion that she was little more than, as a California newspaper put it in 1981, a "frivolous social climber with more political ambition than Lady MacBeth."[1] Early in her White House tenure, Reagan recognized the need to radically alter her image, to appear more caring and less callous. The nation's growing intolerance of drug use and embrace of children's safety presented a remarkable opportunity, and Reagan's staff guided her toward an affiliation with the parent movement, setting the stage for her transformation from a "frivolous social climber" into a committed antidrug warrior with the health of the nation's children in mind. It worked: within a year Reagan's popularity soared as her platform—and parent activism—became a national success.

But as the first lady embraced the movement, she rarely acknowledged the actual effects of the parents' work. Rates of adolescent marijuana use plunged during the Reagan administration's first term, to half of what they were in 1979. Having made the prevention of adolescent marijuana use into a national obsession, parent activists were quick to accept credit for the change. But without rising rates of marijuana to battle, parent activists and the first lady needed a new cause, one that ensured their continued relevance. By 1982, Nancy Reagan and leading parent activists stopped specifically citing marijuana and turned their attention to the larger, more generic problem of "drugs," despite the fact that nearly all levels of adolescent drug use were decreasing at the time. In spite of this lack of evidence, parent activists and the White House continued to suggest that adolescent drug abuse was nothing less than a national crisis. And indeed, they had no choice: without the threat of adolescent drug abuse, the first lady would lose her platform and parent activists would have no reason to continue their work.

Aligning with the Reagan administration brought parent activists to the national stage, but it also laid the foundation for their movement's demise. By 1984, Reagan had placed marijuana at the center of the drug war, switching the federal focus from the treatment and rehabilitation of heroin addicts to law enforcement and militarized interdiction efforts targeting "soft" drugs like cocaine and pot. But he also cut off the tap. As rates of adolescent drug use fell, the president slashed the federal budget for antidrug education and prevention initiatives, leaving parent volunteers to pick up the slack. Without the White House's financial support, leading parent activists quickly realized that their longtime boast that they could resolve the nation's adolescent drug abuse problems without federal assistance was, in fact, nearly impossible. This fracture—between the presentation of the parent movement as an all-volunteer army and the reality of their reliance on federal grants—created tension between leading activists and caused breakdowns along political lines. Those who aligned most closely with the Reagan administration—primarily NFP leaders, who were known to be Republicans—flourished during the early 1980s, thanks to private donations from conservatives. But groups like PRIDE and FIA, run primarily by liberal Democrats, struggled as federal funding began to disappear.

The close relationship between the White House and the parent movement marked a moment of historic proportion, the period when parent activists were able to align their anti-marijuana crusade with the larger social concerns of the time. But the administration's public embrace—followed by selective financial support—ultimately smothered the movement, sparking infighting among movement leaders while administration officials played obvious favorites. The short-term benefits of aligning with the administration blinded parent activists to its costs, and by the end of 1984, when the federal money that had once funded the parents' campaign had almost entirely disappeared, the Reagans continued to benefit from the alliance while parent activists watched as their movement began its ultimate collapse.

•

Three months after Reagan took office, activists gathered again in Atlanta for the third annual PRIDE Southeast Drug Conference. There, standing before a crowd of over 500 parents, teachers, professionals, and doctors who traveled to Georgia from thirty-four states, Keith Schuchard celebrated how far the parents' movement had come and how buoyed she was by the new administration. In her keynote address, Schuchard declared that "the dream we dared to speak of rather timidly three years ago in this auditorium seems well on its way to realization." Since 1978, the PRIDE conference had grown from a single-day event for a handful of drug abuse professionals into a days-long gathering of hundreds of people, all of whom were deeply concerned about adolescent drug abuse.

Most importantly, Schuchard continued, they now had an ally in Washington. Even though she was an avowed Democrat, she asked for the movement's support for "President Reagan, now a victim bearing [the] pain of our society's unraveling." She requested that those in attendance, with the assistance of Reagan's sympathetic administration, "begin a personal effort of family, neighborhood, and community reconstruction." "Let each of us," she urged, "clothe the whole child in the cloth of a decent, law-abiding community that takes pride in its commitment to drug-free excellence of body and mind."[2]

Schuchard celebrated the accomplishments of PRIDE, but she also used the opportunity to promote her other organization, the NFP, which had cohosted the event. In his address on the NFP's background and potential, NFP president Bill Barton echoed Schuchard's enthusiasm for their mission. "Ladies and gentlemen, we have indeed gained credibility," he said. "We know we are correct, and we have gone about our efforts in a logical, straightforward fashion that creates credibility." But Barton also made it clear that, unlike PRIDE, which continued to focus on education and organizing individual parent groups, the NFP was a national umbrella organization, with large-scale legislative goals in mind. "We hope to continue drawing upon the private sector, whose job it will be to work with government, and accomplish in a hand-to-hand fashion the goals and objectives that both we and the government desire," he said. Private funding was key, Barton continued, because there was a distinct danger in relying on federal funds. "We cannot allow ourselves to become funded by government in our general budget," Barton said, "because too often such funding eventually leads to servitude."[3]

One member of the audience was particularly poised to respond to both Schuchard's and Barton's appeals. Ann Wrobleski, special projects director for Nancy Reagan, was invited to the conference by parent activists Pat Burch, Susan Silverman, and Joyce Nalepka, who were the NFP's primary representatives in Washington. Burch, along with Bill and Pat Barton, had met with Wrobleski and the first lady earlier that year, talking for over an hour and a half about the problem of adolescent drug abuse and how the administration could be more receptive to parent activists' needs. The first lady chose not to attend the PRIDE conference, but she sent Wrobleski in her stead, along with a telegram that told attendees she and the president were "behind their efforts 100 percent."[4]

When Wrobleski returned from Atlanta, she was ready to encourage the first lady to do far more than simply send a telegram. Wrobleski had been "taken aback by the fervor of the parents. There was a lot of pain and suffering and anger—at the government, at the so-called drug-abuse professionals. You could taste it," she said. After seeing hundreds of amateur parent activists spontaneously develop into a surprisingly cohesive national movement, she was sure that the first lady had found her calling. "These were people trying to grapple with a problem," Wrobleski said. "People who quite frankly needed a champion."[5]

Nancy Reagan needed a champion herself. In the early days of the new administration, Reagan had developed a reputation for insouciant grandeur even as the United States was falling into a deep recession. The first lady was mocked for her $10,000 inaugural ball gown and her lavish trip to England to witness the marriage of Prince Charles and Lady Diana, as well as for her plans to use $1 million in tax-deductible donations to fund a major White House redecoration. Building on her image as new American royalty, disconnected from the country's struggling citizens, in the summer of 1981 a best-selling "Queen Nancy" postcard debuted, which featured the first lady's face on the body of Queen Elizabeth, complete with ermine robe and crown jewels.[6] By November, a year after her husband swept into office, the first lady was notably unpopular. A Gallup poll revealed that 18 percent of those surveyed gave Mrs. Reagan an unfavorable rating. In comparison, only 8 percent had expressed disapproval of Pat Nixon in March 1969, and only 7 percent disapproved of Rosalynn Carter in May 1977.[7]

Wrobleski was certain that embracing the antidrug cause could help the first lady turn these numbers around. But to become a prominent drug fighter, Reagan needed a staff that could usher her along. Also present at the PRIDE conference was Carlton Turner, a board member of the NFP and the nation's best-known marijuana researcher. Turner, who received his PhD in chemistry from the University of Southern

Mississippi, had been working for ten years as the director of the University of Mississippi's Research Institute of Pharmaceutical Sciences, the only institution in the United States where federally funded research on marijuana took place. Turner had made a name for himself in the world of drug research through his studies of the various strains of cannabis he cultivated on the ten-acre plantation, and his ominous reports about the effects of delta-9-tetrahydrocannabinol (THC) had caught the attention of the parent movement early on. Turner argued that, unlike drugs like alcohol, which pass through the body quickly, cannabinoids (the active components in THC) "stay in the body for days and are stored in every major organ, particularly in the brain. There is no other drug used or abused by man that has the staying power and broad cellular actions on the body as do the cannabinoids." Parent activists, relying on his information to bolster their claims, had invited Turner to join their board of directors shortly after the NFP was formed.

Turner embodied marijuana's transformation from a seemingly innocuous substance to national scourge. Though in 1976 he was quoted in an interview in *High Times* saying that he was neither for nor against marijuana use ("If I were a crusader, it would interfere with my objectivity," he claimed), after a half-decade of research, Turner had become a vocal opponent of adolescent marijuana use, and this transformation bolstered his career. On July 9, 1981, he was appointed the president's senior adviser for drug policy, a nomination that proved the Reagan administration's strong emphasis on marijuana. His appointment to the White House staff forced Turner to resign from the NFP board, but in his resignation letter, Turner reassured his parent activist colleagues that his "intentions are to stay very active in drug abuse prevention work."[8] The man who had wanted to avoid being called a "crusader" in 1976 was, five years later, quick to accept that role, declaring to reporters that he "was hired by the President of the United States to clean up America."[9]

Less than a week later, Turner met with Nancy Reagan, Wrobleski, and several other members of the first lady's staff to discuss "how Mrs. Reagan might fit into drug policy." In his notes on the meeting, Turner wrote that the first lady "was very anxious to get started and obviously had some knowledge about the area. Her intensity was very good." As for where the first lady could begin, Turner focused on the obvious: marijuana. The country was reconsidering its attitude toward the drug, Turner noted. In the wake of the paraquat scare, and with growing understanding of marijuana's dangers "in terms of systems of the body," marijuana no longer seemed like an innocent drug, he wrote. And as the "parents' movement began to pick up steam," decriminalization no longer seemed like the national solution; instead, parent activism did.[10] If Reagan wanted to improve her popularity, Turner continued, the timing was right for an alliance with the populist anti-marijuana crusade.

Given his former affiliation with the NFP, Turner encouraged the first lady to work specifically with that organization. PRIDE and FIA did good work, Turner knew, but the NFP was led by social conservatives like Bill Barton, Pat Burch, and Joyce Nalepka—activists who would be more sympathetic to the White House's larger goals than people like Schuchard and Rusche, who founded the movement but were known Democrats. If the first lady was going to take up adolescent drug abuse prevention, Turner reasoned, she should do so with like-minded friends. With Turner's support, the first lady began working almost exclusively with the NFP, and Pat Burch became the White House's primary parent activist contact.

As the White House moved closer to their organization, NFP leaders also began cutting liberal members from their ranks, in order to accommodate themselves to the Republican administration. Lee Dogoloff, who had joined the board after his departure from the Carter White House, was the first to go. His affiliation with the Carter administration, in Burch's view, made him "a liability," and she directed the decision to quietly fire him from the NFP board in the summer of 1981. Though Dogoloff continued to work in the field of drug abuse prevention by becoming executive director of the American Council on Marijuana (later the American Council on Drug Education), he was disturbed by how quickly the NFP had affiliated—both politically and morally—with the Reagan White House. "For the most part I thought politics were aside," Dogoloff recalled. "I knew that Pat Burch was a Republican, but that was okay because [the NFP] was, from my perspective at least, apolitical. But then they let me go because I was so liberal that she saw me as a threat."[11]

Schuchard and Gleaton were also disturbed by Dogoloff's dismissal, as well as the NFP's immediate right turn. After Dogoloff's termination,

Schuchard and Gleaton resigned from the board of the organization they had cofounded and returned to their work with PRIDE, deepening the divisions now growing between the Atlanta-based activists and those based near DC.[12] Only Sue Rusche and FIA steered clear of the conflicts erupting between the two groups. She remained a welcome presence at both the PRIDE conference and the separate conference soon hosted by the NFP, and FIA stayed true to the movement's goal to remain unaffiliated with either political party, focusing instead on anti-paraphernalia lobbying and organizing additional parent groups.

In November 1981, the first lady hosted forty NFP members, along with numerous reporters, in the White House's State Dining Room, where she announced that adolescent drug abuse prevention would be her primary cause. At the meeting, Reagan spoke fondly of her own role as a mother and promoted parent activism, telling Pat Burch, Joyce Nalepka, and the gathered reporters that she believed "parents are the answer to it all." Reagan warned that "for a long time parents have not been involved the way they should be" in their children's lives, and this was why drug problems, especially problems with marijuana, had plagued the nation. But with the rise of groups like the NFP, Reagan saw the tide beginning to turn. "I think that in the final analysis it's the parents who are going to turn this thing around—I think they're the most potent force there is," she said to thunderous applause.[13] Afterward, as she posed for pictures with activists and took questions from the audience—none of which were about her spending habits—it was clear that Reagan had found her path.

•

The first year of Ronald Reagan's presidency was a remarkable period for the parent movement, as well as the nation's war on adolescent drug use. By mid-1982, driven by positive coverage in the press and the first lady's increasing support of the movement, parent activism had spread across the country; the NFP reported that, just two years after its formation, as many as 3,000 individual parent groups had joined its ranks. And drug use, especially adolescent use of marijuana, had dramatically declined. A report released in February of that year found that fewer seniors in the class of 1981 had reported using marijuana, PCP (phencyclidine), and tranquilizers, or even smoking cigarettes, than had their peers in the previous four years. Even more remarkably, rates of daily marijuana use had plunged from a high of 11 percent in 1979 to 7 percent in 1981. Lloyd Johnston, director of the University of Michigan's "Monitoring the Future" report, which had tracked annual rates of high school drug use since 1975, was buoyant about the results. "From the standpoint of public health," Johnston noted, "there can be little doubt that the sharp decline in marijuana use is good news."[14]

As the assault on youth marijuana use ramped up, however, toleration for ambiguity about marijuana's harms diminished. In February 1982, a four-year, $450,000 federal study by the National Academy of Sciences (NAS) released its results, which suggested that marijuana use was less problematic than originally believed. NAS began its study in 1978, and it acknowledged that short-term marijuana use by schoolchildren was thought to have "serious effects" on behavior and learning—including causing the "amotivational syndrome" that parent activists had feared for years—and that the drug's suspected hazards justified "serious national concern." Still, Dr. Arnold S. Relman, chair of the committee, concluded that the NAS had "failed to find that marijuana was either as safe or as dangerous as some have claimed." Instead, Relman noted, no "conclusive evidence" could be found to suggest that prolonged pot smoking caused "permanent changes to the nervous system or brain." Although its final results were "politically inconvenient," Relman said that "our committee found the present truth of the matter to lie somewhere in between the two extremes, so we give no comfort to those with strong positions on either side of the argument."[15]

Response to the report was quick and negative. Joyce Nalepka, speaking for the NFP, said that the study was little more than a joke. "We are concerned this prestigious organization has not been able to come down with a strong warning, which is what our children need," she told the *Washington Post*. *Time* suggested that "frightened parents" weren't going to ease up on their fight. After "an estimated 60% of high school seniors tried pot" in the 1970s and the drug made "inroads at elementary schools," it didn't matter that current rates of drug use were going down; parent activists were going to continue to "dissuade legislators from further liberalization." Even the *New York Times* paid limited attention to the study. The same month the findings were released, the *Times* declared that "parent networking" was the newest weapon "in the war against teenage abuse of alcohol and marijuana."[16]

The NAS report also did little to stem the first lady's newfound enthusiasm for her chief cause, though it did inspire her to use the more generic term "drugs" when making public addresses instead of referring specifically to marijuana. "Increasingly, unhappy families are unhappy because of drug use by their children," Reagan told the League of Republican Women at a fund-raising fashion show that raised $2,400 for the NFP in March. "And today, there are millions of confused, heartsick families in the nation, and drugs are the reason for their misery."[17]

Later that month, on March 22, the first lady hosted the White House Briefing on Drug Use and the Family, the first event of its kind. Sponsored by ACTION, the federal volunteer agency, and its new leader, the conservative Reagan family friend Tom Pauken, the purpose of the six-hour meeting was, according to Carlton Turner, "to encourage corporate participation in [prevention] programs."[18] The meeting brought together 115 representatives from parent groups, Fortune 500 corporations, and the medical field to meet, network, and establish relationships. After the group examined toy-shaped marijuana paraphernalia and met with representatives from parent groups, Reagan used her opening remarks to reassert the first couple's commitment to the cause. "The White House is committed to this drive against drugs," Reagan said. "My husband's concern has grown along with mine, and I intend to keep the spotlight on drug abuse as long as I'm here."[19]

Money, however, was the meeting's true focus, even as it remained a touchy subject. Despite the first lady's personal fund-raising efforts for the NFP earlier that month, the meeting was meant to create opportunities for activists to take steps to avoid reliance on federal funds by meeting with donors who could assist them with financial support. Bill Barton, who addressed the meeting as NFP president, agreed that the solution to the drug problem lay in the private sector. He argued that he felt "it imperative that we work with, but not for, the Government," and noted that the nearly 3,000 NFP-affiliated parent groups that had formed across the country accepted no federal or state funds (though he neglected to mention the large amounts of money that movement leaders received from the administration).[20] Sue Rusche, who attended for FIA, argued that the meeting wasn't actually about money at all. Instead, she described the event as an attempt to "raise the consciousness" of business leaders, and denied that any explicit financial solicitation had taken place.[21]

The first lady may have been publicly encouraging parent activists to seek private support, but her husband's administration ensured that national parent leaders had federal money to spend as well. In the hands of Tom Pauken, a failed congressional candidate whom Reagan had hand-selected to lead ACTION, that agency became a generous benefactor to parent activists in its own right. Originally formed in 1971 to serve as a "domestic Peace Corps," ACTION had been transformed by 1982 into the White House's drug abuse extension office, handing out grants to antidrug groups that the office had never funded before. In his 1995 memoir *The Thirty Year War: The Politics of the Sixties Generation*, Pauken wrote that he despised how, during the Carter administration, ACTION had "used federal dollars to fund what seemed like virtually every remnant of the New Left apparatus remaining from the turbulent sixties."[22] Under his leadership, ACTION's priorities shifted away from liberal volunteer community engagement groups and toward programs that promoted conservative ideals, like a better public image for Vietnam veterans and, most notably, widespread antidrug education campaigns. Its 1982 budget included over $902,000 for antidrug programs, including a $175,000 grant for PRIDE and $24,000 for the American Council on Marijuana, run by Lee Dogoloff after his departure from the NFP.[23] With the addition of Nancy Reagan's private fund-raising, parent leaders had more federal money during the early years of the Reagan administration than they'd had at any time before, even as parent activists publicly shunned taking government funds and the White House advocated for partnering with the private sector.

Still, it was Nancy Reagan who remained the movement's most prominent supporter, and when she wasn't sponsoring fund-raisers and fashion shows for the NFP, she was attending movement-oriented events. Despite Schuchard's and Gleaton's break from the NFP, PRIDE's conference was still the largest antidrug gathering in the country, and an appearance by the first lady was obligatory if she wanted to preserve her image. On April 2, 1982, Reagan traveled to Atlanta, where she addressed over 600 cheering fans at the fourth annual PRIDE Southeast

Drug Conference. Bolstered by grants from ACTION, it was the group's largest and most spectacular meeting yet. Three days of adolescent drug abuse prevention activities were interspersed with student groups performing musical acts, movies, and grand buffets. There were also celebrity guests. Standing onstage alongside actress Melissa Gilbert (star of television's *Little House on the Prairie*) and Dr. Gabriel Nahas, Reagan commended the movement's work. "I'm very happy to be here among all you concerned parents," she said, "because, while drugs have cast a dark shadow in recent years, the parent movement has been a light in the window—it shines with hope and progress." Even as she stood next to actors and scientists, however, the first lady was the meeting's true star. After her speech, the journalist Michael Massing reported, "members of the audience hoisted her on their shoulders and carried her around the hall as if she had just scored the winning touchdown of a football game."[24]

Six months later, the first lady addressed a similar audience at the first conference organized by the NFP. The meeting, funded in large part by the first lady's donations, was as elaborate as PRIDE's: the group brought together hundreds of people, including parent activists, lawmakers, medical experts, drug abuse specialists, and policymakers, from forty-three states and four nations to Alexandria, Virginia, for its inaugural event. There, Barton and Nalepka thanked the audience for its support and proudly revealed the organization's new logo. Printed on a banner that hung behind the front podium, the NFP's new emblem emphasized its evolving mission of fighting not just marijuana but the danger posed by "drugs" in general. The banner featured an enormous American flag whose bottom stripe drifted downward, with the words "Drugs and Youth: An American Crisis" bordering its edges.

Nancy Reagan addressed the crowd as the keynote speaker. "I know this is your first national conference," she said. "Wouldn't it be wonderful if we never had to hold another one? Well, that day is a few years down the road." Reagan then used her brief remarks to celebrate how far the movement had come. "Looking back at the sixties when this whole drug problem seemed to start, you realize how ill prepared we were," she said. "We were as much babes in the woods as our children, perhaps more so." But in the past six years, since the first parent group formed, "we are making progress," she said. "The parent groups have grown from 1,000 to a little over 3,000. I think the parents have shown the professionals that something can be done on a scale larger than previously believed. What I'm trying to say is, you are a success and you deserve some public gratitude for all that success. I came here today to thank you so much for what you're accomplishing. And to tell you to hang in there—together, we will make it."[25]

•

There was a certain irony to the first lady's remarks about embattled parents and the new logo's declaration of an "American Crisis." Throughout 1982 and into 1983, rates of adolescent use of all drugs rapidly declined; by 1983, rates of adolescent marijuana use were at their lowest in recorded history. The University of Michigan's annual survey report announced that high school seniors' daily use of marijuana had continued to drop during the first two years of the Reagan administration, decreasing from 7 percent in 1981 to 5.5 percent in 1983, while the use of amphetamines, barbiturates, and LSD had dropped markedly as well. The report's authors celebrated these "substantial declines" and argued that they were "an encouraging sign that the downturn, which began in the past couple of years, is real and continuing."[26]

Yet even as rates of use dropped, politicians, researchers, and the national media continued to declare that adolescent drug abuse was nothing less than a national crisis and that volunteer activism was the country's only solution. Writing in *Ladies' Home Journal* in January 1983, Nancy Reagan decried the "epidemic among our nation's youth" that had destroyed so many lives. "Drug addiction is the most democratic of problems," Reagan wrote. "It crosses all social, political, color and economic lines, and celebrities' kids are every bit as vulnerable as ghetto children." But, Reagan concluded, there were solutions to the problem: forming a local parent group, counteracting peer pressure, and even writing to the White House for a list of parent groups. "I'd like to ask everyone—parents as well as students—to get involved," Reagan wrote. "If we close ranks, pull together and share our love and concern, nothing can stop us!"[27]

Leaders of the parent movement also had a vested interest in keeping the battle against adolescent drug use alive. Whereas once they were laughed out of federal offices, by 1983 social science researchers and government officials were lauding parent groups as the most important development in drug abuse prevention in decades. NIDA's associate director for policy development and implementation, R. A. Lindblad, declared that, with the formation of the NFP, "the visible, vocal, contemporary [parent] movement was born. It has spread, not as a fad, but as an organized and committed response to the drug problems of the United States."[28] And in answer to the question posed by their article in the *Journal of Primary Prevention,* "Parent Groups in Drug Abuse Prevention: Is This the Constituency We've Been Waiting For?" the mental health researchers Anne Penney and Emily Garfield argued at length for "yes."[29] If their battle had only been against marijuana, parent activists would have already won. Instead, unwilling to give up the recognition they had worked years to achieve or to abandon their increasingly respected work, parent leaders joined the first lady in continuing to declare that the war on drugs was an essential battle. Their war on marijuana, out of necessity, had evolved.

By autumn of that year, the first lady and leaders of the NFP opened a new front in their battle against drug abuse: television. In October, Nancy Reagan cohosted *Good Morning America* (the same program that had broken the Peter Bourne Quaaludes story in July 1978) for a series of stories about parent activism that encouraged parents from across the country to write to the White House with their questions and concerns about adolescent drug abuse. The first lady then invited cameras into her White House office, where, standing alongside NFP officials Carolyn Burns and Joyce Nalepka in their television debut, she answered some of the hundreds of letters they received, promising to call and personally counsel several parents, who, in their letters, seemed particularly distraught.[30]

Good Morning America brought parent activists into the country's living rooms for the first time, and a month later the activists' mission was broadcast to an even wider audience. On November 2 and 9, PBS stations across the country ran a two-part miniseries called *The Chemical People,* a program dedicated to exposing the problem of adolescent drug use and offering "community task forces" as the solution, which were little more than parent groups by another name. The project was launched nationally with a half-hour-long program called "An Appeal to All Americans," produced from the East Room of the White House on October 27. Cohosted by Nancy Reagan and the actor Michael Landon, this initial appeal promoted the upcoming program and introduced the concept of "town meetings." Over the following two weeks, the "meetings" were local opportunities for group viewing of the miniseries, to be followed by a public discussion on how to stop adolescent drug abuse and the formation of the task forces. *The Chemical People's* producer, Lloyd Kaiser of the Pittsburgh PBS station WQED-TV, declared that a total of 10,675 such meetings had been organized across the country to coincide with the two-part event, and he had high hopes for the cause. Knowing that a young son or daughter was abusing alcohol or drugs was "unthinkable," Kaiser said in the televised appeal, but with *The Chemical People* and new task forces formed nationwide, there would be "no more struggling alone, no more finger pointing, no more denying the problem."[31]

The programs themselves were a sensationalistic and star-studded success, proving how popular the prevention of adolescent drug abuse had become, and how eager celebrities were to enlist in the cause. Each episode was introduced by Nancy Reagan and cohosted by a variety of actors and sports stars, including Bill Bixby, Rita Moreno, Bruce Weitz, Willie Stargell, and Sandy Duncan. The programs primarily consisted of interviews with adolescents and parents whose lives had been disrupted by youthful drug use, along with dramatic re-creations of their stories. With a special emphasis on stopping the use of "soft" drugs like marijuana, the programs ended with discussion prompts for the town meetings and task forces to follow. And while no specific parent groups or activists were featured in the shows, the NFP was hugely influential behind the scenes: Joyce Nalepka helped plan the programs, wrote sections of the follow-up teachers' guide, and officially endorsed the shows to all of the country's NFP-affiliated parent groups. Kaiser also promised Nalepka that her organization could take control of the task forces that formed in the program's wake, effectively linking them all the more closely with the NFP and traditional parent groups.[32]

With the celebrities it featured and the White House's explicit endorsement, *The Chemical People* was one of the most popular PBS programs of the 1980s. Though many viewers watched the programs collectively at town meetings, Kaiser reported that "there were still sufficient viewers at home responding to Nielsen rating service" that in cities like Chicago and Los Angeles, "astonishing ratings doubled the usual proportionate prime time share of their audiences."[33] Many of those who attended town hall meetings also truly believed that *The Chemical People* offered hope. Eighteen-year-old Alan Seawell, who attended a meeting with his mother in Wilmington, North Carolina, told the local newspaper that, after using "marijuana, alcohol, hashish, codeine, LSD, methaqualone, valium and amphetamines" for years, he was now "straight" and hoped that *The Chemical People* would encourage the community to become "involved enough to prevent or curtail area drug abuse." His mother, who told the paper that the program made her relive "a very frightening part of her life," felt the same way. She believed that the program's town meetings could encourage parents to become more involved and help them avoid having to deal with the troubling situation she and her son had experienced. With positive reviews of the programs running in newspapers across the country, parent activists couldn't have been more thrilled.[34]

•

In the wake of *The Chemical People*'s success, and in the midst of the nation's ongoing battle against adolescent drug use, 1983 marked the year when the movement's antidrug, anti-marijuana stance was fully embraced by popular culture, aided by the White House's explicit support. It was a stunning reversal from the "drug culture" of the 1970s that parent activists had lobbied against for years: instead of *Tots Who Toke*, kids could watch *The Chemical People* or read comic books that dramatized their favorite superheroes fighting drug use. That year, in cooperation with the Department of Education, the Keebler Company released three editions of *The New Teen Titans* that featured the Changeling, Cyborg, Raven, the Protector, Speedy, Starfire, and Wonder Girl saving children from drugs, including marijuana, mushrooms, and PCP. Each issue also emphasized the White House's support by opening with a letter from Nancy Reagan, who pleaded with children to join the battle against drug use. If they did, they too could be heroes—"to your mother and father, family and friends, but most of all," she wrote, "to yourself."

Parent activists had other reasons to celebrate too. In the five years since the last decriminalization law was passed, every state except Alaska had recriminalized the possession of marijuana. The Reagan

Revolution didn't only bring conservative Republicans into the House and Senate; it also brought Republicans into governorships and state legislatures across the country. With the tide turning fast against marijuana, and with the Reagan administration threatening to withhold federal drug abuse funds from states that continued to decriminalize the drug, marijuana was quietly recriminalized across the country, with many states making possession of the drug into a felony.

But the White House's public support for parent activism masked a quiet transformation in the federal government's larger war on drugs that would eventually reduce the amount of money available for anti-drug education and prevention programs and leave parent volunteers to pick up the slack on their own. Despite decreasing national rates of drug use, a year earlier President Reagan had used public approval for fighting drug abuse to reorient the drug war's core priorities, and by 1983 the effects of this change were being felt. Moving away from Nixon's and Carter's focus on treating and rehabilitating heroin users, Reagan turned the parent movement's war against marijuana into law, reorienting federal funds away from treatment and education and toward interdiction and law enforcement. Although this new policy direction seemed like a capitulation to parent activists' requests at first, it ultimately forced the movement to work without federal financial assistance, even as the White House's demands for activists' services increased. Most upsetting for parent activists, it was Carlton Turner, the former NFP board member who helped to cement the alliance between parent activists and the Reagan administration, who oversaw this shift and who argued most emphatically that parent groups should begin to go without the federal funds on which they'd grown dependent.

In June 1982, President Reagan signed Executive Order 12368. On its face, the order, which placed Turner in charge of the domestic and international drug abuse functions of all executive agencies, seemed hugely supportive of parent activists' work. At the signing ceremony held in the Rose Garden, the president was lavish with his praise and applauded the "education and prevention efforts" of the parent movement, as well as the "volunteer groups, parents, teachers, students, [and] independent agencies . . . which have been fighting a long, hard battle against the drug problem." Now, however, Reagan wanted "a new approach." With his new executive order, the president sought to align law enforcement and health agencies at all levels, along with volunteer organizations across the country, in order to "mobilize all our forces to stop the flow of drugs into this country." Ultimately, the goal was "to brand drugs such as marijuana for exactly what they are—dangerous, and particularly to school-age youth." For the president, the order was a rejection of "the helpless attitude that drug use is so rampant that we're defenseless to do anything about it. We're taking down the surrender flag that has flown over so many drug efforts; we're running up a battle flag." With "stronger law enforcement, through cooperation with other nations to stop the trafficking, and by calling on the tremendous volunteer resources of parents, teachers, civic and religious leaders, and State and local officials," Reagan concluded, "we can fight the drug problem, and we can win."[35]

Though Reagan would boast that Executive Order 12368 supported the goals and prevention efforts of the parent movement, the primary purpose of the order was quite different: it militarized and expanded the war on drugs, turning a rhetorical battle into an actual war. The order called for an increase in FBI antidrug funding, from $8 million to $95 million by 1984, and expanded the powers of the DEA so that the agency could participate in ever more aggressive interdiction efforts. Meanwhile, it reduced federal investment in addiction treatment, rehabilitation, and even antidrug education efforts in order to free up funds: NIDA's budget was reduced from $274 million to $57 million while the Department of Education's antidrug education budget was slashed from $14 million to just $3 million.[36] Even ACTION's minimal budget for parent activism was decreased: FIA received $100,697 from ACTION between 1982 and 1984, and PRIDE received $682,347. A year later, however, as Reagan's budget cuts went into effect, the total ACTION budget was $300,000 for all drug programs, from parent activism to the myriad other programs the office supported.[37] With deep cuts put into place, parent volunteers were expected to pick up the cost of antidrug education on their own, forcing volunteers to do more with less even as drug abuse prevention became a popular national cause.

As if reduced federal funding wasn't bad enough, the new *Federal Strategy for Prevention of Drug Abuse and Drug Trafficking*, released by Turner's Drug Abuse Policy Office in 1982, was an even greater cause for alarm. On its surface, the strategy praised the "important private efforts" of "the highly successful Parent Movement," which prevented drug abuse "where it really counts: by individuals, in families, and in local communities." The strategy also heaped praise on parent activists for pointing the federal government in the right direction by refocusing Reagan's drug war away from "hard" drugs like heroin and toward common, and therefore more dangerous, drugs like marijuana. Ultimately, it declared that the movement was nothing less than "a dramatic indication of the intense concern across the country and the willingness of people to get personally involved in solving drug abuse problems that touch their lives."

But the next sentence gave parent activists pause. "Significantly," the strategy declared, "the Parent Movement has grown with little financial support from the government." Even though, Turner proudly declared, "the President's budget for 1983 requested almost one billion dollars to support the Federal drug abuse programs," very little of that was earmarked for parent activists—or for drug research, education, prevention, rehabilitation, or treatment. With funding now directed toward an increasingly militarized drug war, the strategy relied on parents to pick up where budget cuts left off. Pointedly, Turner reminded readers that parent groups should be composed exclusively of volunteers, ignoring the leading parent activists who had turned adolescent drug abuse prevention into full-time careers. "Continued growth and success of the Movement is based on parents uniting with each other," the strategy concluded, "knowing how their community works, and maintaining identity as a voluntary organization." The only proper role of the federal government in this area was to provide "leadership, encouragement, and support."[38]

For leaders of groups like PRIDE and FIA, Turner's assertions in the *Federal Strategy* were patently untrue. Small, local parent groups had grown without direct federal assistance, but PRIDE and FIA had received hundreds of thousands of dollars in federal funding over the past few years, and Gleaton, Schuchard, and Rusche were only able to conduct their work—hosting national conferences, publishing newsletters, and organizing parent groups nationwide—with the White House's help. Indeed, these activists argued, national rates of adolescent marijuana use had only fallen because, with Washington's support, they had dedicated their lives to national prevention initiatives. After being the first activists to raise the alarm about marijuana's negative effects, they were deeply dismayed to learn that the government was turning off the tap. Turner and Reagan may have appeased parent activists' demands by publicly celebrating their work and reorienting the domestic drug war to target marijuana, but by cutting funds for antidrug education and prevention programs, they were also burdening activists with considerably more responsibility, all while promoting the idea that their work had been "volunteer-based" all along.

Meanwhile, the first lady's preferred organization didn't face these financial struggles. From 1983 into 1984, aid from Nancy Reagan went directly to the NFP, and as the year went on, the amount of money continued to rise. In January 1984, while the Reagans viewed a performance of *The Hasty Heart* at the Kennedy Center, Mrs. Reagan was handed a check for $10,000 from the play's director, the actor Burt Reynolds, which she earmarked for the NFP.[39] Then, in September 1984, Nancy Reagan traveled to New York City to meet with Sultan Hassanal Bolkiah of the small island nation of Brunei, an oil-rich country that had gained its independence from Britain only earlier that year. Hoping to facilitate a positive relationship with the Reagan administration, the sultan presented the first lady with a check for $500,000, also made out to the NFP. "What you are doing is very important for the world community," the sultan wrote in his accompanying letter. "You are helping people understand the consequences of a life thrown away, how precious life is, and what each individual has to contribute."[40] Even the Reagans' tax records revealed that they had personally donated $4,786 to the NFP in 1984, though they neglected to donate to any other parent group.[41]

The White House's obvious preference for the NFP didn't go unnoticed by other parent leaders. Gleaton was furious that PRIDE, whose founders had also started the NFP, was now receiving almost no federal assistance, direct or indirect. He called and wrote several letters to Turner, trying to plead his case. He referenced his own role in establishing the organization, in recruiting board members, and even in hosting a "wine and cheese reception" for White House staff at the 1981 PRIDE conference, "at no cost to NFP." Now the first lady had made it clear that her only assistance to PRIDE would be in attending the group's annual conference, which PRIDE struggled to put on without federal financial support. The group's work was only beginning, Gleaton argued, and it needed more money if it was expected to succeed.[42]

But Turner was unmoved. Gleaton's memos went unanswered, and with the federal drug budget set, no more money for PRIDE was forthcoming through ACTION. After Reagan was reelected in a landslide in 1984, Turner knew that the first lady no longer needed to be affiliated with all of the leading parent groups to maintain her newfound popularity. Her poll numbers had rebounded because of her partnership with the NFP, which, thanks to her own efforts, was now far better known than PRIDE. And it was private donations, not federal money, keeping the NFP afloat. If PRIDE suffered, Turner reasoned, it was through no fault of his own. The White House had been emphasizing private partnerships for years; it was up to Gleaton to fund his own organization now.

Sue Rusche was beginning to understand this as well. Also upset that the NFP was receiving the majority of the first lady's donations, Rusche called Turner at the White House, shortly after the president was reelected, to complain. But when she asked for additional financial help for FIA, Turner was quick to turn her down. "The only way I could sell the president on supporting the parents' movement was to say that it wouldn't cost anything," he said. "A big reason this administration *likes* the drug issue is that so much of it can be handled by volunteer groups." Then, in a moment of shocking candor, Turner revealed what some parent activists had been fearing for over a year. "You're white middle-class folks," Turner concluded. "You're the last people that need government handouts." It would have been impossible to sum up the White House's position any better.[43]

By the end of 1984, it was clear that the first lady had aligned, both personally and financially, with the NFP, while PRIDE and FIA were left to fend for themselves. But even the NFP's success wouldn't last forever: a new organization was forming across the country, one that would take the concept of adolescent drug abuse prevention and transform it into one of the most popular tropes of the 1980s. Though originally intended to fight adolescent drug use in the inner cities, Just Say No quickly became a national marketing and merchandising campaign, appearing on T-shirts, television shows, and advertisements and in White House public events. And though the first lady helped the group dominate the field of adolescent drug abuse prevention in the early 1980s, when she became affiliated with Just Say No, she quickly forgot about the NFP.

10

THE TRUTH BEHIND JUST SAY NO

JOAN BRANN HAD always been an activist. Born in Oakland, California, in 1930, Brann first took to political organizing in her late twenties, when she supported liberal Democratic candidates in California and beyond. By 1964, she was a pro, canvassing her hometown's housing projects to elect the progressive lawyer Phillip Burton to the US House of Representatives. Brann was an active and eager volunteer, handing out slate cards, leading voters to the polls, and convincing the undecided to vote Democratic. Brann was so committed to the cause that when she came to the apartment of a young mother who claimed that she couldn't vote because she had a meal cooking on the stove and a child asleep in the bedroom, she offered to take over the woman's chores. "I'll watch the baby, and I'll stir the pot," Brann said. "Well, if you'll do that, I'll go vote," the woman replied.[1]

By the mid-1970s, Brann had transformed from an adept canvasser into a well-known community organizer. While working as a program analyst for the San Francisco Housing Authority and raising five children with her husband, Frank, she rallied her neighbors around issues like health care and African American cultural pride.[2] By 1977, she was trailblazing again when she was appointed as the first black director of the US State Department's International Communication Agency reception center in San Francisco, where she was charged with overseeing meetings between foreign professionals and their counterparts in the United States. Iris Jacobson, the director of the State Department's Office of International Visitor Programs, chose Brann over the other candidates for the job—which was traditionally referred to as the "city's top hostess," and whose previous appointees were, according to one newspaper, "sleek with money and privilege" (and, of course, were all white)—as a form of "mini-affirmative action." "If you have a judge visiting from another country and you want to arrange a meeting with a US judge, suppose you have a man judge and a woman judge, or a black judge and a white judge from which to choose. I want the visitor to meet the woman—or the black," Jacobson said. "I want to give them a perspective that women just don't cook meals and give tours. And that blacks don't just carry their luggage at airports or drive cabs." Brann, she felt, would help offer that perspective.[3]

But Brann didn't stay in that position for long. Her reputation for diplomacy and her desire to open doors between Africa and the United States brought her to Washington in January 1980, where she had been appointed director of the African American Institute (AAI). AAI was formed in 1953 to provide African nations with Western technological, political, and philosophical training in order to improve understanding and communication between the continent and the United States. The job seemed a perfect fit for Brann, one that combined her interests in international communication and African culture. While working with AAI, Brann also continued to hone her diplomatic skills. She was appointed to the board of directors of the National Council of International Visitors for the 1981–1982 session, serving as a citizen diplomat for African officials.[4]

But Brann had to return to California less than three years after she first left. Her husband died in June 1982, leaving her widowed in her early fifties, and, after another death in the family, she inherited the house in northern Oakland where she was raised. When she returned to California, she found that life there had dramatically changed. Though Oakland had long held a reputation for being dangerous, Brann had taken pride in her hometown, a friendly community of close-knit neighbors, and enjoyed her large backyard filled with rosebushes. Since she had left for Washington, however, the emergence of a thriving drug trade and the subsequent rise in violence had drastically altered the city's feel. Open-air dealing had become such a problem that newspapers were calling Oakland "the drug capital of the west," and the week she moved back several drug-related murders occurred not far from her home, one of them in a schoolyard where children were playing.[5] When she saw policemen leap over her fence and chase two teenage drug suspects across her lawn, she knew she had to do something. "Up to that moment, I had no idea of the frightening extent of the drug problems in my community," she said. "Then it dawned on me how terrifying it must be for young children to walk to school in such a drug-infested area. I decided to try to do something about it."[6]

What Brann would "try to do" transformed the battle against adolescent drug use for the rest of the decade. Though few people would credit the phenomenon to this fifty-year-old African American grandmother from California, Joan Brann invented the concept of "Just Say No," a movement originally designed to address the needs of the inner-city minority youth who wanted to create environments of positive peer pressure to keep kids away from drugs. Brann formed the first Just Say No club in 1985 with the help of several local children and Tom Adams, a fellow parent activist. The concept quickly spread across the country, becoming one of the most popular, and powerful, antidrug messages of all time.

Brann was more than just the originator of Just Say No. In the mid-1980s, traditional parent groups like PRIDE and the NFP had yet to cater to the needs of urban African American parents, and Brann was one of the first people in the country to recognize and address this obvious oversight. A year before she founded her antidrug club, she had also formed one of the first parent groups for nonwhite, non-middle-class parents, Oakland Parents in Action (OPA), which transformed the concept of traditional parent groups to meet the needs of lower-income minority families by pooling resources and ensuring that working parents received child care and food.

Brann's concept of a club for low-income children to help them stay away from drugs was revolutionary, and her ideas would go on to shape how the White House addressed adolescent drug abuse in Ronald Reagan's second term. Today, when most people think of Just Say No, they think of Nancy Reagan. With her support, Just Say No became the largest nationwide antidrug program of all time, dominating the mid-1980s with children's clubs, pledge drives, and marches, its ubiquitous green-and-white logo—a slashed circle with the words JUST SAY NO printed within—appearing on countless T-shirts, posters, buttons, and flags. It became a pop culture phenomenon, with celebrity endorsements and a club formed on the television show *Punky Brewster*. Most of all it was Nancy Reagan herself, who claimed to have started the Just Say No movement and was its most famous face, beaming with hope and joy as groups of children surrounded her at antidrug rallies, delighting her with cheers of "just say no" when asked what they would do when confronted by alcohol and drugs.

But Nancy Reagan did not create the concept of Just Say No, and the first lady's affiliation with the group whitewashed the movement's Oakland origins and placed it under corporate control, destroying much of what Brann had worked for years to achieve. As the program went national, with over 10,000 clubs formed by 1987, corporations realized the profit potential in advertising to thousands of Just Say No kids, and Nancy Reagan facilitated a marriage between Just Say No and Procter & Gamble (P&G). Brann quickly lost control of her organization: within months P&G staff replaced Just Say No officials, forced Brann's Oakland office to close, and transformed Just Say No into little more than a national merchandising opportunity, turning adolescent drug abuse prevention into a marketing slogan used to sell everything from paper towels and cake mix to clothing and potato chips.

As much as Brann was able to achieve during her lifetime of activism, when her most famous project was usurped by the White House and P&G, she knew that the first lady's support for adolescent drug abuse prevention was little more than a means to a very profitable end. By 1988, as her husband's time in office drew to a close, Nancy Reagan was one of the most popular first ladies in the nation's history, thanks in no small part to her affiliation with Just Say No, while companies from P&G to Frito-Lay had benefited financially and socially from their alliance with the Just Say No brand. The only people who didn't benefit from Just Say No's remarkable national growth were the nonwhite youth of Oakland the program was originally intended to help, whose city continued to struggle with illegal drug use and who were quickly forgotten as Brann's program transformed from a local organization dedicated to helping their families into one of the largest drug abuse prevention phenomena of all time.

•

In September 1984, an Associated Press headline screamed "Children Deal Drugs Openly in Oakland," and warned that kids, "often too poor for summer camp and too young to work, are enticed by drug dealers who pay them $60 to $200 a day to sell their wares." With marijuana joints sticking out of their pockets and cocaine, PCP, LSD, and heroin in their backpacks, children as young as five waved down the cars driving through downtown and yelled to the drivers, "Hey, want to buy some smoke?"[7]

The idea of children openly selling drugs was terrifying, but for many of their parents, there were few other options to make ends meet. Between 1981 and 1988, Oakland lost 12,000 jobs in the traditional manufacturing, communications, utilities, and transportation industries—a massive blow for a city whose population was only 340,000. The national recession decimated downtown Oakland, where department stores closed and were boarded up, with few other tenants willing to fill the empty spaces. Between 1970 and 1990, the city also experienced dramatic white flight: 90,000 white residents abandoned Oakland, removing much of its tax base and further pushing the city into economic ruin.[8] When Joan Brann moved home in 1982 after nearly three years on the East Coast, it was this Oakland that she encountered and wanted to help.

Addressing the city's adolescent drug problem seemed like a reasonable place to start. Brann had heard of parent groups in places like Atlanta and Washington, DC, and she agreed with their premise that the best way to deal with the problem was by focusing on young children to prevent drug use before it began. She was concerned, however, about implementing the same concept in downtown Oakland, a place where no parent group had existed before. Discussing the problem with her neighbors, Brann was put in touch with W. Thomas "Tom" Adams, vice president of the public health research organization Pacific Institute for Research and Education (PIRE) and director of its Pyramid Project, a NIDA-funded antidrug program that provided technical assistance for activists working on prevention efforts.[9]

Adams, a white father who lived in the nearby town of Lafayette, had started his own parent group in the late 1970s, and he was excited about helping Brann expand the concept to her community. But he also recognized that, given Oakland's struggles and Brann's position as an activist for African American rights, a traditional suburban parent group, with its emphasis on constant parent vigilance and tacit understanding that parents had both the time and the financial resources to dedicate to the task, wasn't what she had in mind. Instead, Adams encouraged Brann to write a grant proposal to the San Francisco Foundation, a philanthropic organization that supported local community-building initiatives, to receive funding to start her own activist group catering specifically to the needs of the black working parents in her community.

In her successful application, Brann laid out her concept for Oakland Parents in Action (OPA): "Although a great deal of progress has been made in recent years in developing effective drug abuse prevention programs, rarely are the unique needs of low-income, minority families and youths singled out for particular attention. This project will adapt the successful methods of parent group organizing used in white, middle-class communities throughout the country to low-income, mainly black neighborhoods of North Oakland. The project will test and develop methods that will make the parent group organization approach appropriate to low-income, ethnic neighborhoods."[10] OPA received its grant in March 1984, and Brann went to work immediately, serving as projects director for the group while Adams served as president. Linda Wiltz, another experienced black political activist and Oakland resident, joined OPA as the group's community organizer.

OPA thrived in its first year. Soon Brann and Wiltz had a core group of twenty-four volunteers, ranging from parents and teachers to principals and school board members, who, like other parent activists, watched their children's behavior, collectively enforced antidrug rules, and worked to offer alternative activities so that children wouldn't be tempted by drug use. Unlike traditional parent group meetings, however, the OPA meetings that Brann hosted in her backyard also catered to the community's needs: she served food, provided child care, and offered financial assistance to needy families to ensure that all parents could attend. She saw responding to her volunteers' needs as a core component of OPA's mission. As Brann explained, "Part of what we're doing is helping to strengthen families who want the kind of support we're offering. We're trying to link people together in positive ways that will help families and children. We'll do anything we can."[11]

OPA was enormously well received by its Oakland neighbors. Local parents saw the need for preventing adolescent drug abuse in urban areas where, unlike in the country's suburbs, drugs were visible and rates of use remained high. But parent movement leaders in Washington were less than receptive to the group, dismissive of Brann, and uninterested in her attempts to adapt their concepts in a different way. Adams, who had been a parent activist for over half a decade by the time OPA was founded, had long been critical of the movement's lack of racial diversity. "I was very, very concerned over the fact that there were so few black parents in the movement," Adams said. Brann was already a well-known and committed activist, and she seemed an ideal candidate for the NFP's board. Yet no matter how hard he tried, Adams was not able to convince NFP leadership to allow Brann, a black Democrat, to join its directorship.[12] Even as OPA became the preeminent parent group in the black community—the recipient of numerous awards and grants and the focus of NIDA publications like *A Guide to Mobilizing Ethnic Minority Communities for Drug Abuse Prevention*—NFP leadership remained largely Republican and white, and Brann was never invited to join its staff.[13]

Adams did succeed, however, in getting Brann's fledgling organization some high-profile attention from the White House. That summer Adams contacted Ann Wrobleski, Nancy Reagan's projects director, and noted that, in the first lady's three years of visiting addiction treatment centers and parent groups across the country, she had consistently avoided the inner city. Adams suggested that, if the first lady visited Oakland and saw the kind of work that OPA did, she would be amazed. He touted Brann's program as "a shining light" designed to get parents who had long been neglected by the larger parent movement—black, urban, and lower-class—active in the fight to keep kids off drugs. Most of all, Adams told Wrobleski, if she visited, the first lady would have nothing to fear. Though she was a Democrat, Brann deeply respected the first lady's drug prevention work, and Reagan would be welcomed with open arms.[14]

Wrobleski found Adams's appeals convincing enough to schedule an official trip, and on July 3, 1984, Nancy Reagan conducted her first visit with an urban, nonwhite parent group. As Adams had promised, not only did OPA welcome Reagan, but the event was a lavish, media-studded affair. With dozens of newspaper reporters and cameras watching, 200 Oakland parents, teachers, community leaders, and children greeted the first lady when she arrived at Longfellow Elementary School in North Oakland and presented her with an enormous birthday cake decorated with a map of the United States. Reagan's sixty-third birthday was on July 6, and the parents and children stood around the first lady, serenading her with a song they called "Happy Birthday to America and Mrs. Reagan."

Afterward, Reagan sat with about forty parents and children in classroom 18, where they watched a thirteen-minute antidrug film that had been produced by NIDA. After viewing the film, Reagan told those gathered that drug abuse "is one of the most democratic problems we have. It crosses all lines—economic, social, racial, political—it doesn't make any difference. The dangers are there and they've got to be dealt with. Somebody's making a lot of money off our kids."[15] Then, in what would become a nationally significant statement, Reagan told the crowd, "You have to feel like you're going to win [the war on drugs]. And we will. After all, you know we only make this trip once. I think. So let's make it count and just say no to drugs."[16]

The phrase "Just Say No" has become so inextricably linked with the first lady that it's easy to assume that she used it intentionally while in Oakland. But in fact, Reagan said it in passing, and the phrase would not become a theme for her tenure as first lady until later, after Brann and Adams turned the slogan into a national phenomenon. The history of Joan Brann and OPA makes clear that Just Say No—with its clubs and T-shirts, shows and events—didn't come into being until a year later, in 1985, when a young student named Nomathemby Martini suggested that kids start their own antidrug clubs. It was then and there that the phenomenon was born.

Six months after the first lady visited Oakland, in January 1985, Brann was invited to lead an antidrug assembly for children at the Peralta Year Round Elementary School. Peralta was a low-income, predominantly black school that, less than a decade prior, had battled to stay open. By 1985, though still mostly black, the school was a model of successful public education, with a committed body of parent volunteers and a curriculum that promoted diversity and tolerance. Brann was invited to the school, attended by Angel Wiltz, the daughter of her collaborator Linda Wiltz, to show a video about the first lady's visit to Oakland the previous summer and lead a discussion about drug use. Brann told the gathered children that they were there "to see a film about Nancy Reagan's visit to our school last July. . . . Her visit was quite a day for us. Afterward, we had the film you're about to see made of the occasion. The film is about drug use and we hope that you will think about it long and hard."[17]

The children watched the film with quiet attention. Afterward, there was an open discussion about how drug use affected the children's lives. Affirming that everyone knew someone in their community or family who had used drugs, the children discussed the dangers of drug use and how it was harmful to growing kids. As the discussion came to a close, twelve-year-old Nomathemby Martini—whose first name was derived from the Zulu word for "hope"—raised his hand and offered a suggestion: "In the film, when Mrs. Reagan was leaving the class, she said, 'Now remember, next time somebody asks you to use drugs, just say no.' Well, why don't we start a club against drugs and call it 'Just Say No'?"[18]

Brann was thrilled with Martini's suggestion. A Just Say No club was an ideal form of adolescent activism: with some adult assistance, children could form and run the groups themselves, at Peralta or any other elementary school in Oakland and beyond. The club also combined everything Brann had been working for with OPA—community togetherness, an alternative to drugs, and a safe space for children to gather—but modified to address kids' desires and needs. The other children were enthusiastic about the idea, and by the end of the assembly, fourteen other kids, including Wiltz's daughter Angel and her friend Tarnishia Paul, had formed the first Just Say No club, writing their names and addresses on slips of paper that Brann and Wiltz took to the PIRE office that night.

When Adams arrived at work the next day, he questioned his assistant about the papers on his desk. When she explained that they were contact information for the adolescent members of a new, student-created antidrug club, Adams experienced what he called "an intuitive sense that this might be the answer." Adams had been working for years on antidrug initiatives directed primarily at middle-class parents, helping them work with their kids to ensure that families stayed drug-free.

Though he had had some success, he had never worked directly with low-income children before, nor had he experienced an antidrug initiative that came directly from a child himself. The potential for Just Say No, Adams realized, was that kids themselves could make it cool to avoid drug use, and by appealing to the extremely young, it could also keep kids on the drug-free path for life. "The great promise of the Just Say No clubs was that it's easier to reinforce an already existing norm than it is to change one," Adams said. "When a high school kid is already into drugs and delinquency, it may be too late. That's why we concentrated on kids 10 to 14, catching them before they start."[19]

Realizing the club's potential, Adams, an experienced organizer, took control: he established the Just Say No Foundation with Brann and Wiltz in nearby Walnut Creek and appointed himself as its president and Brann as vice president. With Brann, Adams quickly wrote a how-to guide for adults interested in helping children start a club, printed T-shirts, buttons, and flags featuring the Just Say No logo that he and Brann designed, and made all these items available for purchase through the foundation. Recognizing the importance of letting children be active participants in making their choice, they also wrote a pledge for Just Say No club members to sign: "I know who I am, and I know I want to stay healthy and happy. I can stand up for myself and stick to my decision to live a drug-free life," it read. "I can ask for support from my friends and family. I pledge to say 'No!' to drugs and alcohol. I can help others to say no to drugs and alcohol."[20]

A veteran fund-raiser, Adams also realized that a child-focused antidrug club founded by inner-city kids was a remarkable grant opportunity, and one that the traditional parent movement had neglected to consider. As other parent groups competed for funds and struggled with diminished federal support, Adams made the case for Just Say No to numerous groups in Washington and beyond and was pleased to find a warm response. Shortly after the first club formed, Adams received a $22,000 grant from the US Department of Health and Human Services and a $50,000 grant from the liberal Drug Abuse Fund in Washington, DC. Within a month, he had the National Association of Broadcasters, the Ad Council, and service clubs like the Elks publicizing the clubs to local children. With funds and increased publicity, the concept of Just

Say No quickly spread nationwide, generating excitement and the potential for additional fund-raising and recognition.

He also contacted the White House again. In February 1985, Wrobleski was preparing to help the first lady host an antidrug ceremony for children, and given Reagan's role in inspiring the Oakland children to form and name the first Just Say No club, Adams hoped that Martini, Wiltz, and Paul could attend. Adams explained the concept of Just Say No to Wrobleski, who passed it on to Nancy Reagan, and the first lady was thrilled with the idea. Already sympathetic to Oakland after her positive reception there the previous July, Reagan welcomed the children and used the White House event to promote Just Say No clubs. Meeting in the East Room on February 22, Reagan handed out Just Say No buttons and told the children to keep up their battle against drug abuse. "There may be times when you get a little discouraged and think it isn't worth it," Reagan said. "But keep in mind if you even save one life, it's worth it, so keep going."[21]

By April, with the first lady's support, Just Say No was a national phenomenon. On April 26, thousands of children rallied to show their support for staying drug-free in several simultaneous Just Say No marches held in Los Angeles, Washington, Chicago, and Atlanta. At the Atlanta march, Soleil Moon Frye, the nine-year-old star of the popular *Punky Brewster* television series, was named "national chairkid" of the Just Say No Foundation, and footage of her leading a crowd of hundreds down the street accompanied by bands, martial arts instructors, and balloons closed a special Just Say No–themed episode of her show that aired in October. Nancy Reagan naturally oversaw the march in Washington. Greeting a group of 2,000 youths who had marched from downtown Washington to the South Lawn of the White House, Reagan celebrated their efforts and continued to promote the power of saying no. With the children gathered around her, the first lady had them shout the word "no" three times. "That's wonderful," Reagan said after they were finished. "That will keep the drugs away."[22]

Just Say No quickly took on a life of its own. Clubs formed in every state: the Just Say No Foundation reported that over 5,000 groups had affiliated with the movement midway through 1985. Following the official Just Say No handbook, the youngest club members were taught the dangers of experimenting with drugs like marijuana and the importance of helping their friends, while older children were encouraged not only to resist drug use but also to participate in civic engagement and volunteering opportunities. Newspapers regularly reported that Just Say No members were invited to state capitals, where they were celebrated for their prevention efforts, and schools touted the high membership in their clubs, boasting of students' volunteerism and the subsequent decrease in drug use rates.

Within a year of its founding, Just Say No was no longer directed specifically at inner-city youth—children across the country were embracing the concept as the White House overtly supported the cause. And even sooner, within just a few months, it was also tightly connected to Nancy Reagan, who continued to lead marches and Just Say No rallies, including one in Oakland where, rather than addressing inner-city youth, she appeared alongside players from the San Francisco 49ers and promoted the program in interviews and public addresses.[23]

Young club members in Oakland didn't mind the national recognition their idea was receiving. In fact, inspired by Adams, they began a letter-writing campaign, hoping to generate additional publicity and high-profile support. Angel Wiltz wrote a letter to Abigail Van Buren, whose nationally syndicated advice column, "Dear Abby," appeared in over 1,000 newspapers nationwide. Wiltz's short letter, in which she expressed her desire to help children avoid drug abuse appeared in the column on August 30, 1985, sandwiched between letters from a man in Oklahoma who was uncomfortable about being asked to attend his son's stripper-filled bachelor party and a man from Texas who was unsure about opening his windows during a tornado.

"I am 9 years old and I am a captain in one of the 'Just Say No' clubs, helping other kids to say no to drugs. These clubs are being started all over the country. They were formed last February under Oakland Parents in Action, a program to educate parents in early drug prevention," Wiltz wrote. "Our aim is to get kids to say no to drugs because drugs will mess up their minds, hurt their bodies, ruin their chances in life, hurt their grades, make their parents sad and get them in trouble with the law." Wiltz then asked if Abby would help her promote her club, and she described how to contact OPA for more information. In response,

Abby was brusque but amenable: "Glad to help. Please give me a progress report."[24]

"Dear Abby" reached over 80 million daily readers in the mid-1980s, and Wiltz's letter generated an enormous reaction: over the next few weeks, OPA's office received 2,000 phone calls and 7,000 letters from people wanting to start their own Just Say No club. Given the response, Brann wrote a follow-up letter, in February 1986, in which she reiterated the importance of the clubs and asked Abby to promote OPA's new guidebook, *Just Say No: Stopping Drug Abuse Before It Starts*. "Abby, you have already helped us so much already," Brann wrote. "Will you please help us again and put this in your column?" This time Abby was considerably more enthusiastic, responding, "I just said *yes!*"[25]

With support from the White House and Dear Abby, over 10,000 clubs had joined the Just Say No Foundation by the spring of 1986. Antidrug rallies and marches were regular occurrences in Oakland and beyond, and the program continued to generate rave reviews from the students and parents who participated in it. By May, Just Say No had even earned the approval of traditional parent activists like Sue Rusche. In February 1984, Rusche had signed a contract with King Features to write a twice-weekly syndicated column about drugs, originally called "Striking Back" and then "Straight Talk About Drugs." On May 8, 1986, she used her column to applaud the racial and economic inclusivity of Just Say No. "On May 22, over 5,000,000 children are expected to march through cities and towns across the nation to 'Just Say No' to drugs," Rusche wrote. "Black kids, white kids, native Indian kids, Asian- and Spanish-American kids, kids from the suburbs, kids from the ghetto, kids from rural areas, kids from the inner city, poor kids, rich kids, middle class kids—all will not only pledge to stay away from drugs, but will help their friends do the same by making a commitment to form Just Say No clubs." The movement was powerful, Rusche concluded, because of its inclusivity—which her own movement had neglected to achieve.[26]

As Rusche broke from the traditional parent movement by celebrating Just Say No, it was accounts like hers in which the true origins of the movement became murky. Rusche briefly mentioned OPA and Joan Brann in her article, crediting Brann and Tom Adams with publishing the first official club handbook. But she gave ultimate credit for Just Say No to the National Institute on Drug Abuse, which Rusche believed had originated the concept "with a public service media campaign designed . . . by the Advertising Council." Rusche also credited local Atlanta parent activist Ruby Calloway with the original idea for the Just Say No march, stating that "everybody likes Ruby Calloway's idea. In just a year's time, the Just Say No March has grown from a few thousand kids in a handful of cities to millions of youngsters in hundreds, perhaps thousands of cities."[27]

Indeed, the contributions of OPA and Joan Brann—to say nothing of the participation of children like Nomathemby Martini—were getting lost in the fervor surrounding Just Say No as groups sprouted across the United States and Nancy Reagan began using the slogan constantly in her public addresses. Members of Oakland's African American community were starting to resent the White House's embrace of the program. As Just Say No moved away from its origins, Avery Carter, a community organizer with OPA, told a national conference on preventing alcohol and drug abuse that the black community was "not upset that Nancy Reagan gets credit for starting the Just Say No program. But what does upset us is the fact that many Black people do not know how the program actually started; this has not really been effectively communicated in all the literature that has been developed by some agencies." Carter lamented that the radical origins of Just Say No and OPA—programs that were formed in the same city that birthed the Black Panthers and where Joan Brann started her activist career—were being whitewashed by Punky Brewster and the Reagans. Just Say No "was not Nancy Reagan's concept," Carter concluded. "It grew because our children were migrating to something that was basically not available, not in school, at home, in religious institutions, and in various other places that they were going."[28]

But Carter wouldn't be able to stop the White House from taking control of Brann's organization. On September 14, 1986, Ronald and Nancy Reagan presented the most famous antidrug announcement of their administration. The twenty-minute speech, broadcast on all the major networks, was promoted as the highest-profile antidrug address the Reagans had given, and the buildup to the speech was enormous. The president's spokesman, Larry Speakes, announced the address on

August 5, calling it "an unprecedented event." Not only would it be the first time the president and his wife delivered a speech together on television, but, Speakes continued, "when the chapter on how America won the war on drugs is written, the Reagans want this speech to be viewed as a turning point." Though few other details were provided, Speakes said that "the Reagans hope to make September 14 a special night for the country."[29]

The Reagans' official Just Say No address, filmed in the residential West Hall, featured the Reagans, seated on a loveseat, holding hands and speaking in turn. The residential surroundings emphasized the purpose of the address, which was to show the Reagans talking to the public "not simply as fellow citizens," as the president said, "but as fellow parents and grandparents and as concerned neighbors."

"America has accomplished so much in these last few years," Reagan opened, but "drugs are menacing our society. They're threatening our values and undercutting our institutions. They're killing our children." He then celebrated the first lady's ongoing battle against adolescent drug abuse, lauding the "over 100,000 miles to 55 cities in 28 states and six foreign countries" that she had traveled over the past five years during her visits to drug clinics and prevention groups. "Her personal observations and efforts have given her such dramatic insights that I wanted her to share them with you this evening," Reagan said. Nancy Reagan then addressed the public directly.

"As a mother," she opened, "I've always thought of September as a special month, a time when we bundled our children off to school." But "today there's a drug and alcohol abuse epidemic in this country, and no one is safe from it—not you, not me, and certainly not our children, because this epidemic has their names written on it." As a solution, the first lady offered the concept of Just Say No, briefly mentioning the Oakland children who had founded the first club two years earlier. "Our young people are helping us lead the way. Not long ago, in Oakland, California, I was asked by a group of children what to do if they were offered drugs," she said, "and I answered, 'Just say no.' Soon after that, those children in Oakland formed a Just Say No club, and now there are over 10,000 such clubs all over the country. Well, their participation and courage in saying no needs our encouragement. We can help by using every opportunity to force the issue of not using drugs to the point of making others uncomfortable, even if it means making ourselves unpopular."

The address concluded with the president announcing that "the job ahead of us is very clear. Nancy's personal crusade, like that of so many other wonderful individuals, should become our national crusade." He then outlined six initiatives—from creating drug-free workplaces and drug-free schools to offering treatment and expanding interdiction, to strengthening law enforcement and prevention—and announced that the cost of the drug war would rise to an unprecedented $3 billion. Mrs. Reagan was given the final word: "Now we go on to the next step: making a final commitment not to tolerate drugs by anyone, anytime, anyplace. So, won't you join us in the great new national crusade?"[30] By the time the address concluded, it was clear that the president and his wife wanted Just Say No—conceived, as Nancy Reagan acknowledged, by Oakland schoolchildren—to be the mantra of every American, and the crusade against adolescent drug use one of national concern.

The Reagans' speech brought Just Say No to an even broader national audience, but response to the administration's ideas was tepid. The day after the speech, the *New York Times* published a lengthy report noting that the address "gave no specific remedies for curbing illegal drugs in terms of legislation or orders from the executive branch." The article argued that, even though drug use rates had dropped in recent years, the concept of "just saying no" oversimplified a complex problem by ignoring what made people use drugs in the first place. If the Reagans expected Just Say No to work for adults as well as children, the program would have to address the problems of poverty and crime that lay behind most drug use. Though the speech "marked the most visible effort to date by the Reagans to publicize the effects of drug abuse on the nation," it ultimately reaffirmed the administration's belief that "nothing would be more effective" in the battle against drug abuse than, as the president put it, "for Americans to simply quit using drugs"—which, the paper noted, was unlikely.[31]

Still, the *Times*'s halfhearted response to the speech did little to stem the increasing popularity of Just Say No, or to halt the growing interest of corporations seeking to partner with its campaign. Despite Adams's early success with grant applications, overseeing the thousands of clubs that seemed to form overnight—supplying them with materials and literature, writing guidebooks, and helping to organize national events—was an expensive task, and the Just Say No Foundation was continually running low on funds. So, in February 1987, when Adams was approached by Procter & Gamble, the multinational consumer goods company best known for its cleaning products, packaged food items, and cosmetic goods, with an offer of $150,000 for the "exclusive use" of Just Say No imagery for a "back to school" advertising campaign that fall, he was interested. P&G had already spoken with the White House, and the corporation wanted to partner with both Just Say No and the first lady for a campaign that would place coupons for P&G products like Bounty paper towels and Duncan Hines cake mix alongside a message from Nancy Reagan and an antidrug pledge card for children to sign and return in the mail. For each pledge that was returned, P&G would donate an additional ten cents to Just Say No.[32]

Adams was intrigued by P&G's offer, but also surprised by how quickly the White House had accepted its conditions. Several corporations had tried to partner with the White House and Just Say No before, but the first lady had been reluctant to let her name or image be used to make explicit endorsements. Even the NFP, Reagan's preferred parent group, was barred from using her name and image on its materials.[33] But P&G was different somehow: when Adams arrived at the White House the following month to discuss the partnership, Reagan made it clear that she had already aligned with the corporation. H. R. Weitzen, P&G's manager of promotion and marketing services, told Adams that he would name Mrs. Reagan "Honorary Chairperson of the Just Say No Foundation" in their ads, and P. H. Goldman, P&G's promotion manager, explicitly outlined P&G's interests in a follow-up memo, telling Adams that, because of the first lady's participation, P&G was "excited about the opportunity to teach kids to stay drug-free." Nevertheless, as Goldman reminded Adams, P&G's "primary objective is to build the business. To accomplish this, our relationship must be exclusive in the packaged-goods industry. If the event smacks, even a little, of 'we've heard this before,' our sales personnel and customers will not be moved to support our goal—lots of activity, pledge and product. Any breach of this agreement will preclude P&G's interest in supporting Just Say No in years to come."[34]

After two fund-raising initiatives earlier that month had failed, Adams needed to accept P&G's offer to keep Just Say No in the black, even though it was clear that P&G's motives were little more than to burnish its image and increase sales. In addition, the White House was forcing Adams's hand. When he visited the White House later that month, Nancy Reagan reiterated her support for the partnership and then asked Adams to hire a P&G executive to help run the foundation. Adams was hesitant to go through with the deal: putting a P&G executive on the foundation's staff meant losing control over the organization that he had founded with Brann. Moreover, it seemed antithetical to Just Say No's original purpose, which was to help kids from low-income neighborhoods find alternatives to the crime, violence, and drugs surrounding them—not to sell cake mix or paper towels alongside an antidrug pledge.

Adams stalled for two months, but he soon found out that the White House wasn't playing games. At a subsequent meeting with the first lady in May, she told Adams, in no uncertain terms, "If you don't say yes to P&G, I'm pulling out of Just Say No."[35] Unwilling to lose Reagan's sponsorship and desperately in need of the money, Adams hired former P&G employee Ivy Cohen to serve as the foundation's executive director, ceding some of his control as president to her. Ten months later, in March 1988, Cohen installed Wallace Abbott, senior vice president of marketing at P&G, as chairman of the foundation's board. Though Adams stayed on as president, his position became largely ceremonial, and in just a few months the relationship between Just Say No and P&G had been transformed from a partnership based on advertisement circulars and pledge cards into corporate control of all of Just Say No's major operating procedures—a transformation that occurred with the White House's explicit support.[36]

Still, even Adams had to admit that P&G's partnership with the first lady and Just Say No had launched an extremely successful pledge drive in the fall of 1987. In the buildup to "National Pledge Day" on September 21, when the pledge cards and P&G coupons would be printed in newspapers nationwide, Adams told the *Pittsburgh Press* that he expected to get "10 million children to respond." He also celebrated how far Just Say No had come. "We won't know for several years if it's going to work or not, but we've grown from three clubs to 15,000 in two years.

It's a substantive program, and we're building it as we go along," he said. Adams was especially positive about what Just Say No meant from an activist's point of view. Avoiding any discussion of P&G, Adams was most proud that Just Say No was "the only social movement in the history of this country started by young people this age."[37]

Despite Adams's embrace of the pledge drive, his time with Just Say No was about to end. In May 1988, H. R. Weitzen sent a memo to Wallace Abbott exploring the immediate objectives the foundation was to undertake "in order to develop a more viable national organization." These initiatives, all of which were financial, were directed at Just Say No's Oakland office, and they specifically targeted Brann and Adams. Despite the Oakland office's small size (Brann and Adams directed a staff of five), Weitzen told Abbott to "eliminate the Oakland office activities" in order to "reduce current case demands." He also suggested that Abbott recruit "an experienced and seasoned manager to oversee the Foundation's development as an ongoing entity," clearly suggesting that neither Brann nor Adams was fit for the job. He recommended that Adams step aside as president and serve as a consultant, and that Brann's role as vice president be eliminated. This "restructure" had to be given immediate priority, Weitzen wrote, if Just Say No was to "develop a national management capable of establishing the organization as an effective entity." But Adams knew the truth of the matter lay elsewhere. P&G didn't want to streamline the operations of Just Say No; it only wanted access to its clubs and supporters. Drug-free kids had parents who needed to buy things like paper towels and packaged goods, and Adams knew that the company's ultimate goal was to advertise to them and "build its business," all while appearing to be a good corporate citizen through affiliating with Just Say No.[38]

Brann and Adams were furious about P&G's takeover of their organization. Before they could be forced out of their positions, both resigned from the foundation in August 1988. They soon found support in Washington, where not everyone was as receptive to the takeover as the White House had been. On August 12, 1988, Charles Rangel, chairman of the House Select Committee on Narcotics Control and Abuse, held a press conference decrying P&G's co-optation of Just Say No. Standing alongside Adams and Brann, Rangel introduced them as the organization's founders and said that they were "standing with me today to protest the commercialization of the Just Say No program." Just Say No was being "abused as a sales promotion," Rangel continued, "for profit, by one of America's largest corporations." Though the program was once "the last ray of hope that we would have a national drug prevention policy," because of the corporate takeover, Rangel continued, it was now little more than a "division of P&G to sell soap." This set a dangerous precedent, Rangel argued, and he wanted to alert the public to this abuse.

Rangel believed that P&G had used the name and image of the first lady in its ads "without her knowledge or support," and he decried how P&G had abused "the good names of the first lady and the Just Say No Foundation as a sales promotion." Though he had long been critical of the Reagan administration's policies on drug abuse, Rangel told reporters that he had "always lauded the efforts of the first lady and supported her antidrug efforts." What Rangel did not know was that the first lady had directly overseen the consolidation of Just Say No with P&G. Thus, curiously, Rangel called upon the first lady's staff to "come forward to protect her integrity," but he made no similar calls for P&G to reinstate Brann or Adams or to refocus Just Say No's efforts back on inner-city youth. By 1988, Nancy Reagan was so closely affiliated with Just Say No that even critical Democrats like Rangel sought to protect her when they felt that her prevention programs were being maligned. Remarkably, it was Nancy Reagan—and not Tom Adams or Joan Brann—who generated the most public sympathy in the wake of a corporate takeover of Just Say No, a move that she herself had authorized.[39]

Rangel's complaints went nowhere, however, and by the end of 1988 P&G's usurpation of Just Say No was complete. The foundation never reopened its Oakland office, and Brann and Adams were forced to watch as their foundation morphed, through the power of corporate money, into Just Say No International, spreading its mission across the globe. At its peak in the early 1990s, Just Say No oversaw 25,000 clubs in the United States and twelve other countries, and it had an annual budget of over $5 million. Ivy Cohen continued to lead the organization as executive director, and the first lady, still untarnished by the scandal, continued to support the cause, leading rallies and marches until 1989, when she and her husband returned to California.[40]

The P&G takeover also opened the door for more corporate involvement in adolescent drug abuse prevention. By the end of 1988, companies like Frito-Lay, MasterCard, Members Only, and McDonald's had all used the Just Say No image in their marketing campaigns, and all had experienced a boom in profits as a result. For many, supporting Just Say No was a "win-win." Members Only spokesman Bob Perilla called using the antidrug theme "a boon for business" that increased sales of their clothes while making the company look like "a good corporate citizen." And Beth Currin, senior product manager for Doritos, told the *Washington Post* that "there is a definite halo effect. The antidrug message lends credibility to a product."[41]

Despite its popularity, Just Say No did little to actually decrease youth drug use. In 1988, the year Brann and Adams resigned, the University of Michigan's "Monitoring the Future" survey found that, although rates of adolescent drug use in the United States had dropped over the past seven years, they were still "the highest in the industrialized world." Fifty-seven percent of high school seniors had tried an illicit substance in the past year, and marijuana was still the most commonly used drug. Even more troubling was the growing number of adolescents who were experimenting with cocaine. The survey found that one in six high school students had tried cocaine in the past year, and one in eighteen had tried a frightening new form of the drug, crack. The survey also found that Just Say No was a particularly useless prevention program for adults. Among high school graduates, the report found that over 40 percent had tried cocaine by the age of twenty-seven, when their earning potential had increased and they could afford the more expensive drug. Even more worrisome, nearly 7 percent had tried crack. Though rates of adolescent marijuana use had fallen from their peak in 1979, the report found that a rise in cocaine use among both adolescents and adults suggested that, "in our long parade of popular drugs . . . there will likely be more problems to come."[42]

The program also did nothing for Oakland. By 1988, Brann's hometown was still making headlines for its open-air drug dealing and violence. The year prior, the city had experienced 66 drug-related murders and 180 cases of drug-related arson, most of which were related to the growing crack trade. One resident complained that there were "hundreds of drug dealers" on his street, "many armed with machine guns."[43] As locals fled the violence, which had destroyed businesses and deprived the city's inhabitants of jobs, Brann knew that her transformation from Oakland activist to national leader had been a mistake. Just Say No had started as an honorable idea, she said, but by becoming popular too fast and too soon, it never actually helped Oakland's kids. Addressing a conference of black antidrug activists, Brann warned that they shouldn't repeat her mistakes. "Activists must never lose their identity with the community," she said, "and they should be particularly wary of going uptown either geographically or spiritually."[44]

Adams also recognized the danger of becoming too closely affiliated with the White House. Though Nancy Reagan had played a crucial role in generating interest in Just Say No, partnering with her had also laid the framework for the loss of the foundation to corporate control. When paid professionals replaced volunteers and the cause became identified with specific corporations, Adams knew that grassroots activists couldn't compete with executives and White House officials interested in the profit potential of prevention.[45] Though he remained a fixture at PIRE for several more years, Adams's time with adolescent drug abuse prevention had drawn to a close.

But the biggest failure of Just Say No was that it masked the country's real problem with drug use. By 1988, rates of adolescent marijuana use had been falling in white, middle-class suburbs for nearly a decade, in part because of the success of the growing number of parent activists who could dedicate the time and resources necessary to enforcing antidrug behavior. With rates of adolescent marijuana use already dropping, children's clubs and television shows, while entertaining, had a negligible effect on a problem that was already on the wane.

But, as Joan Brann knew, cocaine use was on the rise, and because of the widespread introduction of crack cocaine in 1986, use was particularly rising in the inner cities, where there were fewer parent groups to keep children away from drugs and the majority of cocaine users were adults. As the largely white, suburban parent movement continued to focus on marijuana and the White House transferred its loyalty to Just Say No, there were few safeguards in place to halt the dangerous new trend. And when parent activists did realize that crack was turning into a national crisis, they also quickly learned that their methods were incapable of handling the problem. Surprisingly, it was crack cocaine that laid the foundation for another reversal in the war on marijuana. With parent activism proving incapable of keeping up with the growing national appetite for illicit drugs and the war on drugs being transformed into a war on crack, the pro-marijuana movement was waiting in the wings, ready to relaunch its legalization battle and reemerge as the protector of smokers' civil rights.

11

CRACK UPDATE

IT WAS A slim pamphlet, covering everything from "Street Names for Crack" and "Crack on the Job" to "Crack Houses" and "Signs and Symptoms of Use." Warning that "crack and cocaine can kill from the very first time they are used," it stated that, with a million Americans using the drug, crack was nothing less than an epidemic. Even more frightening were the drug's effects on kids. Although the majority of crack users were adults, the bulk of dealers were still in school. "Youthful dealers are on average only in ninth grade," the pamphlet warned, and "the school dropouts who deal are an average of 17 years old." It concluded with this dire threat: "Crack is instant death for some, instant addiction for many. The bottom line is don't take the risk. Even once."[1]

Sue Rusche published *Crack Update* through Families in Action in 1986, the year crack cocaine made its media debut. The drug had been seen in Miami and Los Angeles as early as the late 1970s and was being used in New York by the early 1980s, but it wasn't until the summer of 1986 that breathless media reports spread fear of crack nationwide, declaring that the country's newest drug would soon be terrorizing nearly every American home. On television and in newspapers, reporters warned that crack was "instantaneously addictive" and the drug that had already "transformed the ghetto" would quickly move from the inner cities "to the wealthiest suburbs of Westchester county," "destroying our young people" and "spreading into the middle class." For months, terms like "plague" and "epidemic" were used to describe "the most addictive substance known to man," and over 140 stories on the drug—many of which decried crack's effects on pregnant women and the unborn—ran on network news that year alone.[2]

The crack "epidemic" that raged across the country in the summer of 1986 did more than create a new locus for national hysteria and fear, however; it also transformed how Americans viewed the drug war and increased support for the already popular battle. As fears of crack spread, a majority of Americans declared that drug abuse was by far "the nation's most important problem," and over 60 percent said that they would "be willing to give up some freedoms" to fight drug abuse, especially if that meant helping the nation's kids.[3] With midterm elections coming in November, Congress knew that there was both an opportunity and a distinct political advantage in joining the battle against drug use, and by October both chambers had quickly passed the Anti–Drug Abuse Act of 1986, the most wide-ranging and punitive drug measure of the era, which built upon ideas to punish and demonize drug use and drug users that were nascent in much of the Reagan administration's earlier work, and expanded them into federal law.

Today the act is primarily remembered for its intense penalties for crack. A person possessing only five grams of crack—an amount roughly equivalent to the size of two dimes—earned a mandatory five-year prison sentence, whereas someone had to possess 500 grams of powder cocaine, an amount equivalent to over a pound, to receive the same sentence. Cocaine use overall was higher in affluent white communities, but crack was especially common in black urban areas; as a result of the new law's 100-to-1 sentencing disparity, waves of mass incarceration of African Americans followed. Within a few years, drug offenses accounted for two-thirds of the rise of the federal inmate population and more than half of the increase in state prisoners, the majority of whom were black. The effects of the act were also incredibly long-lasting: the number of people incarcerated on mandatory minimum sentences for drug offenses jumped from 41,100 in 1980 to approximately half a million by 2010.[4]

The effects of the 1986 law reached far beyond crack. Marijuana remained a central preoccupation for the Reagan administration and the Anti–Drug Abuse Act of 1986 increased penalties for the drug substantially, especially for its biggest dealers. The possession of 100 kilograms of marijuana (roughly 220 pounds) brought a mandatory sentence of five years in prison; for 1,000 kilos, the sentence was doubled to ten years. The act also increased federal penalties for the cultivation, possession, and transfer of lesser quantities of pot, including up to a year in prison and a minimum $1,000 fine for the first conviction, while subsequent arrests could result in the crime being treated as a felony. Convictions for cultivating and selling greater amounts could result in the harshest sentences dictated by the law, including up to life in prison and $1 million in fines.

Beyond determining mandatory minimums for drug sentences, one of the act's most powerful legacies was the creation of a punitive new environment that emphasized the federal government's interest in preventing, and punishing, drug use. The act provided $1.7 billion in new funds to dramatically expand the drug war, bringing the total drug budget to nearly $3 billion—the most ever allocated to the cause to that date and nearly double the budget from when Reagan first came into office. The bulk of this money was used to increase the federal government's interdiction and enforcement efforts, including nearly $400 million for surveillance, $1.1 billion for state and federal agencies to use in the arrest and prosecution of drug offenders, and $96.5 million for the construction of new federal prisons to house the rising number of inmates. Police officers were also given broad new powers. The DEA was allowed to make warrantless searches and seize assets and property only tenuously associated with drug crimes, and local law enforcement officers were allowed to do the same, selling seized property and keeping the profits to help support their continued antidrug campaigns.

In a reversal from the president's previous cuts for antidrug education and prevention measures, the act also included $200 million for antidrug educational campaigns, which were made available as grants to organizations that sought to warn people away from drug abuse. As elder statesmen in the movement and with some of the closest relationships to the first lady, parent activists seemed primed to get much of this money. But, in a surprising twist, the Anti–Drug Abuse Act of 1986 ultimately sped the downfall of parent groups by increasing competition in the antidrug education field. The $200 million the act promised for education and prevention spurred the development of hundreds of new antidrug prevention methods and groups and created an environment permeated by a ubiquitous barrage of antidrug messages, which appeared everywhere from television, to newspapers, to comic books and the backs of milk cartons, to programs that placed uniformed police officers in elementary schools. No longer the sole place to get information about the dangers of drugs, parent groups were rendered obsolete by the sheer barrage of antidrug information that was quickly made available, and which many Americans found impossible to escape.

As the media declared that crack was ravaging inner cities and that the majority of addicts were black adults, parent groups also seemed incapable of tackling issues beyond kids smoking pot: they were seen as being too suburban, too white, too focused on children, and too middle-class. Like the heroin epidemic of the 1960s and '70s, crack made marijuana seem tame in comparison, and parent activists appeared overly fixated on an issue and a substance that just didn't seem like a problem anymore. Since rates of adolescent marijuana use had already been dropping for years, this may not have come as a surprise, and some parent activists tried to remain relevant by reorienting their methods to target urban cocaine and crack use. But even then, their methods seemed quaint at best, still focused too closely on parents and the family, and dwarfed by national antidrug campaigns. With federal support for the drug war rising and people terrified about crack's effects on kids, 1986 should have been parent activists' crowning moment—a time when, ten years after the first parent group formed, the entire country rallied around their cause. Instead, crack sped the parent movement's downfall, rendering activists irrelevant and obsolete.

If the Anti–Drug Abuse Act of 1986 resulted in the parent movement's death, its other surprising outcome was the pro-marijuana movement's rebirth, inspired in large part by the act's heightened penalties for pot. Though few smokers had over 200 pounds of the drug at their disposal (and arrest rates for marijuana had actually fallen, from over 450,000 in 1985 to 360,000 in 1986, as the nation switched its focus to crack), marijuana users still saw the act's increased punishments, warrantless searches, and asset forfeiture provisions as infringements on their civil rights. After years of being back on their heels, writers and organizers at NORML and *High Times* felt called to action, declaring that smokers who had hidden for years in the "cannabis closet" had to come out and defend their civil rights. The new executive director of NORML, Jon Gettman, saw the act's passage as an opportunity for his organization to return to its activist roots, and he built on marijuana smokers' growing anger and resentment at being compared to, and punished like, crack addicts by working to launch a reinvigorated marijuana activists' revolution.[5] As the nation turned its focus toward crack and parent activism collapsed, smokers were no longer afraid of being vilified for their drug use, and though the phenomena are rarely discussed in tandem, what the *New York Times* called "crack's destructive sprint across America" had the surprising effect of ushering in a new era of marijuana activism and relaunching the battle for smokers' rights.[6]

•

Easy to make and easy to sell, crack was the perfect drug for the 1980s. Jefferson Morley, a white journalist who tried crack for an article in *The New Republic*, argued that in the era of deindustrialization, decrepit cities, lackluster educational opportunities, and rising unemployment in the black community, not to mention the phenomenal amounts of money that could be made in the drug trade, crack made a lot of sense for a certain population. "You can be a moral tourist in the land of crack and still get a sense of how the drug can make sick sense to demoralized people," Morley wrote. "If all you have in life is bad choices, crack may not be the most unpleasant of them."[7]

Crack was also a product of the freewheeling free market of the decade, a capitalist adaptation of product and technique that transformed a substance that was otherwise prohibitively expensive into a readily available and inexpensive high. Back in 1981, when powder cocaine first graced the cover of *Time* magazine, reporter Michael Demarest declared that the "all-American drug" was so intriguing precisely because of its unavailability. With a price of "$2,200 per ounce, five times the price of gold," by 1980 only a small segment of the "upwardly mobile" had used the drug, though they spent an estimated $30 billion on it that year and forty metric tons were expected to be trafficked into the country from South America in 1981.[8] By 1985, however, cocaine's use was expanding far beyond the upper class: the National Institute on Drug Abuse found that 9 percent of the population, or about 22 million people, had tried the drug at least once, and use was only expected to grow.[9]

This increased interest in cocaine eventually led to a glut in the market. By the mid-1980s, reports on cocaine's dangers were beginning to emerge from medical schools and the federal government, transforming the drug's image from a benign and seemingly innocuous high into a dangerous habit that could ruin lives. Inspired in part by television movies that portrayed people whose comfortable existences were destroyed by addiction, as well as the federal Office for Substance Abuse Prevention's massive 1985 public service campaign "COCAINE: The Big Lie," there was a growing understanding in middle- and upper-class white communities of the risks involved with cocaine (and a subsequent decline in use), even as interest in using the drug continued to soar.

Crack was born from this disjuncture. As the middle-class market for powder cocaine was drying up, the production of crack utilized the surplus supply to exploit new markets. Created by mixing cocaine and water with a base (usually a sodium bicarbonate like baking soda), crack made an expensive substance cheap: small "rocks" sold for $5 to $20 apiece. In its new form, crack could also be smoked, making its high both intense and short-lived. Addictive and affordable to nearly everyone, crack brought cocaine to a lower-class market that had rarely had access to the drug before—including the market in America's struggling inner cities, where the drug found its strongest niche among working-class and poor residents. As the media would soon report at length, its use was particularly high among poor urban African Americans—the population that would be targeted the most by the anti-crack provisions of the Anti–Drug Abuse Act.

Neither the parent movement nor the national media were well attuned to the problems of America's black urban poor, and they might have ignored crack entirely if it hadn't been for the notable cocaine-related deaths of two sports stars in quick succession. Most prominent was Len Bias, the promising basketball star from the University of Maryland whose death two days after he was drafted by the Boston Celtics rocked the nation. Bias—tall, good-looking, and talented, a born-again Christian from an intact and loving family—embodied the American Dream, especially for black America. His death from cocaine intoxication on June 19, 1986, at the age of twenty-two turned the drug into a national tragedy. The calamity was compounded when Don Rogers, a twenty-three-year-old football player with the Cleveland Browns, died of a heart attack from cocaine intoxication eight days later, on the night before his wedding.

Despite the fact that both men overdosed on powder cocaine and not crack, the media frenzy that followed equated the two, focusing national attention—and Capitol Hill—directly on the issue of cocaine abuse. The death of Bias was particularly troubling for the nation's lawmakers, who viewed Maryland as a home team. "Congress is predominantly male and very sports-oriented," Representative George Miller said. "Within 24 hours you were hit with a devastating blow."[10]

The deaths of Bias and Rogers jump-started the media frenzy over the dangers of crack, and with congressional elections set for the fall, members of Congress knew they had to act quickly and come down strong on drug abuse. Members of the House and Senate were vehement in their calls for eradicating the nation's drug problem. In July, House Speaker Tip O'Neill called for a bipartisan effort to develop a comprehensive drug law and bring it to the floor by September, an unusually fast turnaround for such a complex set of measures. Leaders in the Senate followed several days later, and as lawmakers jostled over who could be seen as toughest on drug abuse, Jim Wright, the House Democratic leader, pushed for action as quickly as possible. By September, antidrug fervor had grown so strong that "you could put an amendment through to hang, draw and quarter," joked Representative Claude Pepper, a Democrat from Florida. "That's what happens when you get an emotional issue like this."[11]

Bills moved through Congress rapidly, and on October 27, the president signed into law the Anti–Drug Abuse Act of 1986, one of the most sweeping pieces of antidrug legislation in American history. President Reagan declared that the law was the culmination of his and his wife's "national crusade" to educate people against using drugs, and that "today marks a major victory in our crusade against drugs—a victory of safer neighborhoods, a victory for the protection of the American family."[12] Following the trend of the past several years, many in Washington declared that the act would help prevent adolescent drug abuse and strengthen the American family—that, in short, the act would make the parent prevention model the law of the land. "The drug boom is fueled by the demand of our children," Representative Charles Schumer declared at a news conference shortly after the law was passed. "We need to educate our young people to the hazards of drug abuse. Focusing on the supply side alone won't solve that problem."[13]

Thrilled with the new law, parent movement leaders, as the nation's most visible antidrug activists, felt compelled to respond to the crack crisis. In the summer of 1986, Joyce Nalepka, now president of the NFP, issued a call to action in the organization's newsletter, observing that the deaths of Bias and Rogers "should serve as a message to parents everywhere that drugs are killing America's youth." "Today," Nalepka warned, "the drug 'crack' is experiencing an unprecedented and alarming popularity among teenagers. This highly addictive drug is inexpensive and increasingly available on our streets and in our schools. Parents, teachers, clergy, coaches and politicians need to work together to prevent further tragedy."[14] Sue Rusche responded in her nationally syndicated column, asking, "Who really killed Len Bias?" Her answer indicted everyone in America. It was the country's fault that young stars like Bias died because "we don't teach students that drugs are illegal," Rusche wrote. "Nor do we teach them that they'll be held responsible if they break the law. Instead, we play fast and loose with the law and wonder why young people are confused."[15]

But parent activists had little to offer in response to the crisis beyond the parent peer group model they had long championed, and their newspaper articles and vague calls for action paled in comparison to an increasingly widespread flurry of new antidrug programs and products. The Anti–Drug Abuse Act's $200 million in education funding prompted a bewildering number of new groups to join the battle against drugs, and they quickly developed a series of virulent antidrug programs that bombarded schools with books, films, tapes, curricula, T-shirts, bumper stickers, and other gimmicks that sought to perpetuate the idea that all drug use was equally dangerous and that drug users and dealers were nothing less than evil. Supported by the president and much of the country, this "zero-tolerance" approach soon became impossible to escape. The DARE (Drug Abuse Resistance Education) program placed uniformed police officers in elementary and middle school classrooms, while other organizations, including corporate sponsors like Keebler and McDonald's, were inspired by the success of Just Say No and hoped to continue to cash in on the trend. With a massive infusion of private and federal financial assistance, antidrug messages appeared everywhere from comic books to Saturday morning cartoons, to the sides of trucks and on the backs of milk cartons. And though these methods often had little educational cohesion or proven efficacy, marketing, advertising, and education professionals saw the antidrug movement as a lucrative new business. "People are recognizing there is potential money in this field," said Dennis Nelson, director of drug education for the Fairfax County, Virginia, schools. "We're seeing scare tactics, get high on yourself stuff, all kinds of philosophies."[16]

Children weren't the only targets of the antidrug advertising boom. By June 1987, the sheer volume of antidrug campaigns and public service announcements (PSAs) led *Advertising Age* to declare that the offensive against drug abuse was "the single-largest informational effort ever launched through US media." PSAs ran on television constantly— "more than we can put on the air," said George Schweitzer, vice president for communications for CBS—and they featured celebrities like Mr. T, Clint Eastwood, and Pee-wee Herman warning—and sometimes threatening—adults about the dangers of drug use. A far cry from the simple, plaintive message of *The Chemical People,* by 1987, crack had inspired antidrug messages that were as dark and menacing as the specter of drug use itself.[17]

With antidrug messages appearing everywhere from schools to cereal boxes, parent activists simply weren't as necessary as they once were. For years they had been one of the few sources of information about the dangers of drugs, and the White House had relied on them as amateur experts in the field. But a decade after the first parent group formed, antidrug messages were ubiquitous and antidrug education was in nearly every school. Individual parents no longer felt the need to form groups to teach their children about the dangers of drugs or, with rates of suburban marijuana use dropping, to provide the constant vigilance that movement leaders preached. By 1986, the NFP reported, the number of its affiliated parent groups had plummeted from a high of over 7,000 in 1983 to only a couple hundred nationwide. A report released by the Department of Health and Human Services found that groups disbanded or disappeared for a variety of reasons. Some parents quit because their families simply outgrew the movement as their children aged, while others joined the NFP only briefly, since even a short affiliation would allow them to receive tax-exempt status. But other groups fell apart because the movement no longer seemed necessary, and because, as the nation's concerns about drugs changed, the movement seemed reluctant to evolve with the times or adapt its methods to support aging children.[18]

After a half-decade in which they had enjoyed increasing power and influence, not all parent activists were willing to give up their role in controlling the direction of the country's drug abuse prevention programs, however. In a memo to Reagan's chief drug adviser, Carlton Turner, Sue Rusche argued that parent prevention techniques had already solved many of the country's most pervasive drug problems and that, with dedicated funding, she could devise programs to tackle crack as well. "In our view the Reagan administration correctly identified that a vast volunteer movement was needed to bring reduced drug use rates about," she wrote. "But the Administration did not understand that VOLUNTEERISM IS NOT FREE. It takes money—a relatively small amount, but nonetheless money—to support and encourage the parent volunteer effort." Needless to say, she didn't want to share such funding with an increasing number of other prevention groups.[19]

The NFP was hardly in a better position. With its membership and influence dwindling, the group was struggling, even as its leadership largely ignored the problem. If the group had an issue, President Joyce Nalepka argued in the summer of 1986, it was only its "lack of a national identity for our individual and group members because all our groups have different names. We think this can be remedied without major changes." She then urged every group to place the NFP's logo on their stationery and publicity materials. "This should help you at the local and state levels by clearly identifying your group as part of this vital effort and add strength to the national effort," she wrote.[20]

But branding couldn't solve the larger problems haunting the organization. As crack swept the nation and children rallied behind Just Say No, Nancy Reagan began pulling away from parent groups, especially the NFP, and favoring Just Say No instead. She continued to attend the NFP and PRIDE conferences every year, but her appearances in 1985 and '86 were brief, her speeches lasting only minutes—a far cry from when she was hoisted on attendees' shoulders and celebrated as the parents' cheerleader-in-chief. Even more damaging, the money the first lady once funneled to the NFP was now going to other causes. The 1984 check for $500,000 from the sultan of Brunei was the first lady's last major contribution to the organization. By 1986, the White House was funding a far wider range of groups, including the National Therapeutic Riding Center, which received $5,000, and the Youth to Youth organization of Columbus, Ohio, which received $50,000.[21]

In response, the NFP's leaders turned on each other, looking for someone, or something, to blame. Tom Adams, the veteran parent activist and cofounder of Just Say No, later claimed that the qualities that had allowed certain people to emerge as leaders in the field—being strong-willed, articulate, individualistic, and combative—ultimately pitted activists against each other as they competed with other antidrug groups and battled for federal funds. Faced with constant financial insolvency and a mix of strong-willed individuals that "never jelled into a cohesive, cooperative group," Adams argued that the stress of the crack epidemic planted "seeds of conflict" among leaders, even within the same parent group.[22] By December 1986, five months after crack broke into the national consciousness, those "seeds of conflict" ended the career of Joyce Nalepka and set the stage for the destruction of the NFP.

On December 15, in a conference call between twelve of the organization's nineteen board members, it was decided that Nalepka hadn't done enough to curry favor with the White House or to continue to promote parent groups. In a unanimous vote, the board decided that she would be dismissed from her $40,000-a-year job and that Karl Bernstein, a longtime board member, would replace her. "The dismissal was based upon a difference of opinion about the future direction of the organization," chairman Don Delzer told reporters afterward. Board members whom the majority thought would not agree with their decision were not invited to participate in the call.

The aftermath of the decision was tumultuous. Nalepka filed a civil suit, charging discrimination and unfair labor practices, and in protest and solidarity with their ousted president, several other board members resigned, including many of those who didn't participate in the vote. As her case made its way through court, Nalepka's dismissal also placed everything in NFP's Maryland office in flux. The fifteen-person paid staff was left without an official leader while Bernstein prepared to take the role. Meanwhile, the NFP canceled its annual conference and released its last newsletter in December 1986, the same month Nalepka was fired.[23] In the span of a month, what was once the most powerful parent group in the country—one whose members had appeared on television with Nancy Reagan and accepted the first lady's half-million-dollar check—was in shambles. By 1988, after cycling through two more short-lived directorships and losing most of its member groups, the NFP closed its doors, marking the end of the parent movement's time in Washington as well as the waning of the influence of anti-marijuana activists on Capitol Hill.

After the November elections, the fervor surrounding the Anti-Drug Abuse Act also became tempered. A cause that once had been declared "*the* issue" by Senator Trent Lott was forgotten as rates of crack use fell and the nation was distracted by other news, including, most prominently, the Iran-Contra scandal.[24] In early January 1987, President Reagan quietly slashed almost $1 billion from his drug war, eliminating grants to state and local law enforcement agencies and further cutting funds for drug education and treatment, including the limited grants that, through ACTION, were supposed to go to PRIDE and FIA. The White House struggled to explain the cuts to the public, but argued that total drug spending was still two and a half times as large as it was in 1981. Aides noted, echoing Reagan's remarks, that "the [drug] war is best fought with moral rectitude and inspirational leadership, and only secondarily with money."[25]

By early 1987, just six months after crack prompted a national panic, the drug war's landscape had dramatically changed. The battle had been pumped full of millions of dollars, money that militarized the drug war and paid for the hundreds of antidrug messages that were broadcast every day. Drugs and drug users were being demonized in the press, while politicians and celebrities endorsed the need for drug-free kids in television shows, PSAs, and classrooms. Ten years after the first parent group formed, their insistence on drug-free youth had become nothing short of a national obsession. But the parent activists who had been some of the first people to sound the alarm on adolescent drug abuse were themselves rendered obsolete now. There was no need for grassroots coalitions of parents to deliver antidrug messages when comic books and commercials were doing so for free.

The activists who survived the end of the Reagan administration did so by finding alternative paths. Sue Rusche used her column "Straight Talk About Drugs" to become a nationally recognized expert on drug abuse prevention, and FIA remained solvent through private donations and partnerships with nonprofits like the Scott Newman Foundation. Thomas Gleaton focused on PRIDE Surveys, a subsidiary he had co-founded with professors at Western Kentucky University in 1982 that created school surveys to measure students' alcohol, tobacco, and other drug use. Joyce Nalepka continued her fight against adolescent drug abuse privately, founding the organization Drug-Free Youth: America Cares out of her home in Silver Spring.

Others left parent activism entirely. Upset by the movement's infighting and its co-optation by the Reagan administration, Keith Schuchard returned to her career as a literary historian, publishing numerous books on William Blake, Emanuel Swedenborg, and cabalistic Freemasonry.[26] Even as the nation embraced the mission of the parent groups as never before, eleven years after the first ones formed, the leading activists had gone their separate ways.

•

Washington may have been passing increasingly strict antidrug legislation, but as parent groups lost influence on Capitol Hill, the path was being paved for NORML's resurgence. Heralded by *High Times* as the only group that could defend the civil liberties and individual freedoms of marijuana smokers, NORML declared in 1987 that it had new leadership and new direction. In the words of a reporter from the *Atlanta Journal-Constitution*, the group's volunteers had switched "from blue jeans to blue suits" and "changed their image in order to change pot's image." James Bell, leader of NORML's resurrected Atlanta chapter, told the paper, "We're trying to educate people to make them realize they may not like marijuana or people who smoke it, but you don't need to put them in jail."[27]

Leading the charge was thirty-year-old Jon Gettman, who took NORML's helm in November 1986. Gettman, who had previously spent almost a decade working in the paraphernalia business, provided a surprisingly mature and less controversial voice for the rehabilitated marijuana legalization movement. His lack of a law degree or lobbying experience also distinguished him from NORML's previous leaders. Gettman originally began volunteering for NORML as a bookkeeper in 1981, but as NORML cycled through leaders in the wake of Keith Stroup's departure, he rose in the ranks until he was promoted to national director.

Once there, Gettman changed NORML's focus from lobbying to re-energizing its supporters and educating the public, and he defended marijuana use in language not heard since the 1970s. "Marijuana reform will not occur unless we confront it as a moral issue," he wrote in *High Times* in February 1987. "Our only interest is justice. For NORML, and for you if you join us, our cause is just because we are engaged in the moral activity of bringing people together. We are an idea whose time has come."[28] Other activists, including *High Times* senior editor Ed Rosenthal, supported Gettman's approach. "[Jon] is changing NORML from a lawyer's lobbying group into an activist, grass roots movement," Rosenthal told *High Times,* "and it's working."[29]

As an apologetic former paraphernalia salesman, Gettman was the perfect face for reform. Prior to leading NORML, "I spent eight years in the drug paraphernalia business," Gettman wrote in *High Times,* admitting that "the first object of selling drug paraphernalia was, and still is, to make money." Rather than celebrating these sales, Gettman used his new platform to atone for his sins. Gettman recognized that the paraphernalia industry, which he defined as "free-market capitalism at its best," had deeply offended parents and often harmed the children to whom he sold his products. "The problem with the freewheeling paraphernalia market was that we were pandering to an illegal interest in the marketing of our goods," Gettman wrote. "Much like sex is used to sell cars, we were, in retrospect, using drugs to sell knick-knacks. Just as the exploitation of women in commercials offends people, our exploitation of drugs was offensive to some, especially to parents trying to keep their kids away from any drug use, illegal or otherwise."[30]

But Gettman also offered a solution, one that showed just how much NORML had evolved. "I think it is time for marijuana consumers, the merchants of tobacco accessories, parents' groups, and antidrug crusaders to put aside our differences and work together on the issue on which we all seem to agree—keeping drugs out of the hands of kids," he wrote. "Clear statements need to be made that there are some things that adults do that children and teenagers should not do."[31] Gettman even released a pamphlet, called "Drugs & Children," that declared, "NORML is strongly committed to the concept that growing up should be *drug-free.* Meaningful communication within the family based on honest information on the health and social consequences related to all drugs is the best way to *prevent* drug abuse." But the pamphlet went on to argue that "prohibition has failed to *protect* adolescents. It has only created a widely available, unregulated forbidden fruit."[32] A punitive drug war wouldn't keep kids away from pot, he argued. Only legalization and regulation would ensure a truly marijuana-free environment for the nation's kids.

NORML's transformation from a lobbying group into an educational foundation that actively supported drug-free adolescence was a remarkable, and tactical, shift. Like parent activists who argued in the 1970s that more people would oppose decriminalization if they knew the facts about marijuana's harm, Burt Neal, NORML's assistant national director, argued in *High Times* in March 1987 that his organization had "always believed that the American people have yet to hear our side of the story." The more people knew about the harms of marijuana prohibition, he said, the more they would recognize it as an assault on civil rights. "NORML's key function is to educate the public about marijuana and the issues surrounding its use," Neal wrote. "We are an invaluable resource to any journalist investigating the drug issue, and we provide timely and documented information about marijuana, the laws and litigation regarding its use, and the controversies surrounding governmental efforts to discourage its use and cultivation."[33]

Gettman had far bigger plans than simply promoting drug-free youth and emphasizing marijuana's relative safety in comparison to crack. In response to what he saw as flagrant abuses of marijuana smokers' civil rights in the 1986 drug law, Gettman also wanted to launch a reinvigorated activist revolution. Silenced for years by the Reagan administration and the parent movement's war on pot, Gettman saw the 30 million to 50 million regular American marijuana smokers as a powerful bloc—a "sleeping giant" that Gettman wanted to reawaken. In his monthly column in *High Times,* Gettman revived the pro-decriminalization language of the 1970s by declaring that marijuana use was nothing less than a matter of personal privacy protected by basic civil rights. Given the new directives of the Anti–Drug Abuse Act, Gettman wrote, "the DEA thinks it is empowered to make warrantless searches, entrap individuals, smuggle narcotics, seize property, kidnap 'suspects,' and protect cooperative felons to achieve the national security objective of a drug-free America." The escalated drug war, he warned potential activists, was nothing less than "a WAR ON YOU," and in response, he declared that it was "the responsibility of every pot-smoking citizen out there to wake up, organize, and take to the streets! Do not wait for someone to tell you what to do! Just do it!"[34]

High Times supported Gettman's mission, and throughout the late 1980s and into the early '90s it featured dozens of articles about the dangers of the drug war and how it infringed on marijuana smokers' rights. In one of them, Leslie Stackel, a NORML member and *High Times* columnist, called the act's mandatory sentences absurd. "Cultivate 100 pot plants and your punishment runs to six-and-one-half years, the jail time accorded to a life-threatening robber," she wrote. If the rationale for these sentences was to keep major distributors incarcerated longer, Stackel noted, the laws "have proved ineffective at crimping the drug scourge." Instead, they had only been "highly effective at packing the prisons with relatively low-ranking, non-violent inmates," she wrote, including hundreds of casual marijuana smokers.[35] With millions of regular marijuana users in the United States, Stackel and Gettman argued, a widespread, national pro-pot counterrevolution was the only thing that could overturn the act's overly punitive measures.

NORML would have a difficult time launching this counterrevolution, however. The organization's membership remained under 10,000, dropping as low as 5,000 in 1988, far off its mid-1970s peak.[36] Its major mouthpiece, *High Times*, had also lost much of its luster, with circulation dropping from a high of nearly 450,000 readers per issue in the mid-1970s to roughly 250,000 by the late 1980s. And despite Gettman's calls for unity, turnout for his protests in places like New York was disappointingly small: sometimes only two dozen people would come to hear him denounce the nation's drug laws.[37] Gettman knew that, after years of being attacked by the Reagan administration, parent activists, and the national media, many of the nation's marijuana smokers were scared, unwilling to step outside of the "cannabis closet" they were hiding in. This was hardly a surprise: the country had made a radical shift over the past decade, moving from accepting marijuana and its users to declaring that their "culture" was malevolently harming kids. There might have been tens of millions of underground smokers in America, but with the national mood still firmly against drugs, Gettman was unsure how to inspire the country's marijuana users to act.[38]

But things were about to change. Crack's frenzied sweep across the country had knocked marijuana from national headlines for the first time in years, and though NORML's numbers were small and fewer people were reading *High Times,* pot's popularity was rebounding in a surprising, and surprisingly sympathetic, way. Across the country in San Francisco, where the first legalization protest had taken place decades earlier, the HIV/AIDS epidemic was taking a tragic number of lives and the fight for medical marijuana was beginning. As a grandmotherly baker mixed marijuana into the brownies she gave her "kids" to help them combat the painful effects of the disease, the kind of pro-legalization counterrevolution that Jon Gettman envisioned was being jump-started in California, and an unlikely figure named "Brownie Mary" Rathbun was leading the way.

12

"THE FLORENCE NIGHTINGALE OF MEDICAL MARIJUANA"

BORN ON DECEMBER 22, 1922, in Chicago to a conservative Irish Catholic mother, the presciently named Mary Jane Rathbun left home at age thirteen to travel with an activist group throughout the Midwest to support the rights of striking miners and agitate for women's reproductive rights. In 1941, after finishing college, she moved to San Francisco ("to chase men," she later explained), where she embarked on her first career. "I was going to be a psychiatric chick," she told *High Times,* "but I found out I could make more money as a waitress, so I did that for almost fifty years."[1]

By the 1980s, moved by the HIV/AIDS epidemic ravaging her city, Rathbun had stopped waitressing and was volunteering full-time caring for the young men in her neighborhood who were succumbing to the disease. She found that, if she baked marijuana into brownies, she could ease some of her patients' pain and combat the "wasting syndrome" that took so many lives. Baking and distributing as many brownies as she could, the sweet little old lady who cursed like a sailor quickly became known as "Brownie Mary" and, through her activism and numerous arrests, she transformed marijuana into a sympathetic cause. By exuding compassion for the sick, Rathbun was able to transform perceptions of marijuana and gay men struggling with HIV/AIDS—both anathema to much of America at the time—into a powerful force driving the passage of new drug laws.

Robert Randall was born in Sarasota, Florida, in 1948, one of three children in a typical suburban family. After receiving a master's degree in rhetoric from the University of South Florida, he moved to Washington, DC, in hopes of becoming a political speechwriter, but when he failed to secure a writing position, he took a job as a cab driver instead. After being diagnosed with debilitating glaucoma that rendered him nearly blind, Randall had to quit driving and took a position as a community college professor, where his conservative dress, thick glasses, and quiet demeanor made him a favorite of students and fellow teachers alike.[2] As he searched for ways to preserve his vision, he soon found that only marijuana could relieve the pressure in his eyes, and in August 1975, when he was busted for cultivating his own plants, he became the country's first activist for medical marijuana. Working with Keith Stroup at NORML and a sympathetic lawyer, Randall successfully defended his marijuana use in court as a "medical necessity" and later sued the federal government for access to the drug. By 1976, this quiet, bespectacled teacher had become a medical marijuana pioneer.

Though they came from different backgrounds and worked on opposite sides of the country, in the 1970s and '80s "Brownie Mary" Rathbun and Robert Randall changed the face of marijuana activism in the United States. During a period when pro-marijuana activists were back on their heels and the country was embracing Just Say No, first Randall and then Rathbun presented a new side of marijuana to the public—one that showed the drug's ability to heal, often in cases where no other substance could help. Marijuana came to be seen as not just something smoked by long-haired hippies to get high, but as a uniquely beneficial drug that could treat the debilitating effects of numerous diseases, from easing sixty-year-olds' pain and nausea from chemotherapy and preserving friendly professors' sight, to putting enough weight on dying young men so they could live a few more months before succumbing to AIDS.

By 1996, the medical marijuana movement had generated enough support to change state laws. In November of that year, a California ballot initiative that allowed patients and caregivers to access medical marijuana passed with nearly 56 percent of the vote, and with nearly 80 percent support in Brownie Mary's adopted hometown of San Francisco. After two decades of demonizing the drug and its users, the passage of California's Proposition 215 marked the first time since the 1970s that marijuana laws were eased. It also sparked a remarkable new recognition that sick people could be legitimate users of the drug, patients who didn't deserve incarceration for accessing their medication. And the revolution didn't stop there: by 1999, medical marijuana laws had passed in four other states, jump-starting a movement that would result in medical cannabis being available in twenty-eight states and Washington, DC, by 2017.

After years of an increasingly tumultuous antidrug crusade, the country's legal acceptance of medical marijuana was evidence of a quiet sea change in how marijuana users were perceived. As early as 1997, nearly one-third of the respondents to a *New York Times* poll revealed that they knew someone who used the drug for medical reasons, and they didn't want to see them arrested for their drug use. Because of these personal connections, the focus of the debate shifted. No longer fixated only on the victims of drug use, a growing number of Americans knew people who were victims of the overly punitive drug war itself.[3]

In the 1990s, even as the federal government remained committed to its ongoing drug war—Richard Nixon's promise in 1970 to place marijuana only temporarily in Schedule I remained unfulfilled—individual states once again emerged as the places where marijuana laws could change. The movement that Jon Gettman and NORML had spent years trying to revive picked up steam when activists like Mary Rathbun and Robert Randall put the spotlight on people suffering from cancer and AIDS, individuals who needed access to marijuana if they wanted to survive. When marijuana was transformed from a national scourge into a healing balm that brought relief to millions, the pro-legalization revolution was reborn.

•

The story of medical marijuana in America can't be told without Robert Randall, the man whom Keith Stroup called "the father of the movement." Diagnosed with glaucoma while still in his twenties, Randall was told by his doctor that, given the intense intraocular pressure generated by an overabundance of fluid in his eyeballs, he could expect to be completely blind by age thirty. He tried surgery and various prescriptions, but nothing helped, and his eyesight continued to deteriorate to the

point where he suffered complete loss of vision in his right eye and considerable impairment in his left. But in 1973, at the age of twenty-five,
Randall smoked a joint with a friend and noticed that the pressure in
his eyes lessened. As his vision grew sharper for the first time in years,
he made the connection that when "you smoke pot, your eye strain goes
away. More than a recreational drug," Randall realized, "ganja is good
for you." He began smoking pot on a regular basis, and his doctor confirmed that the drug was saving his vision by reducing the pressure in
his eyes.[4]

Randall still had to purchase the drug on the black market, however,
and despite pot's increasing popularity in the 1970s, it wasn't always
available. To keep a steady supply, Randall began growing a few plants
on the porch of his Capitol Hill home. In August 1975, while Randall
and his partner Alice O'Leary were away on vacation, DC police were
raiding a nearby apartment and noticed his plants. They ransacked his
apartment, took his marijuana, and left a note demanding that Randall
turn himself in. Though he could have pled guilty, Randall brought his
case to court, working with the progressive attorney John Karr, who
defended Randall pro bono. For additional legal advice, Randall turned
to Keith Stroup, who pointed him to a 1971 NIDA report on UCLA
ophthalmologist Robert Hepler's government-sponsored research on
marijuana's effects on the human eye. Hepler had discovered what Randall already knew: that marijuana decreased ocular pressure, and that
its effects could preserve the vision of those suffering from the disease.

Prior to his trial, Randall traveled to California to work with Hepler, undergoing ten days of rigorous testing in order to prove that large
doses of marijuana kept his eye pressure within a safe range. Hepler
also testified at Randall's two-day nonjury trial and wrote a sworn affi-
davit asserting that Randall would go blind without regular marijuana
use. When Randall's case was heard before the DC Superior Court in
July 1976, Karr defended Randall's drug use by arguing that, despite
its illegality, marijuana was a "medical necessity"—an argument that
had previously been used in court, but never to defend an illegal drug.
"Faced with the choice of certain blindness or using marijuana to save
your sight," Karr argued, "a reasonable person would use marijuana."[5]

After reviewing the history of marijuana as medicine, as well as the
history of the drug's prohibition in the United States, to the surprise

of many, Judge James A. Washington agreed. "Research has failed to establish any substantial physical or mental impairment caused by marijuana," Washington wrote in his ruling, noting that "medical evidence suggests that prohibition is not well founded." But Washington's favorable ruling was primarily based on the reasonableness of Randall's actions. "The evil he sought to avert, blindness, is greater than that he performed to accomplish it," Washington continued, arguing that, if Randall chose to follow DC's anti-marijuana laws, he would ultimately do himself more harm. Thrilled that Washington had ruled in Randall's favor, Stroup took the decision a step further, arguing that Randall's case established marijuana's medical value and thus it no longer deserved to be a Schedule I drug. The ruling showed "that the 'no medical value' classification is patently untrue," Stroup told the press. "The government has to reclassify it."[6]

Stroup's request fell on deaf ears, but Randall was acquitted and, shortly thereafter, became the country's first legal marijuana smoker. In response to his ruling, Randall filed a petition to receive a sufficient supply of marijuana from the federal government's testing farm at the University of Mississippi (where Carlton Turner was then still leading experiments); by the end of 1976, he was receiving 300 prerolled joints each month, delivered to his local pharmacy in bags marked PROPERTY OF THE UNITED STATES OF AMERICA.[7] Though Randall often joked that the quality of the federal marijuana was "consistently bad, very metallic," it kept his glaucoma in check and he retained what was left of his vision. In 1978, when his eye doctor moved to another state and the federal government tried to shut off his supply, Randall successfully sued the government for reinstatement of his marijuana rights and won, becoming the first—and so far only—person to sue federal authorities for access to pot.[8]

In the years following his successful trial, Randall became an outspoken advocate of marijuana's medical benefits, which he saw extending beyond treatment of glaucoma to treating the effects of cancer, multiple sclerosis, and a host of other diseases. In 1980, he and O'Leary cofounded the Alliance for Cannabis Therapeutics (ACT), a nonprofit that helped doctors and patients navigate the bureaucracy that often prevented them from using the drug therapeutically. With his quiet demeanor, conservative presentation, and emphasis on medical, not recreational, uses of marijuana, Randall traveled to state capitals across the country in support of laws that recognized the drug as a legitimate medicine, and his presentations were often met with success. By 1981, thirty-two states and Washington, DC, had passed bills that allowed marijuana, as long as the federal government supplied it, to be used in the limited treatment of cancer and glaucoma in the context of research programs. Soon Randall had high-profile backers on Capitol Hill. In September of that year, two Republican representatives—Stewart McKinney of Connecticut and Newt Gingrich of Georgia—proposed a bill that would have amended the Controlled Substances Act to allow doctors to use marijuana in direct treatment.

Despite ACT's endorsement and 110 cosponsors, however, hearings on the McKinney-Gingrich bill were never held. Critics, including Representative Henry Waxman, chair of the House subcommittee on health, maintained that the five acres dedicated to marijuana at the University of Mississippi were insufficient to treat the 250,000 people undergoing chemotherapy for cancer at any given time, not to mention the 2 million to 4 million Americans suffering from glaucoma. Though the bill was reintroduced in 1983 and 1985 and received broad bipartisan support, it never passed. Marijuana remained a Schedule I drug, and the federal government refused to supply marijuana to any of the states where bills were passed to permit certain medical applications of the drug. By the mid-1980s, the medical marijuana legislation that Randall inspired was far more symbolic than real.[9]

Meanwhile, another movement for medical marijuana was emerging on the other side of the country. Mary Jane Rathbun had been living in the Castro District of San Francisco since the 1940s, not far from her waitressing job at an International House of Pancakes. There she had watched as her neighborhood shifted in the face of dramatic social change. For decades, the Castro had been a relatively quiet and undeveloped area filled with half-timber construction and large Victorian houses, but by the 1960s it had become home to the city's growing gay population, who were attracted to the Castro by its cheap rents and friendly reputation. First established by the thousands of servicemen discharged from the Pacific Theater during World War II for their sexuality, the Castro boasted its first gay bar, the Missouri Mule, by 1963, and Harvey Milk, the prominent activist and future member of the San

Francisco Board of Supervisors, opened his Castro Camera store and election headquarters there in 1973. Though Rathbun was well into her fifties by the time the Castro became a prominent gay neighborhood, she enjoyed her new neighbors and found that she had much in common with them, including her regular marijuana habit: she had started smoking in 1957, when she was thirty-five.

In 1974, Rathbun's life abruptly changed. Her only daughter, nineteen-year-old Peggy, was killed by a drunk driver, and Rathbun deeply mourned her loss. Divorced and working at IHOP, Rathbun felt disconnected and alone and looked for ways to supplement her waitressing income and interact more with her community. Around the same time, she met Dennis Peron, the marijuana and gay rights activist who ran the Big Top "marijuana supermarket" out of his Castro home. The lanky twenty-nine-year-old and the matronly fifty-two-year-old with glasses and gray hair quickly formed a tight, if surprising, connection, bonding over their shared love of marijuana and San Francisco.

Rathbun began baking "special" drug-laced brownies for Peron, which he sold at his store. Her brownies quickly became the best-selling item at the Big Top, and Rathbun realized that she could make more from baking than from her waitressing job. Soon Rathbun was baking full-time, advertising her wares on the streets of the Castro and selling brownies out of a basket for $2 each. She even had professional business cards made to advertise her "magically delicious" goods. Given the makeup of her neighborhood, the bulk of her customers were young gay men like Peron, and many of them became Rathbun's closest friends. After the death of her daughter, Rathbun began "adopting" her neighbors, calling all the young men her "kids."

By the late 1970s, Rathbun had been transformed from an IHOP waitress into the Castro's beloved "Brownie Mary" and become a fixture of the San Francisco scene: the bespectacled, gray-haired woman who swore like a sailor, wore a BORN AGAIN ATHEIST button on her polyester vests, and had a THANK YOU FOR POT SMOKING sticker on her apartment door. But Rathbun wasn't above the law, and her luck ran out in 1981. That year, in January, she was busted by the police when narcotics officers came into her home and confiscated fifty-four dozen pot-laced brownies, twenty pounds of high-grade marijuana, and half an ounce of psychedelic mushrooms. Even the officers had to admit being impressed with Rathbun's business acumen: by 1981, she was regularly pulling in $500,000 to $1 million a year from her baking efforts.[10]

Rathbun didn't deal with the bust well. "Being arrested took all the fun out of my life," she said after pleading innocent to charges of possessing and distributing marijuana. With no income and ten felony charges pending against her, Rathbun worried about the outcome of her hearing, which was scheduled for later that March.[11] But "because of her age and the sweetness of her character," Peron remembered, "San Francisco fell in love with her. Even the prosecutor was embarrassed by the case."[12] By the time she was sentenced in June, Superior Court Judge Thomas Dandurand had dismissed nearly all of the charges against Rathbun and punished her by ordering her to use her baking skills for good. She received a thirty-day suspended sentence, three years' probation with a search clause, and 500 hours of community service, most of which had to be spent cooking at soup kitchens, retirement homes, and the Salvation Army.[13]

Rathbun completed her 500 hours in record time—just sixty days—and she didn't stop volunteering once her sentence was complete. Instead, it became her new full-time job. She dedicated over forty hours a week to helping others and moved into a senior housing complex to save money. To supplement her meager Social Security income, Rathbun also began her baking business again; selling her marijuana-laced brownies (this time more quietly, without the business cards) generated a sufficient income to allow her to volunteer full-time.

The HIV/AIDS epidemic that spread rapidly across San Francisco would transform Rathbun's life once again. In 1983, Rathbun's volunteer work led her to the Shanti Project, a human services agency founded to provide peer support and guidance for those suffering from terminal diseases. Rathbun started working with Shanti (Sanskrit for "inner peace") just as HIV/AIDS was beginning to ravage her city. In September 1982, the Centers for Disease Control reported that AIDS had already affected 547 people in the United States, killing 232, and 20 percent of its victims were in San Francisco.

A year later, the problem was only growing. In the Castro, as local AIDS hotlines received over thirty calls a day, panic was setting in. Low-grade fever, swollen glands, and general malaise sent scores of people to the emergency room, then later to the hospital for terminal care.

Soon fungal infections, rare cancers, and skin lesions known as Kaposi's sarcoma—all symptoms of a dramatically reduced immune system—were killing dozens, and then hundreds, of San Franciscans every year. By 1983, when Rathbun began working with Shanti, the disease had killed over 2,000 people in the United States, the majority of whom were young gay men, including dozens of her neighbors in the Castro.[14]

Seeing her neighbors suffer and die galvanized Rathbun into serious activism, and she began focusing all of her volunteer efforts on the young men she saw battling the disease. She and Peron were both personally affected by the crisis: Rathbun had lost dozens of her "kids," and Peron's partner, Jonathan West, succumbed to the disease in 1990. Rathbun was also growing increasingly furious at what she saw as the slow response of both the local and federal governments. "The saddest part about this whole epidemic—which is now a pandemic—is that it hit the gay community and the IV drug users first, the disposable people," she later told *High Times*. "So the government didn't give a shit about people with AIDS, they thought it was god's retribution, which was a load of crap."

Soon Rathbun was cooking two nights a week in the first Shanti AIDS house. After using marijuana for years to treat the pain from her artificial knees, she knew the drug was an effective medicine and always brought some along to help ease the residents' debilitating symptoms. "The kids all loved to see the old lady coming," she said. "I'd walk in with a few joints to pass before dinner, and a bottle of wine." But Rathbun did more than simply give her patients drugs. "I did their banking for them, brought them meals, went shopping, picked up their medicine," she said. "You know, did things for them they couldn't do for themselves."

Then Rathbun switched from bringing joints to making her famous brownies. "A lot of kids were dying fast from pneumonitis—pneumonia—and I thought it would be better for them to ingest the pot with brownies than to smoke it," she explained. Soon she was baking forty dozen brownies every few months and distributing them by the dozen to people suffering in her neighborhood. "The ones who are terribly sick, they can eat a quarter or half a brownie when they get up in the morning and it makes them feel a little better about themselves," Rathbun told *High Times*. "It takes about an hour to kick in, and then they say, 'I think I can get up today. I think I can go out and run some errands today.' It gives them back some of the self-respect they've lost by being totally dependent on a visiting nurse or a Shanti person. That's important."[15]

In 1983, Rathbun also began volunteering in the newly opened Ward 86 of the San Francisco General Hospital, the first outpatient clinic in the country dedicated to working with those suffering from AIDS. As a volunteer, Rathbun spent her days delivering blood samples and running stats, as well as providing friendship and comfort to people who often felt abandoned by families and friends. One thing she did not do, however, was bring her brownies into the hospital. "You can't get hospitals or hospices involved," she acknowledged, since doctors and nurses were some of the only people taking HIV/AIDS seriously at the time. By 1986, Rathbun had been awarded a gold plaque and recognized as Ward 86's "Volunteer of the Year," an honor she would go on to win three more times.[16]

Rathbun's luck ran out again when she was raided a second time, in 1992. This time she was caught at a friend's home in Sonoma County, about forty-five miles north of San Francisco. Rathbun was visiting Stephen Rider, one of her "kids," when deputies with the Sonoma County Sheriff's Department, who suspected Rider of dealing marijuana, entered the house with a search warrant. There they caught Rathbun setting up rows of baking pans and folding two and a half pounds of marijuana into brownie batter. Rider was also found in possession of three-quarters of a pound of marijuana, along with packaging materials, scales, and sales paraphernalia. Both were arrested on felony charges of suspicion of possessing marijuana for sale.

This time Rathbun was prepared to defend herself and her actions. "I make my brownies for the worst patients, the ones on chemotherapy and the ones totally wasting away," she told the Associated Press. "I pick out the worst of the worst and turn them on." Her arrest in 1981 was "legitimate," she said, because she "was baking brownies for money." But eleven years later, she no longer had any financial incentive for her work. "People donate marijuana to me and I save and when I have enough I bake twenty dozen," she explained. Then she distributed the brownies for free to patients she had come to know through her work on Ward 86. She acknowledged that the police got lucky. "I happened to be at Rider's at the wrong time," she said. "They came to bust him, and they ran into Brownie Mary."[17]

In the end, the bust made Rathbun's cause better known. After her arrest, the sixty-eight-year-old became a media sensation, the star of countless magazine and newspaper articles, and a guest on talk shows like *Maury* (Povich) and *The Sally Jessy Raphael Show*. There she talked extensively about the toll that AIDS had taken on San Francisco and described how marijuana had helped some of her patients heal. The country was finally beginning to understand the disease, and Rathbun was the perfect spokesperson for the medical marijuana cause. After the high-profile AIDS-related deaths of Keith Haring, Freddie Mercury, and Liberace and the announcement by Earvin "Magic" Johnson that he had HIV, Americans were significantly more sympathetic to a disease that took almost 200,000 lives that year alone. In the face of rising death tolls, a matronly old woman giving brownies to the sick didn't seem like a terribly objectionable offense. With San Franciscans once again rallying around her, all of the charges against her were dropped by December. "Her story was more about compassion than marijuana," Peron said. "Mary touched the hearts of America with her commitment and her passion."[18]

Rathbun's time in the national spotlight also focused attention on several new medical marijuana bills making their way through the California legislature. In early 1991, in reaction to what he saw as the positive effects of marijuana on AIDS patients, Peron had lobbied to have Proposition P, a resolution that declared the city's support for medical marijuana, put on the 1992 ballot in San Francisco. Though it lacked the force of law, given Rathbun's escalating fame and growing public recognition of the drug's benefits, it passed with 80 percent of the vote in November, proving that a growing number of Californians were willing to recognize marijuana's utility as a medicine.[19] In its wake, medical marijuana activists carried out similarly successful campaigns up and down the state, and the widespread support the measures received eventually led to California's Senate Joint Resolution 8 (SJR8), which petitioned President Bill Clinton and Congress to enact legislation permitting marijuana to be prescribed by licensed physicians. With Rathbun giving emotional testimony at the state house in Sacramento, the resolution received overwhelming bipartisan support, and it was sent to Washington on September 2, 1993. Though the federal government did not take action, the resolution's passage in California was another success for Rathbun and Peron.

Proposition P and SJR8 proved that voters and politicians alike were willing to support a patient's right to medical cannabis, and they paved the way for a more progressive bill that permitted patients suffering from almost any ailment to receive a doctor's recommendation to use marijuana for relief. In early 1995, Peron worked with activists Dale Gieringer, director of California NORML, and Dr. Tod Mikuriya, a prominent psychiatrist and marijuana advocate, to draft a ballot proposal for Proposition 215, which he called the "Compassionate Use Act," dedicating it to his late partner Jonathan West. The language of Proposition 215 was specific. It asked Californians to exempt patients and designated caregivers from criminal laws that otherwise prohibited the possession and cultivation of marijuana, and it allowed physicians to prescribe the use of cannabis in treatment and not lose their license as a result. It also did not define or limit which diseases the drug could treat.

After filing the initiative in Sacramento on September 29, 1995, Peron began organizing a signature drive to get his proposal on the ballot the following fall. With financial support from drug reform–supporting billionaires George Soros (who donated $350,000 to the cause through the Lindesmith Center, an organization he founded to promote an end to discriminatory drug laws), Peter Lewis (who gave $300,000), and George Zimmer (who gave $160,000), Peron was able to generate over 750,000 signatures in support of his measure, and state officials announced that Proposition 215 would be on the ballot on November 5, 1996.[20]

The run-up to the election was tense. California attorney general Dan Lundgren, along with the California Narcotics Officers' Association and fifty-seven of the state's fifty-eight district attorneys, actively opposed the bill, warning that state-based medical marijuana was in direct conflict with federal law and that medical treatment shouldn't be determined by popular vote. Supporters saw it differently. "This bill would permit seriously ill patients to use marijuana in their medical treatment," a pro–Prop 215 editorial declared. "It will affect thousands of people suffering from cancer, glaucoma, AIDS and other diseases who do not find adequate relief from legally available medicines."[21]

Ads in support of Prop 215 also ran constantly on television. Seeking to build on Rathbun's growing celebrity, most of them featured older women supporting medical marijuana for benevolent reasons. In one ad, Anna Boyce, a sixty-seven-year-old nurse, placed flowers on her husband's grave and told viewers that marijuana had given J.J., who died of cancer, "an extra year of life. Proposition 215 will allow patients like J.J. use of marijuana without becoming criminals. Vote yes on 215. God forbid someone you love may need it."[22] In another, Jo Daly, a former commissioner of the San Francisco Police Department, told viewers that she supported the law because the "nuclear implosion of nausea" she felt after receiving chemotherapy was only mediated by cannabis. Battling cancer that had spread throughout her body, she wanted medical marijuana legalized because she had "better things to do with my life than breaking the law."[23]

Boyce, Daly, and Rathbun represented the new face of pro-marijuana activism: white, middle-aged, and clearly sympathetic. The emotion with which they discussed the importance of medical marijuana—the lives it could prolong, the pain it could ease—was so convincing that a majority of Californians voted for Prop 215. On November 5, 1996, the initiative passed with 55.6 percent statewide approval (including 78 percent of the vote in San Francisco), making California the first state in the country to legalize under state law, with a doctor's recommendation, the possession and cultivation of marijuana for personal use. After the bill's passage, Peron appeared on television. He lit a joint in celebration and told viewers, "This is a great moral victory. This is about who we are as a people and where we're going as a nation."[24]

More than simply legalizing medical marijuana access in California, the Compassionate Use Act also transformed the way the drug was discussed nationwide. Almost a year after its passage, Michael Pollan wrote in the New York Times that, "before the Prop 215 campaign, Americans had focused exclusively on the victims of drugs; now they were meeting victims of the war against drugs, and these people looked a lot like people they knew."[25] A decade after the country embraced Just Say No, in the wake of the crack epidemic and AIDS, marijuana had emerged as a surprising savior. No longer the "demon drug" denounced by presidents and parent activists, marijuana suddenly offered something few other substances could: relief from a variety of debilitating diseases and treatments, and a source of comfort for America's sympathetic sick. Robert Randall, the original medical marijuana advocate, was particularly supportive of Prop 215's passage. Randall announced that he had been diagnosed with AIDS in 1994, and he went on to declare that "no one is suggesting marijuana is a cure for AIDS or that it is an appropriate medicine for every AIDS patient. But marijuana can significantly improve the quality of life available to those AIDS patients who are unable to eat and suffer severe weight loss." For that, Randall argued, they deserved access to the drug.[26]

The few parent activists who remained active in the antidrug fight, however, vehemently disagreed with the drug's promotion as a medicine and argued that medical marijuana was nothing more than a Trojan horse for the nefarious legalization plans of pro-marijuana activists and legalization-supporting billionaires. In 1997, Sue Rusche, who continued to work with FIA, published the *Guide to the Drug Legalization Movement and How You Can Stop It!* "Drug legalization proponents have shamelessly exploited the sick and dying," she argued, "in order to overturn century-old drug control laws." The practice of placing cancer and AIDS patients at the center of their campaigns—a tactic "first articulated by Keith Stroup," she said—would ultimately be used "as a wedge to open up legal markets for drugs that are now illegal." Rusche also warned that the more people supported medical marijuana laws, the more severe and unintended the consequences would be. Rather than helping the sick and the dying, pro-legalization activists wanted "to enable these criminal activities to become legitimate business activities, leaving owners free to develop huge markets and reap unimaginable profits."[27] When a thriving new drug marketplace developed, Rusche warned, children and families would be back in harm's way.

But the country's anti-marijuana sentiment was on the wane, and Rusche's warnings fell on deaf ears. Instead, pro-marijuana activists across the country built on Prop 215's success, promoting the drug's health effects and proposing medical marijuana ballot initiatives in Alaska, Oregon, and Washington in 1998. All of these measures passed, as did another in Maine in 1999. That many of these states had also passed decriminalization laws two decades prior should come as no surprise; despite the country's expanded war on drugs, voters in certain areas consistently remained sympathetic to the marijuana cause, particularly as the crack epidemic ebbed and the face of the suffering medical marijuana user emerged.

•

As in the 1970s, medical marijuana gained momentum with little assistance from NORML's national headquarters. Despite Jon Gettman's insistence that the group return to its activist roots, it was state activists, rather than NORML's national leaders, who were most effective in passing medical marijuana laws. In Washington, DC, NORML continued to struggle with inconsistent leadership and ongoing financial problems. Gettman was relieved of his duties as executive director in 1989, when NORML's board determined that he had devoted insufficient time to fund-raising. The organization then quickly cycled through three different directors.[28] Don Fiedler, a lawyer from Nebraska, led the group for eighteen months before disagreements with the board led to his resignation, and Gregory Porter, a former volunteer, led the group for the next fifteen. Richard Cowan, a longtime legalization supporter and libertarian conservative who, in 1972, defended decriminalization in the *National Review,* came on in 1992 but left the position in 1996 amid allegations of financial mismanagement and personal issues with board members.[29]

It was only when Keith Stroup returned to the organization that NORML regained a sense of stability. He was invited to rejoin NORML's board in the fall of 1994 and once again became the organization's director two years later. Although Stroup said that his new tenure as executive director was temporary and that he would primarily serve as legal counsel for the group, his return to NORML nonetheless indicated that the group was returning to its roots as a straitlaced defender of responsible adult marijuana use. With Stroup back at the helm, the group rebounded financially as both membership numbers and levels of private support grew. Aided by the experienced marijuana activist Allen St. Pierre, who ran the day-to-day operations of the group, NORML came back to life at the precise time when medical marijuana laws were beginning to sweep the country, and its resurrection aligned with a renaissance of interest in the drug, heralding a moment that was ripe for the return of marijuana lobbying and activism on a national scale.

Stroup was hopeful about what it all meant. Medical marijuana had reoriented the conversation about the drug in the United States. In the parent movement's decade and a half of control over marijuana activism, marijuana had been blamed for everything from "amotivation syndrome" to eventual heroin addiction and death. This conversation had stayed strictly focused on marijuana's effects on kids—the specific risks the drug posed to children and the harmful impact of adolescent drug use on thousands of innocent families across the country. But by the mid-1990s, the conversation had changed. Now marijuana was being discussed in terms of its impact on the lives of the sick and dying, many of whom were aging adults. Stroup knew that this shift in marijuana's national reputation was going to have an enormous impact. "The California initiative was the most important development in the marijuana law reform area since 1978, when the last of the states to decriminalize marijuana decriminalized," he told *High Times* in 1997. "From 1978 to last November, I think it's fair to say, we didn't win a single important political battle. . . . I can't overestimate the importance of this victory."[30]

But that wasn't the only shift that marijuana was undergoing at the time. By the mid-1990s, marijuana had not only reemerged as a medicine that could prolong cancer patients' lives and keep people like Robert Randall from going blind—it was also making steady gains in recreational popularity among the children of baby boomers, whose romantic fascination with the 1960s made them want to relive an era of peace, love, and pot. After over a decade of the drug war and a terrifying media blitz on the dangers of crack, youth who had been effectively turned off by cocaine returned to marijuana as a nostalgic high, one that seemed as harmless and simple as the images of the 1960s and '70s in films like *Forrest Gump* and *Dazed and Confused*. "A 60's revival, a wave of 60's nostalgia, is sweeping the baby-sitter population," the *New York Times Magazine* declared in 1991.[31] Rates of adolescent marijuana use rose while jam bands like the Grateful Dead and Phish brought their tie-dyed tours across the United States, and Woodstock '94 did its best to re-create the feel of 1969. A Bronx tenth-grader summed up his generation's feeling to the *New York Times* in 1994. "Other drugs are dangerous," he said. "Nobody smokes crack. That will destroy you, you get skinny and you're nothing no more. We only smoke weed around here in the '90s."[32]

With marijuana's image vacillating between a benign, amusing high and a medicine that could prolong the lives of the dying, Stroup's predictions for what the California victory might mean proved correct. Over the next three years, activists passed medical marijuana laws in Colorado, Hawaii, and Nevada, and they kept passing them across the country for another decade and a half. By November 2016, medical marijuana had been decriminalized in twenty-eight states and the District of Columbia, and as of March 2016, there were 1,246,170 registered medical marijuana patients in the country, using the drug to treat everything from the effects of chemotherapy to Crohn's disease.[33] With over a million users in a growing number of states, support for the drug was increasingly high. A 2016 Quinnipiac University poll found that 89 percent of Americans supported a person's right to access medical marijuana, even in states where medical marijuana laws hadn't been passed.[34]

But Brownie Mary Rathbun, the woman who had dedicated much of her life to using marijuana to help the sick and dying, didn't live to see these laws sweep the country. On April 10, 1999, Rathbun died of a heart attack at the age of seventy-seven at the Laguna Honda Nursing Home, a public facility for the aged poor. After spending years battling arthritis and a bout of colon cancer, she was weakened and frail. "She got so thin at the end," Peron told *Cannabis Culture* magazine. "I went to move her from the chair to the bed and she was so light, I almost lost my balance. I have seen a lot of people die, and it always hurts me, but this was too much. I really couldn't handle it."[35]

In the wake of her death, Rathbun was honored across her city. San Francisco General Hospital, where Rathbun had served in Ward 86 for sixteen years, held a memorial service for its most famous volunteer. J. B. Molaghan, a nurse-practitioner, told the *Los Angeles Times* that Rathbun "was a legend around here." She was "refreshingly irreverent," he said, a deeply compassionate grandmother-figure who adopted everyone, calling patients, nurses, and doctors alike "honey" and "sweetheart."[36] A candlelight vigil was held in the Castro District, where more than 300 people gathered to view photographs and newspaper articles commemorating her life and listen to speakers who recalled fond memories of everyone's foul-mouthed "mom." There, Terence Hallinan, San Francisco's attorney general, called her "the Florence Nightingale of the medical marijuana movement." He also promised that, because of the influence of Brownie Mary, as long as he was in his position, "nobody is going to prosecute in the city and county of San Francisco anyone who uses and cultivates marijuana with a legitimate doctor's recommendation."[37]

Hallinan kept his promise, and San Francisco has remained consistently open to medical marijuana users since 1996. Despite the increasing national popularity of the drug, however, rates of arrest for marijuana possession spiked in the aftermath of the passage of the nation's first medical marijuana laws, peaking in 2007 when 872,721 marijuana arrests were made, comprising 47.5 percent of all drug arrests in the United States that year.[38]

With hundreds of thousands of marijuana arrests made annually, a new argument has begun to develop in recent years, one that combines marijuana and civil rights and includes far more than just the sick and the dying. Inspired by Dennis Peron, Robert Randall, and Brownie Mary Rathbun, as well as civil rights scholars like Michelle Alexander, a new generation of grassroots activists has taken up the legalization cause, arguing that nothing less than full legalization can mediate the gross injustice of a system that overwhelmingly arrests African American men for a drug whose use is widespread among all races. With millions of black men behind bars for possession of a drug that blacks and whites use in equal amounts, a growing grassroots movement is calling foul, demanding marijuana's complete recreational legalization as the only means to achieve a sense of desperately needed social justice—not only for the sick and dying, but also for those who didn't want to live their lives behind bars.

13

A SOCIAL JUSTICE ISSUE

IN THE LATE 1990s, Michelle Alexander experienced an awakening. One morning, as she ran down the street trying to catch a bus, she saw a bright orange poster stapled to a telephone poll. In large bold print it read, THE DRUG WAR IS THE NEW JIM CROW, but Alexander didn't believe it. As director of the Racial Justice Project of the American Civil Liberties Union (ACLU) in northern California, Alexander had spent years organizing grassroots activists and building coalitions to support civil rights, and she was long familiar with the conditions of racial bias in America. But "even in the face of growing social and political opposition to remedial policies such as affirmative action, I clung to the notion that the evils of Jim Crow are behind us," she later wrote. The drug war wasn't the cause of a new racial caste system, she thought. How could it be, when drug laws kept people safe? Even though she knew that incarceration rates were considerably higher for blacks than for whites, Alexander thought that "the problems plaguing poor communities of color, including problems associated with crime and rising incarceration rates, [were] a function of poverty and lack of access to quality education"—the same roots of crime and incarceration that she had already recognized and blamed for years. Except in cases of addiction, Alexander thought, drugs had never entered the picture.

Not long afterward, Alexander learned she was wrong. The longer she worked with the ACLU, and the more she spoke with local activists, the more she realized that the war on drugs was precisely what the sign had said. Like Jim Crow, the drug war was an enormous, complicated system of social control that overwhelmingly targeted African Americans. It separated blacks from whites and alienated individuals from both mainstream culture and the mainstream economy. But unlike Jim Crow, the drug war didn't separate the races in public spaces and schools; instead, it separated blacks from whites by placing a growing number of people in jail. Those who had committed drug crimes, even simple crimes like the possession of small amounts of marijuana, were labeled "criminals" who deserved to be locked up. And despite rates of drug use being consistent regardless of race, it was African Americans who were overwhelmingly thrown into prison for drug crimes—often for years, decades, or life.

The more Alexander looked into the connection between the drug war and mass incarceration, the more disgusted she became. Over three decades—the exact period during which the drug war escalated from a rhetorical battle to an actual war—the US penal population had exploded from around 300,000 in 1970 to over 2 million by 2000, with drug convictions accounting for the majority of those arrests. Rates of American incarceration were up to ten times greater than incarceration rates in other industrialized nations, and in some states black men were admitted to prison on drug charges at twenty to fifty times the rate of white men. By 2000, the United States had imprisoned a larger percentage of its black population than South Africa had at the height of apartheid. At the dawn of the twenty-first century, Alexander realized, one-third of all young African American men were in the confines of the criminal justice system—either incarcerated, on probation, or on parole. "The American penal system," she concluded, "has emerged as a system of social control unparalleled in world history."

Most troubling for Alexander was how a drug charge could haunt a person for life. People with felonies on their records, particularly those who had committed drug crimes, were systematically excluded from state and federal benefits. Even after they had supposedly paid their debt to society and were released from prison, they could still be denied the right to vote, not allowed to serve on a jury, and barred from accessing welfare programs like food stamps and public housing. This systematic exclusion from basic social benefits, Alexander realized, had resulted in a growing, and permanent, undercaste that kept African Americans at

a permanent disadvantage and created generations of entrenched poverty that haunted the families of those charged with drug crimes.

Unlike traditional Jim Crow, however, this new system of
incarceration-based segregation was touted as being ostensibly "color-
blind." Rather than focusing on skin color, it targeted and punished
"criminals" who used and sold drugs, labeling them as dangerous
threats to American safety. As a result, the initiatives that resulted in
mass incarceration were popular with both politicians and voters, who
often didn't realize the laws' racist effects. Regardless, the outcome was
the same: once African Americans were labeled "criminals," the old
Jim Crow–style practices of exclusion and segregation could be rein-
stated. "As a criminal, you have scarcely more rights, and arguably less
respect, than a black man living in Alabama at the height of Jim Crow,"
Alexander argued. "We have not ended racial caste in America; we
have merely redesigned it."[1]

Now a professor of law and race and ethnicity at Ohio State University, Alexander published her findings in her 2010 book *The New
Jim Crow: Mass Incarceration in the Age of Colorblindness*. Though she
wasn't the first person to make these claims, Alexander's book method-
ically broke down the ways in which the war on drugs was a war on civil
rights, and it was a groundbreaking success. Supported by Alexander's
impassioned public speeches, *The New Jim Crow* sold 175,000 copies
in its first two years, and Alexander went on to appear in numerous
documentaries decrying the racist effects of the drug war, including *The
House I Live In* (2012) and *13th* (2016), both of which received glowing
reviews.[2] Her work has inspired a new generation of grassroots activists
to take on the challenge that Alexander argues for in her book: reforming the criminal justice system while working toward racial equality in
the United States. "Nothing short of a major social movement can successfully dismantle" the new Jim Crow, Alexander wrote, and "all who
care about social justice should fully commit themselves to dismantling
this new racial caste system."[3]

The New Jim Crow launched a wave of awareness—and action—
about the effects of institutionalized racism in the war on drugs, and no
intoxicant has inspired more action than marijuana. Between 2001 and
2010, 8.2 million people were arrested for pot, and 88 percent of those

arrests were for the simple possession of small amounts. By 2010, the year Alexander's book was published, marijuana arrests were so common that one was made every thirty-seven seconds, for a total of over 750,000 that year alone. Marijuana arrests also embodied Alexander's argument about the drug war's segregationist effects: despite blacks and whites using the drug at roughly equal rates, blacks were up to four times more likely to be arrested for marijuana than whites, and in some counties they were up to 30 percent more likely to face prosecution for the drug. In 2010, the black arrest rate was nearly three times the white arrest rate for possession of pot.[4]

Given these alarming statistics, activists soon made marijuana legalization—not decriminalizing the drug, reducing fines and penalties, or changing policing tactics—their primary response to Alexander's call to dismantle a racist criminal justice system. Activists focused on legalization because of both marijuana's twenty-year reputation as an effective prescription medication as well as its growing social acceptability. In 2014, 44 percent of adults told a Gallup poll that they had tried marijuana at some point in their lives, and 11 percent reported that they were current cannabis users. These rates—the highest Gallup has ever reported—showed either "an increase in the percentage [of people] who have tried the drug, or an increased willingness to admit to having done so in the past," the report explained.[5] With millions of people admitting to using the drug, activists argued that it was going to get increasingly difficult to justify users' incarceration, especially when the racist breakdown in arrest rates was made clear.

This push for legalization has been both remarkably powerful and remarkably fast. By November 2016, only four years after the first states legalized the drug, grassroots activists in eight states and the District of Columbia had successfully promoted ballot initiatives that fully legalized recreational marijuana use. (Colorado and Washington approved legalization in 2012; Alaska, Oregon, and Washington, DC, in 2014; and California, Maine, Massachusetts, and Nevada in 2016.) Though legalization hasn't continued on as rapid a pace as decriminalization had in the 1970s, when a dozen states decriminalized over a period of five years, it has continued to gain ground, and the drumbeat for its expansion has been steady.

This is because the benefits of legalization—particularly financial ones—have been made overwhelmingly clear. As trailblazers in the movement, activists in Colorado and Washington report that their initiatives have been enormously successful, especially in terms of generating tax revenue. Colorado reported that it sold nearly $1 billion in legal marijuana in 2015, returning $135 million to the state—money that has gone on to provide everything from funds for school construction to increasing residents' access to health care—and in 2016 that sales figure was matched in the first ten months of the year alone, bringing in over $150 million in taxes by October.[6] Washington reported similar results: between 2014, when the first stores opened, and 2016, legal marijuana generated over $1 billion in sales and returned over $250 million in excise taxes.[7] For cash-strapped states, the legalization and taxation of marijuana has enormous appeal: activists claim that by bringing money that once went into the black market back into legal circulation, taxes from legalized marijuana can close budget loopholes and increase services. Polls also show that a majority of the country's residents would willingly support such a shift: in October 2016, a Gallup poll found that the number of Americans nationwide who supported legalization had reached 60 percent—the highest in the nation's history.[8]

Still, when discussing the financial benefits of the burgeoning marijuana marketplace, many activists have continued to emphasize that the most important aspect of legalization is righting racial and social wrongs—even if evidence of this effect is unclear. When legalization was discussed in California prior to its successful November 2016 vote, it was widely defended on this basis. In June of that year, lieutenant governor Gavin Newsom told the Cannabis Business Summit that he supported legalization because "our purpose is social justice, to right the wrong of abject failure which is our war on drugs in the United States of America."[9] And Diane Goldstein, a retired twenty-year veteran of the Redondo Beach police force and a registered Republican, wrote in October 2014 that she believed that the legalization initiative was "one of the best things California can do to improve public safety." In Colorado and Washington, Goldstein wrote, the increased regulation and oversight of legalized marijuana sales had reduced teen use, while dangerous street gangs and cartels had watched their revenues drop as the marijuana market was placed "in the hands of sellers licensed and regulated by the government"; she wanted to see similar controls put into place in California. But most of all, Goldstein supported legalization because it was "a tremendous step toward social justice. Despite being equally likely to use marijuana and less likely to sell it than whites, African Americans are disproportionately arrested for marijuana crimes. The war on drugs has become the latest social mechanism that disenfranchises blacks and other people of color. Any move we make toward ending it furthers the cause of equality."[10]

By pointing out the vast discrepancies between black and white arrest rates, pro-legalization lieutenant governors and retired police officers have been joined by the most diverse generation of marijuana activists in American history. Like Brownie Mary, many are elderly people who want access to legal marijuana for their aches and pains, while others, young and politically aware, are demanding that the country live up to its promises of equality. And unlike the racially homogeneous marijuana campaigns of the past, demands for legalization in the twenty-first century have united activists who are black, brown, and white, urban and rural, and conservative and liberal in the fight for expanded marijuana civil rights. In the years since the first legalization initiatives were passed, this pro-legalization constituency has been joined by groups as diverse as a coalition of Protestant ministers and Jewish rabbis (the Clergy for a New Drug Policy is particularly active in Chicago) to the Black Lives Matter movement, all of whom argue that legalization is an essential aspect of increased social justice and civil rights.[11] Calls for legalization have even made it into presidential campaigns: in 2016, Senator Bernie Sanders became the first major candidate to incorporate changing marijuana laws into his platform since Jimmy Carter in 1976. Combined with the rest of his promises—such as addressing wealth inequality and instituting a living wage—legalizing marijuana was a logical extension of Sanders's larger demands for civil rights.

The Democrats may have lost the 2016 election, but marijuana won big, passing in four more states and spreading legalization to a total of 68 million people—over 20 percent of the population—from coast to coast. The 2016 election and the ballot initiatives that were passed in 2012 and 2014 prove that social justice has become the most powerful incentive to transform marijuana laws in American history. After decades of vacillation, this new generation of pro-legalization grassroots activists has pushed the pendulum of public approval back toward marijuana's acceptance, and these activists have been extraordinarily successful in their campaigns. Outright legalization of recreational marijuana use—an unprecedented transformation from the days of both decriminalization and Just Say No—marks by far the most tremendous shift in drug laws since the federal Prohibition of alcohol, and many supporters believe that their luck will continue, and that national and federal legalization are inevitable—at most, only a few years away.

But legalization has also raised some important questions—about the health and safety of those living in legalized states, about the effects of commercialization and business interests in a newly legal marketplace, and, most importantly, about its ability to actually alter the racial dichotomy of drug arrests. On many of these counts, it's still too early to tell what the long-term effects of legalization will be. In the meantime, a growing understanding of the racist aspects of arrests, along with increasing acceptance of marijuana's use, have already transformed the boundaries of what we think about marijuana in this country, and the role it can play in American society.

Knowing the history of marijuana activism in this country, however, it shouldn't come as a surprise that the nation's near immediate embrace of legalization has also inspired a new generation of anti-marijuana activists to form. These activists—many of whom are younger and more politically aware than the parent activists who came before them—wonder if decriminalization wouldn't achieve the same thing, decreasing the number of racist arrests without legalizing an increasingly potent drug. For them, the potential dangers of legal marijuana are, like pro-legalization proponents' evidence in support of the measures, economic: developing alongside the booming marketplace in legal pot is a new generation of marijuana products, including vaporizers, dabs, edibles, concentrates, topicals, and tinctures that are designed to appeal to an increasingly sophisticated marijuana user and to expand the number of ways to experience the drug's effects. Numerous companies are jumping on the "green rush," working to profit off a marketplace that, some analysts predict, will soon generate $50 billion a year. Given that legalization has been implemented without assistance or oversight from the federal government, anti-legalization activists worry about the lack of consistent regulation and the potential for conglomerates to form. Citing the increased numbers of children hospitalized for eating marijuana edibles, they fear that easy access to an increasingly potent drug poses a far greater threat to public health than the threat criminalized marijuana poses to civil rights.

In short, the battles over marijuana the country experienced in the 1970s are once again coming into sharp relief, though this time with the added wrinkle of states legalizing, and not simply decriminalizing, recreational use of the drug. Just as in the 1970s, states vary in how the new laws are being implemented: the maximum allowed potency of products varies by state, and there are no widespread standards for marketing or package design, particularly of edibles that look like candy and could be appealing to children. States also vary in how residents can access the drug: people in California and Oregon are allowed to grow their own plants, while residents of Washington State cannot. And just as in the 1970s, the federal government continues to consider marijuana a Schedule I drug, making a drug that is legal on one level still illegal on another. This paradox at the heart of marijuana policy has hardly been solved by state-based legalization, but it has shown that, after forty years, Americans once again see changing marijuana laws as both a symbol and a means to an end. For those who equate legal marijuana with social justice and civil rights, legalization is a profitable and positive opportunity to emphasize privacy and individual rights. For opponents of the measures, legalization is a frightening regression toward attitudes that privilege adult intoxicant use over the health and safety of the nation's kids.

And just as in the 1970s, activists once again see the nation's capital as the site where the battle over marijuana laws is taking shape. Washington, DC, legalized recreational marijuana use in November 2014, but unlike in the eight other states where marijuana is legal, government-sanctioned sale of the drug remains illegal, forcing users to navigate the "gift" economy and causing the city government to lose out on potential tax windfalls. It's also the site where pro- and anti-legalization forces have rallied: every group from NORML to the pro-legalization Marijuana Policy Project to the antidrug Project SAM (for Smart Approaches to Marijuana) has offices in or around the city, and marijuana activists continue to come to Washington to voice their concerns. In essence, DC represents America's battle over marijuana in miniature, and as one of the most diverse areas in the country where the drug is legal, it's a good place to see how legalization is playing out. Official Washington may still consider marijuana a Schedule I drug, but in November 2014 voters in the city voted to legalize marijuana in an attempt to end the New Jim Crow.

•

Caught somewhere between a city and a state, with a population of roughly 650,000 (making it larger than Wyoming's or Vermont's), Washington, DC, is a unique place to live and raise a family. It's the site of some of the country's most impressive spectacles: the presidential inauguration every four years, enormous political protests taking over the National Mall, and various festivals and large events that fill the city's avenues and streets. But beyond the neoclassical beauty of the monuments and government offices downtown, DC is also a living, breathing city, with many residents who have lived here their entire lives—residents who, in November 2014, voted two-to-one to legalize the use of recreational marijuana in their city.

Since the law's passage, DC has become the site of one of the country's most bizarre experiments with legalization. Unlike in other legalized states, there are no retail marijuana stores here, and there won't be anytime soon. You can grow up to six plants at home (three mature, three immature), but you can't sell young plants or even seeds. You can possess up to two ounces of smokable pot, but you can't buy or sell any actual buds. Instead, marijuana has to somehow show up in your possession, either given as a gift or perhaps placed under your pillow by the Marijuana Fairy at night. If you do have marijuana or paraphernalia on you, you can only use it in certain areas, like your private residence. You're not allowed to smoke outdoors even in residential areas, and since over 25 percent of the District's sixty-eight square miles, including the National Mall and numerous parks and office buildings, is federal property, getting caught smoking or holding there remains a federal crime.

Cannabis users and sellers have found numerous ways to overcome these challenges, however. The law has a "transfer" clause, which allows adults age twenty-one and older to transfer marijuana between users as long as they don't accept payment for the drug, and several new businesses have found creative ways to profit off this legal loophole. There's HighSpeed, a juice delivery company that offers a "gift" of several grams of marijuana with every order of a $55 or $150 apple juice or lemonade, while Kush Gods has employees drive around the city in luxury cars emblazoned with giant pictures of weed, accepting "donations" in return for marijuana "gifts."[12] In a city where, Michelle Alexander found, three out of every four poor, young black men can expect to be imprisoned at some point in their lives, marijuana legalization has turned into a lucrative venture for those willing to place their business, and potentially their personal freedom, on the line.[13] (The owner of Kush Gods, a young black man named Nicholas Cunningham, has repeatedly been busted by the police.[14]) But it has also turned Washington into one of the primary sites of debate over what exactly legalization means, and a place where marijuana continues to exist in legal limbo between federal law and states' rights.

As in nearly every other state that has passed new marijuana laws, the concept of social justice made legalization extremely popular in Washington. In the lead-up to the passage of Initiative 71, which legalized marijuana in the city, Washington's most visible pro-marijuana activist, Adam Eidinger, emphasized that the law would promote racial and social justice. A career activist and owner of Capital Hemp, one of the few paraphernalia shops in the area before legalization was enacted, Eidinger was the chairman of the DC Cannabis Campaign, which drafted Initiative 71 and sent volunteers across the city to collect over 57,000 signatures to place it on the November 2014 ballot. Armed with a DC flag on which the stars had been replaced with marijuana leaves and the words LEGALIZATION ENDS DISCRIMINATION added underneath, Eidinger and his army promoted legalization as a means to end the city's overt targeting of marijuana use by black residents and the most obvious way to rectify racial disparities in the city's drug laws. In a city that was 49.5 percent black in 2015, Eidinger argued, statistics revealed that, prior to legalization, African Americans were almost eight times more likely to be arrested for marijuana than whites, and over 90 percent of those arrested for pot that year were black. If marijuana were legal, Eidinger argued, "we could tell the police, 'Guess what? It's not even a crime. You don't have to write a ticket.'"[15]

Very quickly, others began to agree. By October, a month before the vote, the DC branch of the NAACP endorsed the bill. "The NAACP DC Branch strongly advocates to end the war on drugs, which has caused significant damage to our communities," said Akosua Ali, NAACP DC's president. "Endorsement of Initiative 71 does not mean that the NAACP is pro-marijuana, but we view Initiative 71 as a step toward ending discriminatory drug policies."[16] Even DC police chief Cathy Lanier believed that the city's marijuana laws were doing more harm than good. In March 2015, a month after legalization went into effect, Lanier said that "all those marijuana arrests do is make people hate [the police]. Marijuana smokers are not going to attack and kill a cop. They just want to get a bag of chips and relax. Alcohol is a much bigger problem."[17]

In November 2014, almost 65 percent of the city's voters approved recreational marijuana legalization, passing the legislation by the largest majority in the country. (The eight states that also legalized pot between 2012 and 2016 passed their initiatives by margins of 50 to 57 percent.) Afterward, supporters declared that DC's shift would herald major changes to marijuana laws nationwide. Bill Piper, director of national affairs at the Drug Policy Alliance, saw Initiative 71 as a bellwether for the rest of the country. Unlike laws that had passed in majority-white states like Colorado and Washington, Piper said, "I think DC is probably going to set off a chain of events in which communities of color generally and cities in particular take on the issue of legalization as a racial justice, social justice issue in a much stronger way than they have so far."[18] Keith Stroup, still serving as legal counsel for NORML's DC-based national headquarters (which actively supported Initiative 71), told the *Washington Post* that "the nation's capital has an exaggerated impact" on national laws. "If Washington, DC, can legalize marijuana and the sky doesn't fall, things will get a lot easier in these other states," Stroup said.[19]

By February 2016, a year after legalization went into effect, it appeared that many of the predictions of Initiative 71's supporters had come true. Arrests for marijuana possession in the city had plunged a shocking 98 percent, dropping from 1,840 in 2014 to just 32 in 2015. Between 2010 and 2015, arrests for possession fell 99.2 percent, arrests for possession with intent to distribute dropped 85.5 percent, and distribution arrests dropped 71.8 percent. While no statistics on the racial identities of those arrested were released, Piper called the decrease "an enormous victory for District residents" and hoped that "law enforcement continues to responsibly enforce the new law and completely eliminates any racial disparity in arrests."[20]

But legalization has created new issues in the District as well, some of them expected and others less so. Alongside a substantial decrease in arrests, marijuana use in the nation's capital has grown, and it has become surprisingly brazen. Hani Ahmed, a community activist in Southeast Washington, told the *Washington Post* in May 2015 that he was surprised by how overt many District residents were about their drug use, despite the continued illegality of smoking in public. "Everybody and their mama thinks they can smoke outside," he told the paper. "I've seen youngins smoking and walking past the police." In the Northwest section of the city, an anonymous government contractor who dealt marijuana on the side noticed "evolving behaviors" among his customers: "People who wouldn't smoke at all before are trying it now," he said. "People who were closet smokers are now way out in the open."[21]

Even dealers are more open about hawking their wares. A month after DC approved legalization, Congress, which maintains control over the District's laws, enacted a spending prohibition that barred the city from creating a system for legally buying, selling, and taxing marijuana, effectively outlawing marijuana stores (though it should be noted that the legal purchase and sale of marijuana were not included in the original text of Initiative 71). The result has been to supercharge the informal market in cannabis sales. Some have taken advantage of the city's "transfer" loopholes to create systems like those used by High-Speed and Kush Gods. Other dealers recognize that, if they carry less than two ounces on them, they are still protected by the city's legalization laws so long as they aren't caught in the act of selling. Armed with business cards, clever marketing campaigns, and a surprisingly open attitude, more DC residents are becoming small-time dealers to take advantage of what Stroup called the city's "green rush." An anonymous dealer told the *Washington Post* that the laws were actually working in his favor. With carrying the drug legally protected and no need to pay the heavy fines and taxes levied on marijuana in other legalized states,

DC's legalization law was, for him, "a license to print money." Rather than eradicating the black market, he said, the law could be called "the dealer-protection act of 2015."

Stroup criticized the DC law for its obvious oversights. "If you're going to legalize marijuana, you also have to legalize the supply because you want to get rid of or at least limit the black market," he told the *Washington Post*. "Right now [DC has] done the exact opposite." More marijuana was being bought and sold, Stroup said, but the city received none of the tax dollars the drug's legal sale might raise. And unlike the practices in other legalized states of having intensive security measures in pot shops and checking customers' IDs, DC's black market has no age restrictions, almost ensuring that rates of adolescent drug use will rise. Already in 2014, according to a survey from Project Know comparing regular alcohol and marijuana use among twelve- to seventeen-year-olds across the country—a report released the same year DC voters opted to change their law—DC was the jurisdiction with the highest number of adolescents reporting marijuana use in the past thirty days. With no ability to regulate its black market, Washington's legalization law has little power to make those numbers change.[22]

Despite its uneven implementation and unexpected effects, however, legalization remains extremely popular both in the District and in other legalized states. Indeed, the laws are so popular that, in November 2016, four more states voted to legalize recreational marijuana use, making 68 million Americans residents of areas where marijuana—along with its correlated markets in edibles and paraphernalia—is legal. In support of their choice, many voters cited the same economic and social justice reasons that prompted legalization's passage over the previous four years.

But beyond arguments for social justice, what is unprecedented about the legalization debate today is that it acknowledges that people use marijuana for fun, just as they drink alcohol or smoke cigarettes. Unlike in the 1970s, when decriminalization was defended as protecting an adult's right to privacy, or in the 1980s and '90s, when medical marijuana was defended as a necessary drug for the sick, in the 2010s support for legalization has grown because voters recognize that, despite fifty years of prohibition, millions of Americans continue to smoke pot. Rather than spending money to prosecute and incarcerate millions of people, legalization allows states to save money by legitimizing this action, while recouping enormous sums in tax dollars in return—all while taking steps to remedy racist arrest rates and increase the potential for equality in the criminal justice system. It's a compelling argument, and in the history of marijuana activism, it is by far the most influential and powerful one yet.

But questions remain about the effects of legalization on racial equality and the impact of the increased availability of marijuana on public health. Recent studies have shown the inconvenient truth that legalization may repair unequal arrest rates in the short term but that, after years of implementation, racist trends arise again and again. More troubling is that, despite active measures taken by states to bar children from marijuana shops, adolescent marijuana use in legalized states is rising, if only slightly. In Washington State, rates of marijuana use increased roughly 3 percent for eighth- and tenth-graders between 2012 and 2014, and there was a slight increase in marijuana use by high school seniors as well. In a 2015 survey in Oregon, one in ten eighth-graders and one in five eleventh-graders reported using marijuana in the past twelve months, a slight increase from the previous year.[23] There is also a growing feeling among adolescents that marijuana use is relatively benign. The University of Michigan's "Monitoring the Future" report found that, in 2014, only 35 percent of nineteen- to twenty-two-year-old high school graduates thought marijuana use was dangerous, down from 55 percent in 2006. The study also noted that daily or near-daily use among college students had risen to 5.9 percent, the highest rate since 1980.[24]

For anti-legalization activists, this is precisely where the danger lies. A new generation of anti-marijuana activists, including men like Kevin Sabet and Will Jones III, see legalization's implementation as inherently dangerous for America's youth, and they've come to Washington to help stop legalization in its tracks. Taking the mantle of anti-marijuana activism from the parent activists of the 1970s and '80s, Sabet and Jones form the new front of the anti-marijuana campaign, one that is more politically and racially aware than parent activists were in their day. Attending to issues beyond marijuana's impact on kids, they acknowledge that racist arrest rates are a real problem, but Sabet and Jones also argue that there are alternative ways to decrease the incarceration of casual marijuana smokers, while reducing the use of marijuana as a whole.

Sabet is the most prominent personality in this new wave. Born and raised in the affluent Los Angeles suburb of Anaheim Hills, Sabet comes from a family of devout Baha'i and has no personal experience with alcohol or drug use. Intoxicant abuse by both adults and kids was rampant in Anaheim Hills, however, and Sabet began to acknowledge its negative effects even as his community "conveniently ignored it," he said. Fascinated by the community's struggle with the intersection of denial and what was actually happening, he took to writing about drug abuse in his local school newspaper. His articles attracted the attention of antidrug activists across the country, including Sue Rusche, who invited him to several FIA conferences when he was a teen. This introduced him to the larger antidrug movement and secured him a prominent place within it as a member of a young new generation working to discourage drug abuse.[25]

Sabet went on to study political science at Berkeley in 1997. It was only a year after medical marijuana had been legalized in the state, but Sabet was disturbed by the number of dispensaries that had already opened up and the general feeling that, as he put it, marijuana use was "no big deal." He formed Citizens for a Drug-Free Berkeley on his second day at the school ("I've always liked a challenge," he said) and was twice elected to the school's senate. With Citizens, Sabet showed up at nightclubs with a CAT scan of the human brain on ecstasy, warning that the drug caused irreversible neurological harm.[26] As a student senator, he also fought to close People's Park, the food and clothing distribution point for the homeless near Berkeley's campus, because of the illegal drug use Sabet saw going on there.[27]

By 2000, Sabet's work had piqued the interest of Barry McCaffrey, President Clinton's chief drug adviser. That summer, Sabet served as a research associate in the Office of National Drug Control Policy. He graduated from Berkeley in 2001 and then went to Oxford to pursue a master's in public policy. His thesis, entitled "Defining American Drug Policy: Is All Policy Local?" brought him back to Washington in 2002, where he briefly worked for George W. Bush's drug adviser John Walters. Then he returned to Oxford to receive his PhD in public policy in 2007, with a dissertation titled "Toward Reducing Total

Harm: Analyzing Drug Policies in Baltimore and New York." Shortly after Barack Obama took office, Sabet served as a session adviser for Obama's drug czar Gil Kerlikowske, but by that point, with initiatives working their way toward the ballot in Colorado and Washington, he worried that marijuana wasn't getting the attention it deserved. "The issue was too dichotomized, even in 2009, 2010," Sabet said. "There was no voice talking about it in a non-moral way."[28]

After the nation's first legalization votes in 2012, Sabet decided to start that discussion himself. Moving away from moral arguments about whose civil rights were being violated by marijuana laws, Sabet began to focus on the potentially harmful public health outcomes of legalization. His biggest fear was the commercialization of the industry: that Big Marijuana could develop in the same vein as Big Alcohol and Big Tobacco. "If we were a country with a history of being able to promote moderation in our consumer use of products, or promote responsible corporate advertising or no advertising, or if we had a history of being able to take taxes gained from a vice and redirect them into some positive areas, I might be less concerned about what I see happening in this country," Sabet said in 2015. "But I think we have a horrible history of dealing with these kinds of things."[29]

Instead, Sabet feared that the government was putting legalization before public health in the rush to correct social injustices and benefit from tax revenues, while voters supportive of new marijuana laws were unwittingly promoting the interests of private industries. This was particularly dangerous for children, Sabet argued, whom he feared were going to become the cannabis industry's primary targets. Speaking at an event at the Pasadena Recovery Center in California in June 2016, Sabet told his audience that they should "be real. The marijuana gummy bear industry is targeted directly at kids. I might enjoy eating gummy bears at the movies every now and then, but I am not the target. Big Marijuana knows that drugs are the double-edged sword of brain development. The simple truth is that addiction starts young."[30] For millennial voters too young to remember Joe Camel and Big Tobacco's other pitches to kids, the ramifications of legalization— the edibles packaged to look like regular foods, the implicit appeal to children with a wide variety of marijuana candies—were particularly worrisome, Sabet said, especially with rates of hospitalization up 150 percent in Colorado since 2014 for children who mistakenly consumed cannabis edibles.[31]

His growing fears over marijuana legalization led Sabet to found Project SAM with Patrick Kennedy, the son of Senator Edward Kennedy, in January 2013. SAM, whose offices sit directly outside of Washington, DC, in Alexandria, Virginia, is adamantly opposed to legalization and calls itself "an alliance of organizations and individuals dedicated to a health-first approach to marijuana policy," as well as a bipartisan group dedicated to "commonsense, third-way" beliefs based on "reputable science and sound principles of public health and safety."[32] According to Sabet, SAM offers Americans an alternative to the dichotomy of legalization or criminalization. "Twenty percent of the population is absolutely for legalization," he explained, "and SAM can't reach them. Another twenty percent is absolutely opposed, and SAM doesn't have to reach them either. So SAM is for the sixty percent of people who don't fit easily into either category— people who want to know more before they vote either for or against a new law." His organization, Sabet continued, wants to offer voters "a different tone."[33]

Project SAM's goal is to stop the wave of legalization votes and urge the country to have a conversation about what legal marijuana's public health effects might be before rescheduling or federally legalizing the drug. Sabet recognizes why people are voting for legalization—that it appears to be a way to achieve social justice by ending the high rates of incarceration for pot—but he disagrees that legalization is the way to go. Sabet believes that real social justice instead will involve a holistic approach to marijuana policy, one that incorporates education, prevention, and early intervention, while discouraging all forms of illegal drug use. And while he recognizes that arrest rates have a racial bias, he doesn't believe that piecemeal, state-by-state changes are the best solution to these problems. Ballot initiatives are "too complex," Sabet said. "Arrests, probation, they vary from state to state and lots of little laws won't change the big picture. Ballot initiatives prevent the discussion of real outcomes and allow too much industry money to influence people's votes." Instead, we need to "promote health and not just change policing," he said.[34]

Unlike antidrug activists of the past, Sabet isn't a hard-liner. In 2015 he told Vox, "I absolutely think we should remove criminal penalties for [marijuana] use. I absolutely think we should not be penalizing someone with an arrest record so they can't get a job." In a far cry from Nancy Reagan and the days of Just Say No, Sabet believes that decriminalization, with its "relatively nonviolent underground market," is a reasonable solution for the "8 percent of Americans who use marijuana," he said. He even supports medical cannabis, telling Vox that "there are clearly some medical benefits for some people from the components in marijuana—in isolation or when taken together. The question is how we deliver that in the safest way, where there's a lower potential for abuse." Still, Sabet believes that an understanding of marijuana's true medical benefits is still years away, and that research may already be too corrupted by private interests. An investment by the government of real time and money in nonpartisan research into cannabis's medical properties, Sabet said, would prevent private industry from influencing the medical marijuana market by only funding research sympathetic to its claims.[35]

Like Sabet, anti-legalization activist and Washington, DC, native Will Jones III believes that the biggest danger of legalized marijuana is that private industry will dominate the field, especially in historically majority-black areas like Washington. As an African American, Jones was driven to activism when the question of legalization was put on Washington's November 2014 ballot and received widespread support. Fearful of legalization's potential effects, Jones founded an organization, Two. Is. Enough., which argued that having two legal intoxicants already—alcohol and tobacco—was more than sufficient. Rather than a civil rights issue, Jones saw legalization as "just another way to sell vice to the African-American community. I see a disproportionate amount of liquor stores and tobacco advertising targeted toward us," he said, "so what is of huge concern is we're seeing a third industry that's ready to follow in those footsteps."[36]

Jones was also quick to point out that support for legalization in the city was far higher among whites than blacks. While 74 percent of DC's white population supported legalization, only 56 percent of black residents did, and only 40 percent of black residents over age fifty supported the bill. It's not that African Americans didn't see the problem with marijuana arrest rates, Jones argued. In a city that was 49.5 percent black in 2015, statistics reveal that, prior to legalization, African Americans were almost eight times more likely to be arrested for marijuana than whites. But Jones and his supporters don't think that was a convincing enough reason to support legalization, and indeed, they saw the city's uneven implementation of legalization as an example of another deep racial divide. Whites will specifically benefit from Washington's legalization law, Jones said, because it stipulates that marijuana can only be legally consumed in a person's private residence. For middle-class white people, many of whom live in single-family homes, that wasn't a problem. For those caught smoking in public, however, like lower-class African American residents of housing complexes or those who smoke on federal land, arrest rates will continue to rise. It is "naive and troubling to argue that legalizing marijuana will end racial injustice," Jones told the *Washington Post*. Legalization will not transform racist cops or prevent them from targeting black communities. Instead, Jones continued, legalization was little more than a means for large national corporations to exploit black communities and prey upon innocent black kids.[37]

Despite high-profile endorsements from prominent black leaders like retired judge Arthur Burnett and Howard University Department of Psychiatry chairman Dr. William B. Lawson, Two. Is. Enough. couldn't convince enough of the city's voters to oppose legalization, and the organization folded shortly after the vote. But Jones has remained a committed anti-marijuana activist and continues to speak out against legalization, writing articles for other new anti-pot organizations that have formed in the wake of widespread passage of legalization laws. These organizations include Moms Strong, a "support group" headquartered in California and Arizona that, much like PRIDE before it, is dedicated to "unmasking the marijuana charade" and informing and educating families with children harmed by marijuana use.[38]

Sabet, Jones, and Moms Strong may be attempting to build a new anti-marijuana platform, but Keith Stroup believes that their fears about Big Marijuana are overblown. He pointed to the voters in Ohio who resoundingly rejected the state's 2015 legalization initiative, which would have restricted cultivation to ten already selected growers and properties. That kind of oligopoly didn't sit well with voters, Stroup said, nor does it sit well with most state legislators who are essentially starting from scratch when it comes to making new kinds of marijuana laws. Instead, Stroup continued, most people, including marijuana activists and state lawmakers, would prefer to see the marijuana industry follow the wine model. Although there are a few major players in the wine industry, most vineyards are small, family-owned operations, and Stroup argues that states could easily write size limitations for growers and distributors into their laws, keeping the scale of the market manageable and monopoly-free. Even the major players who have entered the marijuana market—the estate of Bob Marley and Willie Nelson, for example—have pledged to ensure both the quality of their product and their commitment to sustainability and social justice.[39]

But Stroup's predictions about the potential scale of legalization may be naive. By 2016, legal marijuana was the fastest-growing industry in the country. Forbes put revenue for legalized marijuana sales at $7.1 billion in 2016, and Bloomberg expects that number to grow to $50 billion by 2026 as state-based legalization expands and a growing number of users turn to a legal supply. For comparison, that makes the 2016 industry already larger than Dasani bottled water, Oreos, and Girl Scout cookies, and by 2026 it will match—and eventually outpace—the size of America's booming wedding industry.[40] Musicians long associated with cannabis use may be the biggest players in the industry today, but activists like Sabet and Jones argue that it will be difficult to keep major corporations at bay for long.

Critics also fear that the "green rush" will do little to achieve social justice, the reason many voted for legalization in the first place. Amanda Chicago Lewis, writing for *BuzzFeed News,* reported in March 2016 that the legal cannabis industry inherently benefits whites by excluding from employment anyone with a previous criminal record for marijuana—the bulk of whom are the same young African American men whom legalization was supposed to protect. Lewis wrote about Unique Henderson, a young black man who, after Colorado first legalized medical marijuana in 2009, sought to work at a dispensary. But Henderson couldn't get such a job because he already had two drug possession felonies on his record and people convicted of marijuana crimes are barred from working in marijuana shops. Henderson's white friend, who had never been arrested for drugs, easily got hired, demonstrating that America's history of racist arrests will continue to haunt many African Americans long after legalization laws have been put into effect. Lewis also found that the number of black-owned dispensaries was small. Though no official statistics are kept on the race of business owners, Lewis conducted interviews on her own and reported that "fewer than three dozen of the 3,200 to 3,600 storefront marijuana dispensaries in the United States are owned by black people—about 1%."[41]

If African Americans aren't benefiting from the marijuana marketplace, are they at least benefiting from changes in drug laws? For all the social justice arguments being made in support of legalization, Jon Gettman, the former director of NORML and now a professor of criminal justice at Shenandoah University, found that, for the most part, they were not. African Americans account for 3.9 percent of Colorado's population, but in 2014, two years after legalization was passed, black people still comprised 9.2 percent of the arrests for marijuana possession and were thus 2.4 times more likely to be arrested for marijuana than whites. And although marijuana-related charges decreased by 80 percent overall in Colorado between 2010 and 2014, racial disparities in marijuana arrests didn't substantially change. In fact, for some offenses, especially public consumption, Gettman found that racial disparities actually rose.[42]

Statistics like these have done little, however, to stop today's activists from using social justice as a reason to support legalization measures across the United States. In Massachusetts, one of four states to legalize recreational marijuana use in 2016, Carol Rose, executive director of her state's chapter of the ACLU, expressed her support for the ballot initiative by arguing that "criminalizing marijuana disproportionately hurts poor people and folks of color." Citing Michelle Alexander's *The New Jim Crow* and noting that the new law includes measures to prevent marijuana companies from marketing to children and allowances for cities and towns that want to stay "dry," Rose argued that a vote for legalization was "a vote for public health and social justice."[43] Nearly 54 percent of Massachusetts's residents agreed and voted to allow legalized marijuana that November. Rose's organization celebrated by tweeting that the law's passage was "a win for social justice, public safety, the economy and public health."[44]

But there's a certain irony to *The New Jim Crow* inspiring support for marijuana legalization. Even as her book incited activists across the country to fight for legalization as a matter of social justice and civil rights, Michelle Alexander never made this argument herself. Her book is not solely about legalizing marijuana. Instead, it sounds the alarm about the negative effects of incarcerating a majority of nonwhite Americans for a variety of generally nonviolent crimes and calls for an end to the use of the prison system as a means of segregation and social control. Alexander notes that the drug war has resulted in an unprecedented wave of arrests (which she ties primarily to the war on crack), but she also cites high arrest rates for other nonviolent crimes, including traffic violations, welfare fraud, and "one strike and you're out" legislation. Legalization, which she mentions only once in her book, and decriminalization, which she argues may be a financial imperative in an era when "the financial crisis [is] engulfing states large and small," are just two parts of the solution she proposes, not the whole.

The real solution, Alexander argues, is a transformation in how people of color are perceived in the United States. "A flawed public consensus lies at the core of the prevailing caste system," she writes. "When people think about crime, especially drug crime, they do not think about suburban housewives violating laws regulating prescription drugs or white frat boys using ecstasy. Drug crime in this country is understood to be black and brown, and it is *because* drug crime is racially defined in the public consciousness that the electorate has not much cared about what happens to drug criminals—at least not the way they would have cared if the criminals were understood to be white." For Alexander, it is this "failure to care, really care across color lines," that lies at the heart of this system of control. Police busting more blacks for weed than whites is just a symptom. If the problem is, at its core, an issue of public consensus and caring, Alexander acknowledges, legalization may not be enough to solve it.[45]

With measures in place for the last five years, it's becoming increasingly clear that legalization hasn't immediately resolved the problems of racial disparities and civil rights violations that it was originally touted to help. There are still discrepancies in marijuana arrests, and jobs in the legalized marketplace have primarily gone to whites. The irony of legalization's rollout isn't lost on Alexander. Speaking to the Drug Policy Alliance in 2014, she said that "in many ways the imagery doesn't sit right. Here are white men poised to run big marijuana businesses, dreaming of cashing in big—big money, big businesses selling weed—after forty years of impoverished black kids getting prison time for doing precisely the same thing." Though Alexander was "thrilled" that states are no longer incarcerating as many people for marijuana, there were still larger problems to solve. "I think we have to be willing, as we're talking about legalization," she said, "to also start talking about reparations for the war on drugs, how to repair the harm caused." Until that becomes a larger part of the conversation, Alexander argued, the debate over legalization and social justice remains incomplete.[46]

Even if legalization hasn't immediately solved America's deeply entrenched problems with racism, pro-marijuana activists still claim it's a good first step in addressing the larger issues that Alexander brings up. And building on legalization's attempts to increase racial equality in the criminal justice system, activists claim that there are other undeniable benefits to legalization, including the tax dollars raised, the arrest rates lowered, the money saved by no longer prosecuting marijuana possession crimes, and the lost business for traffickers and cartels. After a half-decade of implementation, it's clear that many in the United States can happily coexist with legal marijuana, with support for legalization clocking in at 60 percent and many reports claiming that national rates of adolescent use of the drug are stable or dropping.[47] As more people become aware of the nation's problem with the mass incarceration of African Americans for drug offenses, it's also clear that the arguments in favor of legalization have generally been more persuasive than those of the anti-marijuana activists, whose fears about the potential commercialization of the industry and threats to public health feel somewhat dated and out of touch with America's growing embrace of the drug.

But that may be precisely the problem. Marijuana is still a drug—one that remains in Schedule I, and therefore illegal on the federal level—and the state laws governing it can swiftly be changed. Without rescheduling or federally legalizing marijuana, a state ballot initiative that legalizes marijuana can be overturned by a new ballot initiative to recriminalize the drug. Americans are not typically a very patient people, and if legalization does begin to result in increased rates of adolescent drug use, or if more children are hospitalized after eating weed-laced food, we can expect legalization initiatives to come to a sudden and abrupt halt, just as decriminalization did in the 1970s. And if racially disparate arrest rates persist, or even increase, in legalized states, we can also expect the newest wave of anti-marijuana activists to declare that legalization is an oversimplified response to the complex problem of racism in the United States. Legalizing one drug, as Alexander argues, will not overturn what is fundamentally a problem of public consensus and understanding, and numerous activists like Kevin Sabet and Will Jones III will argue that, rather than helping people of color, legalizing marijuana has only compounded the problem.

In short, America's current embrace of marijuana legalization is as tenuous as support for decriminalization was in the 1970s, though with several important updates. Just as in the 1970s, arguments in support of changing marijuana laws are still predicated on an adult's right to use, without fear of arrest, a drug that many claim is less harmful than alcohol or tobacco, though today this argument has gained strength from pointing out that blacks and whites use marijuana in equal numbers but African Americans face a far greater threat of arrest and incarceration. Also as in the 1970s, the country seems increasingly comfortable with pot. In the wake of an opioid and heroin crisis that has rattled communities across the country and that killed over 30,000 people in 2015 alone, marijuana once again seems relatively harmless in comparison, just as marijuana decriminalization laws were passed in the wake of a heroin overdose epidemic that took thousands of lives from 1967 to 1976.[48]

But also as in the 1970s, it would be unwise to claim, as some pro-marijuana activists do, that legalization is "unstoppable" and that a majority of states will change their laws, forcing the federal government to change its stance too.[49] Activists believed that the tide was about to turn in the early and mid-1970s, only to watch their progress disappear with the rise of the parent movement and its growing affiliation with the Reagan administration. Today, with a new administration in the White House that is overtly suspicious of recreational legalization, and a small but growing coalition of anti-marijuana activists staking their claim, the history of marijuana activism tells us that only one thing is certain: absolutely nothing is guaranteed, and the pendulum of public opinion on marijuana can always swing back again, as the cycle of activism begins anew.

CONCLUSION

Lessons Learned

I STARTED RESEARCHING marijuana activism in 2010, two years before the first legalization laws were passed. I was a doctoral student looking for a topic that offered something new, an area of history that was previously unknown. I had been interested in drug history for years because I was fascinated by how studying the use of illegal and taboo substances was a lens into everything that excited me about American culture: underground art, literature, and music; political protest and cultural rebellion; and psychological experimentation and the belief that humans can tap into greater powers of the mind. I also loved the idea that the history of the late twentieth and early twenty-first centuries could be viewed through the perspective of drug use, revealing new stories that showed the integral role of illicit substances in shaping the country's direction and beliefs.

Few of the many books I read about drug history, however, said much about a group of parents in suburban Atlanta who influenced the Reagan administration's execution of its war on drugs. Those that did either gently mocked the movement or dismissed the parents' impact as irrelevant. But the more I looked into the parent movement's history, the more I realized that these claims were untrue: parent activists were far more powerful and effective than previously believed. Telling their story seemed like a good place to start, and a way for me to add something new to the already rich field of American drug history. Four years of research into archives and documents later, along with interviews with over two dozen people, my dissertation presented a new history of the parent movement, outlining its rise and fall as well as its impact on the battle over marijuana rights. These parents were hardly irrelevant, I argued; indeed, they were some of the most powerful grassroots activists in American history.

But the story didn't end there. As legalization laws were passed in 2012, 2014, and 2016, I also began to understand that the history of anti-pot parents was only part of the larger story. The parent movement didn't form in a vacuum, but in response to widespread advocacy for decriminalization and to what these parents viewed as decriminalization's negative effects. Today's new legalization movement didn't form in a vacuum either. Legalization of recreational use of marijuana is now promoted as a response to blatantly racist arrest rates caused by Reagan's drug war—the very battle that parent activists helped to mobilize. And those original protests for decriminalization in the 1970s formed in response to specific provocations at the time: Nixon's rising war on marijuana users, the Shafer Commission's pro-decriminalization report, and, of course, the Vietnam War. It is this back-and-forth, this give-and-take, that lies at the heart of the larger history of marijuana activism, I realized. No American marijuana movement has started without being inspired by the other side. The history of the parent movement was a good place to start, but it was only a small segment of a far richer, more convoluted story.

This book is the product of three more years of research, interviews, and attention paid to all forms of marijuana activism, from those who fought to extend marijuana rights to those who have battled to keep the door to the cannabis closet firmly closed. I was fortunate that many of the people involved in over fifty years of marijuana movements—from activists to White House officials to legislators and lawyers—are still alive and that many were willing to talk to me. Although everyone looked at the situation differently, they all had one thing in common: regardless of whether they supported or opposed the use of the drug, each passionately believed that marijuana is extremely important to the fate of the country. More than any other legal or illegal substance, marijuana is a drug that makes people *care,* that inspires them to take to the streets. There has been nothing like it—at least not since the end of the federal prohibition on alcohol—that has inspired such passion or such political ambition. Cannabis, I realized, has groupies.

There was one question that I asked at the end of each interview: what lessons have you learned over the years (and sometimes decades) in your movement? Reactions varied, and many of them are already contained here. But a few other responses seem relevant in this period of intense uncertainty, when the future of marijuana seems more nebulous than ever. What follow are six important lessons drawn from the five decades of history chronicled in *Grass Roots*. This advice could help the activists of today—whatever their views of marijuana—build on past successes while avoiding the potholes that have destroyed the momentum of previous movements.

Lesson 1: Make your argument as sympathetic as possible.

The face at the center of the marijuana debate has changed repeatedly throughout the years. From otherwise law-abiding college kids smoking pot in the '60s, to innocent children serving as "guinea pigs" in the nation's dangerous experiment with decriminalization in the '70s, to the sick and dying in the 1980s and '90s, to the African American men being unfairly incarcerated in the 2000s—activists who have made successful arguments for or against marijuana laws have always centered their claims around a sympathetic figure, one who requires new drug laws in order to more safely navigate the world.

The utility of a sympathetic argument may seem obvious, but it's one of the most important lessons this history reveals. Marijuana, and the activism surrounding it, has rarely been about the drug itself. Instead, debates over cannabis have always centered on the people who use it and whether they're benefiting from the drug or being harmed by it. The focus of this argument has shifted over the years, from adults to children and back again, but regardless of who is at its center, activists have always declared that those who would benefit most from a change in marijuana laws are those who are suffering the most. The concepts of freedom, justice, and dignity have been integral in discussing who deserves to be imprisoned for marijuana and who deserves to be protected from its use. Whether it's an adult's right to use the drug in the privacy of his or her home or a child's right to grow up drug-free, the people at the center of successful marijuana debates are defended as those most deserving of social justice.

The new wrinkle that legalization brings to this story—the possibility that some entrepreneurs might become millionaires in an industry that, when illegal, sent millions of people to prison—makes the argument for sympathy more important than ever. If pro-legalization activists want to spread new laws nationwide, they need to ensure that these laws are framed in a way that benefits others besides the businesspeople cashing in on a trend. And if anti-legalization activists want to protect children or specific groups, they need to make sure that their arguments show the potential dangers for the innocent within a newly legalized industry. Abstract arguments and statistics are useful, but they don't sway voters as powerfully as images of a suffering child, a hospitalized patient, or an incarcerated father do. To be effective, arguments for or against marijuana must continue to show—as parent activists, Brownie Mary, and Michelle Alexander have done—how the drug affects real people and how new laws can help or hinder real people's lives.

Lesson 2: It's all about the money.

There is nothing more important to the success of a grassroots movement than consistent access to sufficient funds. With the right level of funding, activists can publish newsletters, put on events, and communicate with (and increase the number of) their followers. Without it, movements shrivel and die. For example, when NORML's supporters became overconfident after Jimmy Carter's election and dropped their memberships, the group was left struggling for funds, forcing its dependency on Peter Bourne. And when the Reagan administration stopped funding the parent movement, parent activists were forced to compete with a growing number of other antidrug groups for a shrinking amount of federal and private money. Being strapped for funds intensified internal infighting and backbiting so much that the movements self-destructed, leaving bitterness and anger in their wake. Even though today the Internet has made communicating with supporters far easier and cheaper than it was when NORML and parent activists began publishing newsletters forty years ago, it remains the case that no movement can survive without access to consistent, and sufficient, funds.

Money also lies at the heart of every one of the country's new marijuana laws. Decriminalization and legalization are currently popular because of their effects on state budgets. If states no longer have to prosecute marijuana crimes, expenses for courts, prisons, and jails all substantially decrease. Press coverage has touted the tax benefits for states that have implemented full legalization, noting that the money has been used to build schools, offer antidrug education for children, and even increase access to health and dental care for residents. It's hard to argue with the numbers: states are bringing in millions in tax dollars that were previously going to the illegal dealers, and they're using that money to improve infrastructure and local services. This new revenue stream has buoyed the pro-marijuana activists' cause and become a major argument for legalization in other states, especially those that are struggling financially.

The growing anti-legalization movement is concerned about money too. Antidrug activists like Kevin Sabet warn that, despite the tax benefits of legal marijuana sales, Big Marijuana and cannabis companies will care little about public health if it stands in the way of making a profit. As the fastest-growing industry in the United States, the sheer scale of the marijuana market has spooked even some industry giants, causing them to work against the legalization tide. Pharmaceutical manufacturers—including OxyContin producer Purdue Pharma and Abbott Laboratories, which produces Vicodin—have funneled thousands of dollars to anti-legalization groups like Project SAM that lobby Congress to keep marijuana a Schedule I drug. By lobbying against marijuana's increasing medical use, these companies are trying to protect their interests and their profits. States that have legalized medical marijuana have seen a substantial drop in prescriptions written for opioid painkillers—up to 1,800 fewer doses prescribed annually—as a growing number of people turn to marijuana instead.[1] Fueled by the participation of everyone from anti-legalization pharmaceutical companies to pro-legalization billionaires like John Sperling and George Soros, the twenty-first-century battle over marijuana activism is gearing up to be the best-funded one yet.

Undoubtedly, there have been real financial benefits to the legalization of medical and recreational marijuana in terms of states' ability to use new tax revenues to rebuild crumbling infrastructure and to save money by no longer criminalizing people who use the drug. But it's important to note that, even though there were financial benefits to decriminalization in the 1970s too, they did little to ensure the laws' continued viability. Profits that are celebrated today can become demonized tomorrow if the market becomes too wild and unregulated, or if legalization results in spiking levels of adolescent drug use, as happened forty years ago. The battle over marijuana will be fought with real money in the coming years, and grassroots activists must ensure that they're equally well funded if they hope to participate in this increasingly high-stakes fight.

Lesson 3: Be prepared to watch your progress disappear.

It has happened time and again. A period of intense hatred of marijuana (the 1930s, the 1950s, the late 1970s into the 1980s) births a moment when the drug suddenly seems all right (the 1960s and early to mid-1970s, the 1990s, today). In both moments, laws change, as does use. Then acceptance births opposition, which births acceptance, and the cycle begins anew.

Marijuana's shifting reputation doesn't occur in a vacuum. It's important to remember that the moments when marijuana was most explicitly accepted or condemned have generally aligned with periods when Americans have either used or not used another drug. The heroin epidemic of the 1960s and early '70s paved the way for widespread support for decriminalization of marijuana; pot seemed less dangerous than heroin when 1,000 New Yorkers overdosed on the latter in 1971 alone. But by the late 1970s, when the heroin epidemic had died off, marijuana was an easy target for fear. Without the specter of another, far deadlier drug, and with rates of adolescent marijuana use rising, parent activists were able to reorient the drug war to target pot smokers instead, since marijuana seemed like the greatest threat at the time.

This lasted until the mid-1980s, when crack cocaine knocked marijuana from the headlines and became the target of national panic instead. When the crack scare was combined with effective activism surrounding pot's use by the sick, the nation's first medical marijuana laws were passed. In a similar twist, the opioid abuse epidemic—which started with prescription drugs but has now spread to more powerful narcotics like heroin and fentanyl—once again makes marijuana seem tame in comparison, and, when combined with an effective campaign for social justice and civil rights, has helped pave the way for legalization today.

Ultimately, marijuana becomes more acceptable when headlines declare that Americans are abusing other, generally harder drugs; it has historically been during these moments when activists succeed in softening the nation's marijuana laws. But when there are few other "scare drugs" available to take the focus off marijuana—and when the drug becomes associated with other social scourges, like the counterculture, adolescent addiction, or dangerous criminals—pot once again becomes "public enemy number one" and laws that have increased access to it are often quickly overturned. These broad shifts in public opinion show how transient marijuana laws can be, and how little control activists have over extenuating factors. Despite rising rates of approval for legalization, most Americans remain ambivalent about marijuana (if 60 percent of Americans support legalization, that still leaves 40 percent of the country who either denounce the action or simply don't care), and external factors continue to play a large role in altering public attitudes toward the drug.

One of the greatest obstacles activists also need to remember is that all changes in marijuana laws have occurred at the state level—mostly through ballot initiatives, which present another set of problems. By working exclusively with voter-driven initiatives, activists limit themselves to roughly half the country: only twenty-six states and the District of Columbia allow citizens to place initiatives on the ballot, while voters in places like Pennsylvania, Connecticut, Minnesota, and Texas don't have that option. State laws, being responsive to public opinion, can also be changed quickly when, given the right number of signatures, the winds start to shift and a new generation of activists seek to convince voters to make a change; a ballot initiative that increases access to marijuana can be overturned later by another initiative that recriminalizes the drug, making progress subject to voters' whims.

Meanwhile, even as marijuana laws have changed repeatedly at the state level, no group has been able to dislodge federal prohibitions on pot. After nearly fifty years, marijuana remains a Schedule I drug, and discussions at the federal level have been relegated to how thorough and tough law enforcement efforts should be, and how much weight should be put behind prohibition legally, financially, and intellectually. In this sense, anti-marijuana activists have an easier path: with federal law and most states already on their side, they only need to convince legislators to keep the status of marijuana unchanged. Pro-legalization activists have to fight the dual battle of working to change marijuana laws state by state (with some states easier to target than others) while also maneuvering to make the federal government less of a hindrance in their efforts.

Five decades of marijuana activism history show that whoever makes the most of external factors can influence public opinion and ultimately help shape new laws, at least in the short term and, usually, at the state level. This history also shows how quickly a group's progress can be overturned, however, as soon as the prevailing winds shift and a new movement rises in response to new trends in drug use and shifting marijuana laws. If activists want to be successful in this environment, they have to be prepared for the long term. They must understand that success is neither inevitable nor unstoppable and that outside factors will continually arise that either help or hinder their progress. And even when progress disappears, they must remain committed to the cause. If a group can withstand the changing winds of Americans' vacillating feelings about marijuana and continue to do their work, they stand the strongest chance of making long-lasting changes to the country's drug laws, whether at the state level or, perhaps someday, at the federal level as well.

Lesson 4: Don't rely too heavily on the White House.

Relying on the Carter administration was the downfall of NORML in the 1970s, and dependence on the Reagan administration caused the destruction of the parent movement in the 1980s. When activists rely too heavily on their relationship with a single administration, their achievements can quickly disappear, whether because their biggest supporter leaves the administration in scandal (as Peter Bourne did in 1978) or because their biggest cheerleader usurps their movement (as happened with Nancy Reagan in the mid-1980s). No administration has ever developed a flawless relationship with marijuana activists, and an important lesson of the past is that even good relationships with the White House can lead to the activists' message being misused or overturned.

Activists should also understand that a new administration can quickly reverse whatever progress had previously been made. When Bill Clinton entered office in 1993, his admittance that he had tried the drug (though he noted he "didn't inhale") signaled a changing vision of marijuana in America. Under the first baby boomer president, Clinton's administration moved away from the Just Say No attitudes of the Reagan and George H. W. Bush administrations and oversaw, without controversy, the first shifts in state medical marijuana laws. This different approach effectively ended the parent movement's legacy of influence in Washington and slowly paved the way for DC's acceptance of legalization as well. Similarly, when the first legalization laws passed in Colorado and Washington, James Cole, a deputy attorney general in Barack Obama's administration, released a memo in August 2013 acknowledging that, although marijuana was still illegal under federal law, the federal government would practice "prosecutorial discretion" in states that had legalized the drug: the Justice Department would not interfere with the new laws as long as states upheld federal priorities like keeping the drug away from minors and preventing grow operations from opening on federal lands.

But a memo is not law, and legalization wasn't the only measure that people voted for in November 2016. The legacy of the Obama administration's agreement not to meddle in legalized states is at serious risk in the Donald Trump administration. His attorney general, former Alabama senator Jeff Sessions, is vociferously anti-marijuana. While serving as attorney general of Alabama in the 1980s, he famously joked that he thought the Ku Klux Klan was "okay until I found out they smoked pot." More recently, Sessions said that "good people don't smoke marijuana" and that the drug is "not the kind of thing that ought to be legalized." As for the president, his stance is unclear. While campaigning, Trump told the Conservative Political Action Conference (CPAC) that he thought recreational use was "bad" and that legalized states like Colorado had "a lot of problems going on right now." But he also supported states' rights to handle things on their own, particularly in the realm of medical marijuana, which Trump claimed to support "100 percent."[2]

With this new administration's opposition to the legalization of recreational marijuana, we are once again forced to confront how tricky an overreliance on Washington can be, and how difficult it is for activists to navigate the country's state and federal divide as they work to change laws surrounding a drug that is legal in eight states while remaining illegal on the federal level. After five years of seemingly endless victories, a new administration has come into office with the power to enforce a federal law that could wipe out activists' state-based successes. Whether this is good or bad news for marijuana activists today, the message is inescapable that the ongoing tension between the federal government and the states over the drug is simply a continuation of a historical trend, and that neither side should become too comfortable with the direction of the White House, since that, too, can rapidly change.

Lesson 5: Respect your opposition.

Marijuana is the only drug in American history whose legality has slipped back and forth, from illegal to legal to illegal and back again, all through the work of dedicated activists. Cocaine has never inspired such enthusiasm, nor has heroin, meth, or LSD. Alcohol runs a close second, but even though infamous activists like Carrie Nation used hatchets to smash saloons in their dedication to prohibition in the late nineteenth century, since the passage of the Twenty-First Amendment in 1933 few have questioned alcohol's legality.

Marijuana has inspired decades of dedication because the drug is loaded with meaning and because it often means many things at once. If for one person marijuana represents freedom—whether that means freedom from government interference or just freedom to do what she wants—for someone else it means fear—fear that a driver high on pot could be dangerous on a highway, or fear that America isn't the country he thought, or hoped, it would be. As the debate over marijuana grows more complicated, arguments for and against the drug have become more entrenched. Whether or not activists agree with their opposition's conclusions, they must recognize that the other side's beliefs about the drug are as legitimate as their own, because they're based in the same sense of concern. Parents in the 1970s didn't rally against marijuana because they hated hippies—indeed, many of the original parent activists were liberals themselves, voting Democrat and concerned about civil rights. Instead, they decried decriminalization because they were worried about the safety of their kids. In the same vein, activists fighting to extend marijuana rights to the sick and dying, or to keep a disproportionate number of African Americans out of prison, aren't in the battle because they want everyone to get high; they're fighting because the drug has proven medical benefits, or because racist arrest rates stand in opposition to everything this country represents to them.

If activists don't respect the views of their opposition and instead denounce or mock the views of the other side, they run a far higher chance of self-destructing—as happened to the pro-marijuana movement in the 1970s when it didn't take the parents' position seriously, or as when parent activists in the late 1980s demonized marijuana users before turning on themselves. Such lack of respect also becomes dangerous when a new administration enters office and activists prove unable to adapt their arguments to meet the prevailing public tide. When a drug comes loaded with this much baggage, and when debates over the drug shift as rapidly as they have done historically with marijuana, activists must be careful about what they say if they ever hope to convince their opposition. As described under lesson 1, activists' arguments about marijuana need to be sympathetic, not only to the people whom their efforts are striving to protect, but to their competition as well.

Lesson 6: Keep a sense of perspective.

The last lesson comes from Lanny Swerdlow, a registered nurse who founded the Brownie Mary Democratic Club in Riverside, California, in 2012. Swerdlow, a marijuana and gay rights activist, was deeply inspired by how Brownie Mary brought marijuana to HIV/AIDS patients in the 1980s. Building upon her legacy, Swerdlow now represents the interests of cannabis users to Democratic representatives across his state, working to ensure that medical marijuana patients have safe access to their drug and promoting legalization of recreational use as a way to decrease racist arrest rates. In the five years after the first group formed, Swerdlow has overseen the growth of six additional Brownie Mary clubs, all of which are affiliated with the state's Democratic Party and actively promote marijuana rights.

Swerdlow's clubs were vocal in their support of Proposition 64, which legalized recreational marijuana use in California in 2016. There is a lot about California's law that Swerdlow likes. He appreciates that it legalizes the use and sale of marijuana for adults over twenty-one. He likes that it levies two taxes on the drug, one on cultivation and one on the retail price. And he likes that the bulk of the tax dollars raised will be used to fund drug research, treatment, and enforcement, as well as programs that support youth education and environmental protection.

But what Swerdlow likes most about the law is that it allows Californians to grow up to six marijuana plants of their own. Like Amorphia in the 1970s, Swerdlow sees personal cultivation as a necessary element of all proper legalization initiatives, and he hopes that citizens of other states are given the same right in the future. Swerdlow believes that personal cultivation is important not only because marijuana grows wild across the United States, but also because personal cultivation addresses so many of legalization opponents' fears. "If people can grow their own pot," Swerdlow said, "it cuts down on fears of Big Marijuana or monopolies forming. It cuts down on fears of the drug being contaminated or laced. And it cuts down on the cartels and the black market too."

More than that, Swerdlow sees personal cultivation as a key aspect of legalization because he believes that it will be difficult to bar access to a drug that most Americans could grow in their backyards and which millions of Americans clearly want to consume. Despite all the years of activism and anger, changing reputations and punishing laws, skyrocketing arrest rates, and powerful grassroots movements sweeping the country, millions of Americans are still regular marijuana users, whether some activists and authorities like it or not. For Swerdlow, the country's ongoing fight over marijuana has inspired his career as an activist, but it's also given him a deeper sense of perspective. Despite America's ongoing fear of the drug, Swerdlow has promised to keep the fight for personal cultivation and the extension of marijuana rights alive. When I asked him why, he laughed.

"Why not?" he said. "After all, it's just a plant!"[3]

ACKNOWLEDGMENTS

Most authors tend to follow the Malcolm X model and claim that everything good in their manuscript is due to those who offered assistance, while sole ownership of any mistakes falls on the authors themselves. This is the same caveat I will place on my own work. It is because of the aid and cooperation of so many benevolent individuals that this book may be worth anything at all. Mistakes, misunderstandings, omissions, or blunders are solely my own responsibility.

I'd first like to thank my team at Basic Books, who have been nothing short of amazing. Ben Platt first saw the potential of this story, and Brian Distelberg took me across the finish line. Brian's kindness, intelligence, and sharp editorial insights have transformed this work—it is a far stronger, more focused book because of him. My agent, Rayhané Sanders, is a superhero. Rayhané, you are Wonder Woman, defending literature and reading against all enemies. Thank you all for believing in my work.

I am deeply grateful to all the people who took time to help me with my research, talking with me and answering my questions about grassroots activism. I spoke at length with Allen St. Pierre, NORML's former executive director, and Keith Stroup, NORML's founder, who were approachable, generous, and funny individuals who added much depth to my work. That they allowed me to poke around in their files—and use their photocopier—was an enormous boon. I am also grateful to the federal officials and White House advisers who agreed to speak with me about my work. Robert DuPont, Peter Bourne, and Lee Dogoloff were enormously helpful in guiding my thinking and sharing their memories and experiences. I am also grateful to activists Dana Beal, Lanny Swerdlow, Lowell Eggemeier, Jon Gettman, Mike Aldrich,

Stephen Kafoury, and Kevin Sabet, all of whom kindly answered my endless questions when a strange writer had the temerity to call them.

I am deeply grateful to the parent activists who shared with me their stories, their histories, and their archives. Sue Rusche and Keith Schuchard founded the movement, and their generosity and willingness to speak with me early in my research was my first indication that this project could be worthwhile. Joyce Nalepka was open and honest about her experiences, and I thank her for her willingness to talk. My deepest gratitude must go to Thomas "Buddy" Gleaton, who bent over backwards to help me with my manuscript. Buddy did everything from scanning old newsletters and mailing me the thumb drive to agreeing to multiple interviews and checking in just to see how I was doing. He is a perfect example of how to be generous, warm-hearted, and helpful; I can only hope to model his benevolence to others someday.

I also want to apologize to everyone whose stories didn't make it into this manuscript. The story of marijuana activism in America is far larger than any one book can tell. There are so many voices and participants that I was unable to include them all. Instead, I encourage you to tell your own stories. This book cannot, and should not, be the sole history of marijuana activism in America. Now is the time to raise your voice and let your contribution be known. And if you want to tell me your history, I am always happy to know more. I plan on continuing to collect stories from marijuana activists of every stripe. Please feel free to contact me and share.

This book is based on dissertation research that I began in 2010, and I would like to thank the faculty of the American Studies Department at George Washington University for supporting my research and writing efforts, especially Tom Guglielmo and Melani McAlister. I would also like to thank the writer Martin Torgoff, whose book *Can't Find My Way Home: America in the Great Stoned Age, 1945–2000* was an enormous influence on my desire to become a drug historian. Deepest appreciation is reserved for my adviser and friend Herr Professor Leo Ribuffo. Because of his constant support, his hilarious emails, his sound advice, his time for "tea and crumpets," his Christmas parties, and his unswerving faith in both me and my project, he is more than an adviser: Leo is family for life.

Most importantly, I have to thank my friends and family for supporting this project from the start. To my dear friends who have listened to me talk about pot for seven years, thank you for your patience and kindness; I am so lucky to have you in my life. I am also incredibly fortunate to be a Dufton and a Mercer. To Dad, Harriet, Lynette, Mike, Ronda, Adam, my six nieces and nephews, Joan, Henry, Sarah, and Greg, as well as all of my grandparents, aunts, uncles, and cousins, I can only say thank you for letting me write a book about pot and not immediately labeling me the family freak. Your patience and love have been outstanding; how lucky I am to be your kin.

Finally, this book is dedicated to the two most important men in my life: my husband, Dickson Mercer—soul mate, best friend—and our son, Henry, who was only three weeks old when I returned to work on this manuscript. Dickson and Henry, my sun rises and sets because of you, and my world is a brighter place because you exist. I love you more than words can say.

NOTES

Introduction: A Higher Calling

1. Jack Herer, *The Emperor Wears No Clothes: The Authoritative Historical Record of Cannabis and the Conspiracy Against Marijuana*, 11th ed. (New York: AH HA Publishing, 2000), 3. The fact that Franklin grew hemp and also owned a mill that turned it into paper has fueled the myth that both the US Constitution and the Declaration of Independence were written on hemp paper. Although early drafts of these documents may have been written on hemp, the final versions were written on parchment, a paper derived from animal skins.

2. For marketing campaigns of opiates and cannabis tinctures directed at women, see Sarah W. Tracy and Caroline Jean Acker, *Altering American Consciousness: The History of Alcohol and Drug Use in the United States, 1800–2000* (Amherst: University of Massachusetts Press, 2004).

3. Herer, *The Emperor Wears No Clothes*, 3.

4. In his 1917 report, written after traveling to eleven Texas cities, US Treasury Department aide Reginald Smith recommended that marijuana be made illegal; see Jill Jonnes, *Hep-Cats, Narcs, and Pipe Dreams: A History of America's Romance with Illegal Drugs* (Baltimore: Johns Hopkins University Press, 1996), 128.

5. Harry J. Anslinger with Courtney Ryley Cooper, "Marijuana: Assassin of Youth," *American Magazine*, July 1937.

6. Martin Booth, *Cannabis: A History* (New York: St. Martin's Press, 2003), 200.

7. *Hemp for Victory*, directed by Raymond Evans, produced by the United States Department of Agriculture, 1942.

8. The transcript for the 1951 film is available at the McGraw-Hill Education website: http://www.mhhe.com/media_library/hssl/HHP/hhp_video transcripts/fahey/terrible_truth_1951_transcript.pdf.

9. Allen Ginsberg, "The Great Marijuana Hoax," *The Atlantic Monthly*, 218, no. 6, November 1966, 104–112.

10. Martin Torgoff, *Can't Find My Way Home: America in the Great Stoned Age, 1945–2000* (New York: Simon & Schuster, 2004), 42.

11. Bruce J. Schulman, *The Seventies: The Great Shift in American Culture, Society, and Politics* (New York: Da Capo Press, 2001), 16.

12. Ibid., 17.

13. Michael Aldrich et al., *Preliminary Report: Fiscal Costs of California Marijuana Law Enforcement, 1960–1984* (Berkeley: Medi-Comp Press, 1986). Given the effect of racist drug laws and policing over the past thirty years, it's also interesting to note that, in 1967, more than half of those arrested for marijuana in California were white.

14. "LeMar to Get Pot Ballot A-Boiling," *The Berkeley Barb*, April 29, 1966, 9.

Chapter 1: "Forward, All Smokers!"

1. California NORML, "50th Anniversary of the First Pot Protest," California NORML, August 16, 2014, http://www.canorml.org/history/50th _Anniversary_of_First_Pot_Protest.html.

2. Torgoff, *Can't Find My Way Home*, 237–238.

3. Martin A. Lee, *Smoke Signals: A Social History of Marijuana—Medical, Recreational, and Scientific* (New York: Scribner, 2012), 97–98.

4. Quoted in Ginsberg, "The Great Marijuana Hoax." Ginsberg also drew heavily from these reports for his *Atlantic Monthly* article.

5. Charles Perry, *The Haight-Ashbury* (New York: Wenner Books, 2005), 20; "LeMar to Get Pot Ballot A-Boiling," 9.

6. Granary Books, Ed Sanders Archive, "Peace Eye Bookstore, 1964–1970," http://www.granarybooks.com/collections/ed-sanders/peace-eye.html.

7. "Demonstration Held to Protest the Law Against Marijuana," *New York Times*, December 28, 1964; Mary Perot Nichols, "Allen Ginsberg and Peter Orlovsky—Legalize Pot!" *The Village Voice*, December 31, 1964.

8. Editors of LEMAR, "Down with Prohibition," reprinted in *Marijuana*, edited by Erich Goode (1969; New Brunswick, NJ: Aldine Transaction, 2009), 140. Note that Goode cites the date of this editorial as March 1965, but he is incorrect: this editorial appears in the first newsletter, published in January.

9. Torgoff, *Can't Find My Way Home*, 112–113.

10. Ginsberg, "The Great Marijuana Hoax."

11. Mike Golden, *The Buddhist Third Class Junkmail Oracle: The Art and Poetry of d. a. levy* (New York: Seven Stories Press, 1999).

12. Fiedler was not immune to being persecuted for marijuana activism. In April 1967, he and his wife Margaret were arrested in a raid of their Buffalo home for "permitting marijuana to be smoked" in their house. Though Fiedler and his wife had neither been smoking nor had marijuana in their possession, Erie County city judge H. Buswell Roberts sentenced Fiedler to six months in the county penitentiary for offering a poor "standard of permissiveness for his students." In 1969, Fiedler published *Being Busted,* a half-memoir, half-meditation on the event. See "Prison Term Set for Leslie Fiedler," *New York Times,* May 1, 1970, C17; Christopher Lehmann-Haupt, "Leslie Fiedler Dies at 85; Provocative Literary Critic," *New York Times,* January 31, 2003.

13. Michael Aldrich, personal communication with author, September 4, 2015; "Dope Meet," *The* (Austin, TX) *Rag,* January 27, 1969.

14. Don McNeill, "The Youthquake and the Shook-Up Park," *The Village Voice,* June 8, 1967, 1.

15. Don McNeill, "A Long Way to Go from May to December," *The Village Voice,* January 4, 1968.

16. McNeil, "The Youthquake and the Shook-Up Park," 21.

17. Ibid., 21, 31.

18. Dana Beal, personal communication with author, September 1, 2015.

19. Stephen A. O. Golden, "Police Look On as Hippies Stage a Park Smoke-In," *New York Times,* July 31, 1967, 23.

20. Lyndon B. Johnson, "Address on Vietnam Before the National Legislative Conference," September 29, 1967, The American Presidency Project, http://www.presidency.ucsb.edu/ws/?pid=28460.

21. "Protest: The Banners of Dissent," *Time,* October 27, 1967.

22. Eric Pace, "Jerry Rubin, 56, Flashy Radical Dies," *New York Times,* November 20, 1994.

23. Norman Mailer, *The Armies of the Night: History as a Novel, the Novel as History* (New York: Plume, 1995), 120.

24. Joseph A. Loftus, "Guards Repulse Protesters at the Pentagon," *New York Times,* October 22, 1967, 1; John Herbers, "Youths Dominate Capital Throng," *New York Times,* October 22, 1967, 58.

25. Jerry Rubin, *Do It! Scenarios of the Revolution* (New York: Simon & Schuster, 1970), 79, 82, 88.

26. Ibid., 81–82.

27. David Lewis Stein, *Living the Revolution: The Yippies in Chicago* (Indianapolis: Bobbs-Merrill, 1969), 35.

28. Jon B. Gettman, *Crimes of Indiscretion: Marijuana Arrests in the United States* (Washington, DC: NORML, 2005), 48.

29. Paul Krassner, "'60s Live Again, Minus the LSD," *Los Angeles Times,* January 28, 2007.

30. Dana Beal, personal communication with author, September 1, 2015.

Chapter 2: It's NORML to Smoke Pot

1. Keith Stroup, *It's NORML to Smoke Pot: The 40-Year Fight for Marijuana Smokers' Rights* (New York: Trans High Corp., 2013), 21–23.

2. T. Rees Shapiro, "Dorothy M. Newman, Real Estate Agent," *Washington Post,* November 19, 2010.

3. Ben Fong-Torres, "Revolution: and, They Are Wild," *Rolling Stone,* January 21, 1970; Patrick Anderson, *High in America: The True Story Behind NORML and the Politics of Marijuana* (New York: Viking Press, 1981), 86–87.

4. Anderson, *High in America,* 84.

5. Stroup, *It's NORML to Smoke Pot,* 31.

6. Ralph Nader, "The Burned Children: 4,000 Fatal Fabric Fires," *The New Republic,* July 3, 1971.

7. Ralph Nader, *Unsafe at Any Speed: The Designed-In Dangers of the American Automobile* (New York: Grossman, 1965).

8. Stroup, *It's NORML to Smoke Pot,* 33.

9. Ibid., 34.

10. Ibid., 38.

11. US House of Representatives, *Decriminalization of Marijuana: Hearings Before the Select Committee on Narcotics Abuse and Control,* 95th Cong., 1st sess. (Washington, DC: US Government Printing Office, 1977), 335.

12. Stroup, *It's NORML to Smoke Pot,* 39.

13. Brooks Jackson, "Marijuana Lobby Is Washington's Feeblest," *Nashua* (NH) *Telegraph,* October 11, 1971, 2.

14. Stroup, *It's NORML to Smoke Pot,* 38.

15. Ramsey Clark, *Crime in America: Observations on Its Nature, Causes, Prevention, and Control* (New York: Simon & Schuster, 1970), 96.

16. Anderson, *High in America,* 87; Blair Newman, "Amorphia," *Ann Arbor* (MI) *Sun,* May 28, 1971.

17. Blair Newman, "The Prospects and Potentials of Legalized Marijuana: Playboy Corporation vs. the People," *The* (Austin, TX) *Rag,* April 3, 1972, 8.

18. Fong-Torres, "Revolution: and, They Are Wild."

19. "Are You Ready for ... Amorphia!" *Marijuana Review,* October–December 1969, 16.

20. Newman, "The Prospects and Potentials of Legalized Marijuana," 8.

21. Stroup, *It's NORML to Smoke Pot,* 64.

22. Ibid.

23. Michael Chance, "The Inside Story: POThibition," *High Times,* July, 1978, 48.

24. Anderson, *High in America,* 89–90.

25. Brooks Jackson (Associated Press), "Washington's Feeblest Lobby in Uphill Struggle for Legalization of Marijuana," *The Southeast Missourian,* October 11, 1971, 3.

26. Newman, "The Prospects and Potentials of Legalized Marijuana," 9.

Chapter 3: Marijuana: A Signal of Misunderstanding

1. Richard Nixon, "What Has Happened to America?" *Reader's Digest,* October 1967, 49–54; Malcolm McLaughlin, *The Long, Hot Summer of 1967: Urban Rebellion in America* (New York: Palgrave Macmillan, 2014), 1.

2. Common Sense for Drug Policy (CSDP), "Nixon Tapes Show Roots of Marijuana Prohibition: Misinformation, Culture Wars and Prejudice" (research report) (Washington, DC: Common Sense for Drug Policy, March 2002).

3. "Insecurity and Old Values," *Sarasota* (FL) *Herald-Tribune,* March 21, 1971, 2E.

4. "Marijuana: The Law vs. 12 Million People"; "For the Long-Distance Runner Who Got Caught—A 20-Year Sentence"; "One Way or Another It All Goes Up in Smoke"; and "Should It Be Legalized? 'Soon We Will Know'"; all in *Life,* October 31, 1969, 25–35.

5. Richard Nixon, "Special Message to the Congress on Control of Narcotics and Dangerous Drugs," July 14, 1969, The American Presidency Project, http://www.presidency.ucsb.edu/ws/?pid=2126.

6. CSDP, "Nixon Tapes Show Roots of Marijuana Prohibition."

7. *Newsweek,* editorial, September 7, 1970, 22.

8. Lee, *Smoke Signals,* 121.

9. Ibid.; National Commission on Marijuana and Drug Abuse, *Marihuana: A Signal of Misunderstanding: The Official Report of the National Commission on Marihuana and Drug Abuse* (New York: New American Library, 1972), 2. Note that this report uses the Mexican spelling of the name of the drug. "Marihuana" was used by the federal government in its

official publications through the mid-1980s. For the sake of consistency, I use its current spelling, "marijuana," throughout this book.

10. Anderson, *High in America*, 93.

11. In 1972, 24 million Americans saying they had tried marijuana at some point in their lives would have been nearly 12 percent of the population (209.9 million at the time).

12. *Marihuana: A Signal of Misunderstanding,* 61, 42, 96, 73, 130.

13. Anderson, *High in America*, 94–95.

14. Clayton Fritchey, "Can 24 Million Americans Be Wrong?" *Lewiston* (ME) *Evening Journal,* April 4, 1973.

15. *Sarasota* (FL) *Herald-Tribune,* editorial cartoon, March 30, 1973, 6A.

16. Gettman, *Crimes of Indiscretion,* 48.

Chapter 4: "You Won't Have to Be Paranoid Anymore!"

1. Stephen Kafoury, personal communication with author, October 22, 2015.

2. Anderson, *High in America*, 120.

3. "Drugs, Alcohol Panel Named," *Eugene* (OR) *Register-Guard,* February 15, 1973, 10C.

4. Stephen Kafoury, personal communication with author, October 22, 2015.

5. Anderson, *High in America*, 122.

6. "House Defeats Bill to Decriminalize Pot," *Eugene* (OR) *Register-Guard,* June 13, 1973, 3E.

7. Anderson, *High in America*, 123.

8. Stroup, *It's NORML to Smoke Pot,* 80.

9. Ibid., 81.

10. Emily Langer, "Thomas E. Bryant Dies at 75; Led the President's Commission on Mental Health," *Washington Post,* December 13, 2011.

11. Stroup, *It's NORML to Smoke Pot,* 82.

12. Associated Press, "Oregon's Pot Law Changed," *Ocala* (FL) *Star-Banner,* January 15, 1975, 10C; Martha Angle and Robert Walters, "Oregon's Marijuana Experience Reviewed," *Sarasota* (FL) *Journal,* April 4, 1978, 6A.

13. Edward M. Beecher and the Editors of *Consumer Reports* magazine, *The Consumers Union Report on Licit and Illicit Drugs* (New York: Consumers Union Reports, 1972).

14. "The Law: Grass Grows More Acceptable," *Time,* September 10, 1973.

15. James J. Kilpatrick, "A Conservative Approach to the Pot Question," *Washington Star-News,* December 5, 1972.

16. William F. Buckley, "End the Pot Penalties," *Washington Star-News,* November 10, 1974.

17. Carroll Kirkpatrick, "Nixon Resigns," *Washington Post,* August 9, 1974, A1.

18. William E. Leuchtenberg, *The American President: From Teddy Roosevelt to Bill Clinton* (New York: Oxford University Press, 2015).

19. Domestic Council Drug Abuse Task Force, *White Paper on Drug Abuse: Report to the President from the Domestic Council Drug Abuse Task Force* (Washington, DC: US Government Printing Office, 1975), i, 9, 55.

20. Ibid., 38, 39, 42, 52–53.

21. "The Law: Grass Grows More Acceptable."

22. US Senate, Judiciary Committee, *Marijuana Decriminalization: Hearing Before the Subcommittee to Investigate Juvenile Delinquency,* 94th Cong., 1st sess., May 14, 1975 (Washington, DC: US Government Printing Office, 1975), 5.

23. Ibid., 58, 49.

24. Ibid., 239.

25. Jon B. Gettman, *Crimes of Indiscretion: Marijuana Arrests in the United States* (Washington, DC: NORML, 2005), 48.

26. Tad Bartimus, "Alaska Court Studies Case on Marijuana," *Gettysburg* (PA) *Times,* October 17, 1974, 8; Jill Burke, "Irwin Ravin, Alaska Marijuana Rights Activist, Dies," *Alaska Dispatch News,* April 12, 2010; Michael Armstrong, "Homer Legend Irwin Ravin Dies," *Homer* (AK) *News,* April 14, 2010.

27. Anderson, *High in America,* 202.

28. Bill Turrant, "Decriminalize Pot, Says Founder-Director of Group," *Boca Raton* (FL) *News,* April 8, 1977, 3.

29. Stroup, *It's NORML to Smoke Pot,* 82, 84.

Chapter 5: "I'm Like a Bottle Maker During Prohibition"

1. "Earnings Drop 30% at Bethlehem Steel," *Washington Post,* January 27, 1977.

2. Anderson, *High in America,* 176.

3. *Orpheus,* July 1968, 3.

4. Dean Latimer, "Sex & Drugs & Tom Forçade: My Eight Years with *High Times* (and Then Some)," *High Times,* June 1982.

5. Thomas Forçade, "Publishing Statement: On the Principles Behind Publishing *High Times*," *High Times*, November 1976.

6. *Stone Age*, Winter 1978, 13, 63.

7. Ibid., 20.

8. Abe Peck, "The Rolling Paper Review: The Past, Present, and Future of the Paraphernalia Industry and the Weed That Made It Possible," *Rolling Stone*, January 27, 1977, 43.

9. Joshua Clark Davis, "The Business of Getting High: Head Shops, Countercultural Capitalism, and the Marijuana Legalization Movement," *The Sixties: A Journal of History, Politics, and Culture* 1, 2015.

10. Anthony Astrachan, "Pot Luck," *New York Times Magazine*, March 21, 1976; Peck, "Rolling Paper Review," 43.

11. Anderson, *High in America*, 177–178.

12. Associated Press, "Rosalynn Carter Not Upset over Sons Trying Marijuana," *Gadsden* (AL) *Times*, September 3, 1976, 3.

13. Folder: "Written Answers to Questions from Publications," Box 31, Ron Nessen Papers, Gerald R. Ford Presidential Library, Ann Arbor, MI.

14. Clare Crawford, "Should Carter Win, the King of the Hill Might Be Mary if It Isn't Her Husband, Peter Bourne," *People*, September 20, 1976.

15. Unsurprisingly, this simple title did not please Bourne, a man of extensive education and copious interests. Bourne preferred the more expansive Special Assistant for Mental Health, Drug Abuse, International Health, and the White House Fellows Program, though this title did not get approved. See Michael Massing, *The Fix* (Berkeley: University of California Press, 1998), 139.

16. United Press International, "Bourne Says Marijuana Not a Hazard to Health," *Beaver* (PA) *County Times*, May 14, 1977, A14.

17. Clare Crawford, "Ex-Presidential Advisor Bourne Breaks His Silence on the Fuss That Cost Him His Job," *People*, September 18, 1978.

18. Frank Browning, "The Drug Stops Here," *High Times*, April 1980, 42.

19. Jack Anderson, "Carter Flipflops on Pot," *Mid-Cities* (TX) *Daily News*, April 2, 1979, 2.

20. Jimmy Carter, "Drug Abuse Message to the Congress," August 2, 1977, The American Presidency Project, http://www.presidency.ucsb.edu/ws/?pid=7908.

21. Quoted in "Smoke-Ins Sweep Nation," *High Times*, February 1978, 86; see also Shelly Levitt, "The White House Smoke-In," *High Times*, October 1977, 51–53; "Hot Off the Wire from Smoke-In Central," *High Times*, August 1978, 28.

22. Levitt, "The White House Smoke-In," 51.

23. Shay Addams, "Legal Pot—The Civil Rights Fight of the '80s," *High Times*, April 1979, 6. Anti-marijuana activist Sue Rusche responded to this notion by noting that "the drug lobbies' calculated attempt to equate the 'rights' of people to use illicit drugs with the rights black people fought for a decade ago corrupts not only the very soul of the civil rights movement but the soul of the nation as well." See Sue Rusche, *How to Form a Families in Action Group in Your Community* (Atlanta: DeKalb Families in Action, 1979), 6.

24. "How You Can Get Rich" (advertisement), *High Times*, December 1977, 137.

25. Laurie Johnston, "Children, in Test, Buy Drug Trappings Freely at 'Head Shops,'" *New York Times*, March 30, 1978.

26. Los Angeles Times Newswire, "Toys Encourage Marijuana Use?" *Tuscaloosa* (AL) *News*, October 17, 1979, 33.

Chapter 6: Atlanta, 1976

1. All quotes from Marsha Manatt, *Parents, Peers, and Pot* (Rockville, MD: National Institute on Drug Abuse, 1979), 2–3.

2. Ibid., 3.

3. Massing, *The Fix*, 148.

4. "Grass Grows More Acceptable," *Time*, September 10, 1973.

5. Manatt, *Parents, Peers, and Pot*, 1.

6. Keith Schuchard, email to author, August 18, 2012.

7. Manatt, *Parents, Peers, and Pot*, 66, 11.

8. Ibid., 29.

9. Lloyd D. Johnston et al., *Highlights from Drug Use Among American High School Students, 1975–1977* (Rockville, MD: National Institute on Drug Abuse, 1978).

10. Gabriel G. Nahas, *Keep Off the Grass: A Scientific Enquiry into the Biological Effects of Marijuana* (New York: Pergamon Press, 1979).

11. Dudley Clendinen, "Buoyant Antidrug Parley Gains a Global Alliance," *New York Times*, March 24, 1986, A17; Massing, *The Fix*, 144–145.

12. Dan Baum, *Smoke and Mirrors: The War on Drugs and the Politics of Failure* (New York: Little, Brown, 1996), 17–19.

13. "Press Briefing, Marihuana and Health Report, 1975, by Robert Du-Pont," Mss 81-9a, Folder 12: "1974–79, DuPont, Dr. Robert: Correspondence," Box 17, Richard Bonnie Papers, Statements and Miscellaneous

Papers, University of Virginia Law School Library, Special Collections Library, Charlottesville, VA.

14. All quotes in this paragraph are from "Drug Wars: Part 1," *Frontline*, PBS, October 9, 2000.

15. Ibid.

16. Robert Furlow, Associated Press, "Her Personal War on Teen Drug Abuse Began at Daughter's 12th Birthday Party," *Miami News*, May 30, 1978, 48; Massing, *The Fix*, 153.

17. Marsha "Keith" Schuchard, PhD, "The Family Versus the Drug Culture," First PRIDE Conference, Georgia State University, May 25, 1978 (transcript provided to author by Thomas Gleaton, May 22, 2012).

18. Associated Press, "Teen-Agers Cite Parents' Use of Alcohol, Tobacco," *The* (Charleston, SC) *News and Courier*, May 28, 1978, 9-C.

19. Keith Schuchard, "What Is PRIDE?" *PRIDE Newsletter*, June 1979, 7.

20. Rusche, *How to Form a Families in Action Group in Your Community*, 1.

21. Anderson, *High in America*, 302.

22. All quotes from Rusche, *How to Form a Families in Action Group in Your Community*, 12.

23. Massing, *The Fix*, 145.

24. Rusche, *How to Form a Families in Action Group in Your Community*, 33.

25. Ibid., 57.

26. "Paraquat, Paranoia, and Paramilitary Pot," *High Times*, September 1978, 6; Mark Thellman, "Carter's Home State Outlaws Dope Press," *High Times*, August 1978, 33.

27. Joanne Onano, "Sale of Drug Paraphernalia Is Now Big Business," *Sarasota* (FL) *Herald-Tribune*, December 11, 1978, 11A.

28. Rusche, *How to Form a Families in Action Group in Your Community*, 59; Elizabeth Luckow, "Drug Paraphernalia Legislation: Up in Smoke?" *Hofstra Law Review* 10, no. 1, article 12, 1981.

29. Massing, *The Fix*, 150.

30. *High Times*, "Paraquat, Paranoia, and Paramilitary Pot."

31. Michael Antonoff, "Those Mothers Are Trampling Adult Rights," *High Times*, July 1980, 8.

Chapter 7: The Downfall of Peter Bourne

1. "Drug Wars: Part 1," *Frontline*.

2. Massing, *The Fix*, 147.

3. Anderson, *High in America*, 272.

4. Crawford, "Ex-Presidential Advisor Bourne Breaks His Silence."

5. Stroup, *It's NORML to Smoke Pot,* 96.

6. Anderson, *High in America,* 12, 13, 23.

7. Ibid., 19–22.

8. Peter Bourne, interview with author, October 14, 2015.

9. Gordon Chaplin, "Cocaine in Washington," *Washington Post,* June 5, 1977.

10. Stroup, *It's NORML to Smoke Pot,* 100–101.

11. United Press International, "Impact Statement Urged in Marijuana Spraying," *The* (Nashua, NH) *Telegraph,* January 30, 1978, 14.

12. Henry A. Waxman, "Addle Headed Policy on Paraquat," *Milwaukee Journal,* May 3, 1978, 21.

13. Daniel Schorr, "Paraquat Is Carter's Cross," *Eugene* (OR) *Register-Guard,* July 6, 1978, 17A.

14. Jack Anderson, "Fat Cat Bureaucrats Abuse Drug Abuse Agency," *Ocala* (FL) *Star-Banner,* January 8, 1979, 4A.

15. Nancy Lewis and Joseph Albright, "An Aide's Broken Romance and Bourne's Broken Career," *Miami News,* July 25, 1978, A1.

16. "Drug Wars: Part 1," *Frontline.*

17. Anderson, *High in America,* 274–275.

18. Charles B. Seib, "The Cocaine Incident: There's More to the Story," *Washington Post,* July 26, 1978, A27.

19. Stroup, *It's NORML to Smoke Pot,* 101.

20. "Nation: The Wrong Rx for Peter Bourne," *Time,* July 31, 1978.

21. Pat Lewis, "Bourne Lived Glamorous Life Before Fall," *Spokane* (WA) *Spokesman-Review,* July 25, 1978, 11; "Bournes Are Known Social Gadflies," *The* (Lexington, NC) *Dispatch,* July 26, 1978, 17.

22. United Press International, "Impact Statement Urged in Marijuana Spraying."

23. Jurate Kazickas, "Irked by Drug-Use Rumors About White House—Bourne," *Pittsburgh Post-Gazette,* September 30, 1978, 21.

24. Associated Press, "Text of Peter Bourne's Resignation Letter," *St. Petersburg* (FL) *Times,* July 22, 1978, 16A.

25. United Press International, "Impact Statement Urged in Marijuana Spraying"; United Press International, "Reaction: 'Able' to 'Outrage,'" *Reading* (PA) *Eagle,* July 21, 1978, 3.

26. Associated Press, "Carter Says There's No Vendetta Against Soviets," and Associated Press, "President Mutes Bourne Questions," *Reading* (PA) *Eagle,* July 21, 1978, 3.

27. Mary McGrory, "Damage Control in Bourne Case Is Ineffective," *Sarasota* (FL) *Herald-Tribune,* July 26, 1978, 7; Baum, *Smoke and Mirrors,* 116.

28. Frank Browning, "Pot Heads Abandon Carter," *The* (Bend, OR) *Bulletin,* February 27, 1980, 6.

29. Jack Anderson, "Pot Issue Blackens White House," *Lakeland* (FL) *Ledger,* March 31, 1979, 9A.

30. Gettman, *Crimes of Indiscretion,* 23–24.

31. Frank Browning, "The Drug Stops Here," *High Times,* April 1980, 47.

32. Anderson, *High in America,* 23.

33. "Carter's Cocaine Conspiracy," *High Times,* November 1978, 6.

34. Stroup, *It's NORML to Smoke Pot,* 102–103.

35. Ibid., 103.

36. Associated Press, "Bourne Works for UN Now," *Tuscaloosa* (AL) *News,* April 27, 1979, 3.

37. Crawford, "Ex-Presidential Advisor Bourne Breaks His Silence."

38. Peter Bourne, "Kids Shouldn't Get Stoned," *High Times,* September 1978, 76. Interestingly, Bourne's article was followed by a piece from thirteen-year-old Monica Choate titled "Everybody Must Get Stoned," in which she argued that, "compared to the time most kids spend watching TV, a few hours smoking pot can't really hurt them all that much. Anyway, this quack of a doctor has a lot of nerve telling kids what's good for them." See *High Times,* September 1978, 77.

Chapter 8: The Coming Parent Revolution

1. Associated Press, "US Investigates Toxic Marijuana," *Wilmington* (NC) *Star-News,* December 5, 1977, 4-A.

2. All quotes from Lee Dogoloff, interview with author, May 30, 2012.

3. Massing, *The Fix,* 149–150.

4. Carol Krucoff, "Families: Grappling with Teen-Age Drug Abuse," *Washington Post,* February 2, 1981, D5.

5. Elizabeth Becker, "Capital Centre: Mecca of Sports, Haven for Pot Smokers," *Washington Post,* March 25, 1976, F1.

6. Barry Bearak and Richard Meyer, "Drug Furor: Overdue or Much Ado?" *Los Angeles Times,* October 20, 1986, 9.

7. Senate Judiciary Committee, Subcommittee on Criminal Justice, *Drug Paraphernalia and Youth: Hearing,* November 16, 1979 (Washington, DC: US Government Printing Office, 1980), 3, 110, 112.

8. US House of Representatives, Select Committee on Narcotics Abuse and Control, *Drug Paraphernalia: A Report of the Select Committee on Narcotics Abuse and Control* (Washington, DC: US Government Printing Office, 1980), 1, 5, 9, 12, 3, 6.

9. Senate Judiciary Committee, *Drug Paraphernalia and Youth,* 113.

10. David Gelman, "New Look at Marijuana," *Newsweek,* January 7, 1980, 42; Elisabeth Coleman Brynner, "New Parental Push Against Marijuana," *New York Times Magazine,* February 10, 1980.

11. Bill Barton, "National Federation of Parents: Background and Accomplishments," in *National Parents' Movement for Drug-Free Youth: PRIDE Southeast Drug Conference Proceedings, 1980 and 1981* (Atlanta: Georgia State University Press, 1981), 141.

12. Marsha Keith Schuchard, "The National Parents' Movement for Drug Free Youth," in *National Parents' Movement for Drug-Free Youth: PRIDE Southeast Drug Conference Proceedings, 1980 and 1981,* 69.

13. Meeting minutes, Thomas Gleaton, April 3, 1980, Folder: "PRIDE [II] (5)," Box 55, Carlton E. Turner Files, Ronald Reagan Library, Simi Valley, CA.

14. Ibid. For his numerous volunteering positions, Barton was awarded the Naples' Outstanding Citizen of the Year Award in 1979. See "Personalities in the News," *Sarasota Journal,* June 11, 1979, 2A.

15. Bob Kramer to media, Press release, May 8, 1980, Folder: "PRIDE [III] (2)," Box 55, Carlton E. Turner Files, Ronald Reagan Library, Simi Valley, CA.

16. "National Federation of Parents Convenes in DC," *PRIDE Newsletter* 2, no. 4, June 1980, 1–2. In other resolutions, the NFP "2. Calls upon parents and professionals, government and private groups to cooperate and work together in preventing and dealing with drug usage by youth; 3. Stresses that all adults dealing with youth should be regularly provided with the latest information on the effects of drugs on children and youth and on effective resources and ideas for prevention and intervention"; . . . and "6. Calls upon national, state, county and local government agencies to be encouraged to support strongly the efforts of parent groups and the prevention and early intervention programs."

17. Peggy Mann, "Marijuana: Part 2," *Scouting,* October 1981, 76.

18. Ellen Hume, "Network of Antidrug Parents Formed," *St. Petersburg* (FL) *Times,* May 9, 1980, 14A.

19. Stephen H. Newman, "Parents vs. Marijuana," *New York Times,* June 12, 1980, A31.

20. Lloyd Johnston, Jerald Bachman, and Patrick O'Malley, "Student Attitudes About Drugs Shifting" (press release), University of Michigan, Institute for Social Research, April 27, 1980.

21. Jeane Westin, *The Coming Parent Revolution: Why Parents Must Toss Out the "Experts" and Start Believing in Themselves Again* (New York: Rand McNally, 1981), 233–245, 257, 269–270.

22. Ibid., 269–271.

23. Jimmy Carter, "Crisis of Confidence," July 14, 1979, Carter Center, https://www.cartercenter.org/news/editorials_speeches/crisis_of_confidence .htmlhttp://www.pbs.org/wgbh/americanexperience/features/primary -resources/carter-crisis/.

24. Lee Dogoloff, "The Impact of the Parents' Message on White House Drug Policy," in *National Parents' Movement for Drug-Free Youth: PRIDE Southeast Drug Conference Proceedings, 1980 and 1981*, 15–19.

25. Frank Browning, "Pot Heads Abandon Carter," *Bend* (OR) *Bulletin*, February 27, 1980, 6.

26. Jimmy Carter, "The State of the Union Annual Message to Congress," January 16, 1981, The American Presidency Project, http://www.presi-dency.ucsb.edu/ws/?pid=44541.

27. Lee Dogoloff of the Drug Abuse Policy Section of the Domestic Policy Staff, oral history interview, November 26, 1980, Oral Histories, Exit Interview Project, Jimmy Carter Presidential Library, Atlanta, GA.

Chapter 9: "The Most Potent Force There Is"

1. Wanda McDaniel published a four-part series in the *Los Angeles Herald-Examiner* titled "Nancy Reagan: The Woman Who Would Be Queen" in December 1980. This quote is from the first article, published December 8, 1981, *Los Angeles Herald-Examiner*, D1.

2. Keith Schuchard, "The National Parents' Movement for Drug Free Youth," in *National Parents' Movement for Drug-Free Youth: PRIDE Southeast Drug Conference Proceedings, 1980 and 1981*, 69–76.

3. Bill Barton, "National Federation of Parents: Background and Accomplishments," in *National Parents' Movement for Drug-Free Youth: PRIDE Southeast Drug Conference Proceedings, 1980 and 1981*, 141–144.

4. Mark Zaloudek, "Ex-Stars' Stories of Addiction Highlight Drug Conference," *Sarasota* (FL) *Journal*, April 22, 1981, 10A.

5. Massing, *The Fix*, 158.

6. Donnie Radcliffe, "'Queen Nancy'; Majesty on a Postcard," *Washington Post*, September 8, 1981, C1.

7. Associated Press, "Mrs. Reagan Turns Attacks into Jests," *New York Times*, November 6, 1981, A17.

8. Carlton Turner, letter to Bill Barton, June 29, 1981, Folder: "Parents for Drug-Free Youth, Silver Spring, MD," Box OA 15003, Drug Abuse Policy Office Files, 1981–1987, Ronald Reagan Library, Simi Valley, CA.

9. Massing, *The Fix*, 159; Ed Rosenthal, "Interview: Carlton Turner," *High Times*, February 1982, 35–40, 64, 70–72.

10. Carlton Turner to Drug Policy Office, internal memo regarding meeting with Mrs. Reagan, July 15, 1981, Folder: "Mrs. Reagan's Report (1)," Box 57, Carlton E. Turner Files, Ronald Reagan Library, Simi Valley, CA.

11. Lee Dogoloff, interview with author, May 30, 2012.

12. Thomas Gleaton, interview with author, August 19, 2012.

13. Associated Press, "Mrs. Reagan to Parents: 'Be Tough' on Drugs," *New York Times*, November 10, 1981, B14.

14. Lloyd Johnston, "American Youth Are Becoming More Moderate in Their Drug Use" (press release), University of Michigan, Institute for Social Research, February 24, 1982.

15. Cristine Russell, "Panel Finds Marijuana's Health Hazards Justify 'Serious National Concern,'" *Washington Post*, February 27, 1982, A2.

16. Baum, *Smoke and Mirrors*, 162; "Law: The Potshot That Backfired," *Time*, July 19, 1982; Patricia Teasdale, "Parent Networks Catching On," *New York Times*, February 7, 1982, K11.

17. Lois Romano and Donnie Radcliffe, "Causes & Courage: Two First Ladies, Two Luncheons," *Washington Post*, March 20, 1982, C1.

18. Betty Cuniberti, "First Lady's War: Teens' Drug Use," *Los Angeles Times*, March 24, 1982, F1.

19. "Mrs. Reagan's Opening Remarks at White House Briefing on Drug Use and the Family, The East Room, Monday, March 22, 1982," Box 2: "Addresses—Nancy Reagan 3/22/1982: White House Briefing on Drug Abuse and the Family," Ronald Reagan Leadership Collection, Eureka College, Eureka, IL.

20. Enid Nemy, "Drugs' Economic Impact Outlined at White House," *New York Times*, March 23, 1982, A16.

21. "Nancy Stars at Anti-Pot Klatch," *High Times*, June 1982, 24.

22. Paul Burka, "Right, but Wrong," *Texas Monthly*, May 1995.

23. "Nancy Stars at Anti-Pot Klatch," *High Times*, 24.

24. Massing, *The Fix*, 163.

25. Mrs. Reagan's remarks, NFP conference, October 11, 1982, Folder: "Mrs. Reagan (1 of 3)," Box 57, Carlton E. Turner Files, Ronald Reagan Library, Simi Valley, CA.

26. Lloyd Johnston, "Use of Marijuana and Other Illicit Drugs by American High School Seniors Continued to Decline in 1983" (press release), University of Michigan, Institute for Social Research, February 7, 1984.

27. Nancy Reagan, "Let's Get Our Kids Off Drugs," *Ladies' Home Journal,* January 1983.

28. R. A. Lindblad, "A Review of the Concerned Parent Movement in the United States," *United Nations Office on Drugs and Crime Bulletin on Narcotics,* July–September 1983, 41–52.

29. Anne Penney and Emily Garfield, "Parent Groups in Drug Abuse Prevention: Is This the Constituency We've Been Waiting For?" *Journal of Primary Prevention* 4, no. 3, Spring 1984, 173–179.

30. Chuck Conconi, "Personalities," *Washington Post,* October 21, 1983, D3.

31. Lloyd Kaiser, ed., *The Chemical People Book: A National School-Age Drug and Alcohol Abuse Campaign* (Pittsburgh: QED Enterprises, 1983), 144.

32. Lloyd Kaiser, letter to William Pollin, June 28, 1984, Folder: "Chemical People," Box 14, Carlton E. Turner Files, Ronald Reagan Library, Simi Valley, CA.

33. Kaiser, *The Chemical People Book,* 153.

34. Cathy Grant, "'Chemical People' Brings Back Bad Times for Teen," *Wilmington Morning Star News,* November 4, 1983, 1B.

35. Ronald Reagan, "Remarks on Signing Executive Order 12368, Concerning Federal Drug Abuse Policy Functions," June 24, 1982, The American Presidency Project, http://www.presidency.ucsb.edu/ws/?pid=42671.

36. Michelle Alexander, *The New Jim Crow: Mass Incarceration in the Age of Colorblindness* (New York: New Press, 2010), 49.

37. Pat Burch, letter to Carlton Turner, May 15, 1984, Folder: "Parent Groups—Sue Rusche, et al. 05/16/1984, 1:15pm," Box 51, Carlton E. Turner Files, Ronald Reagan Library, Simi Valley, CA.

38. The White House, Office of Policy Development, Drug Abuse Policy Office, *Federal Strategy for Prevention of Drug Abuse and Drug Trafficking, 1982* (Washington, DC: US Government Printing Office, 1982), 49, 42.

39. Chuck Conconi, "Personalities," *Washington Post,* January 16, 1984, B3.

40. Donnie Radcliffe, "Washington Ways," *Washington Post,* October 2, 1984, E1.

41. Associated Press, "Reagans Pay Heavy Taxes, but Not Bushes," *The* (Spokane, WA) *Spokesman Review,* April 13, 1985, A2.

42. Thomas Gleaton, memo to Carlton Turner, July 11, 1983, Folder: "PRIDE [II] (5)," Box 55, Carlton E. Turner Files, Ronald Reagan Library, Simi Valley, CA.

43. Baum, *Smoke and Mirrors*, 193.

Chapter 10: The Truth Behind Just Say No

1. John Jacobs, *A Rage for Justice: The Passion and Politics of Phillip Burton* (Berkeley: University of California Press, 1997), 166.

2. National Institute on Drug Abuse, *A Guide to Mobilizing Ethnic Minority Communities for Drug Abuse Prevention* (Rockville, MD: NIDA, 1986), 6.

3. Marlene Cimons, "Foreign Visitors in US: Changing the Welcome Mat," *Los Angeles Times*, October 7, 1977, I1; Peter Smark, "A Black Activist Takes on the Social Climbers," *The Age*, October 4, 1977, 24.

4. *National Council for International Visitors Newsletter* 36, no. 3, June 1982, 6.

5. NIDA, *A Guide to Mobilizing Ethnic Minority Communities for Drug Abuse Prevention*, 6.

6. "Empowering Children to 'Just Say No,'" *Sufism Reoriented Neighborhood Newsletter*, Fall 2009, 5.

7. Tori Minton, "Children Deal Drugs Openly in Oakland as Officials Trade Charges," *Schenectady* (NY) *Gazette*, September 3, 1984, 3.

8. Chris Rhomberg, *No There There: Race, Class, and Political Community in Oakland* (Berkeley: University of California Press, 2007), 184.

9. The Pyramid Project was conceived in 1975 by Dr. Robert DuPont, when he was still the director of NIDA, to provide information and technical assistance to state and local drug abuse prevention programs. The $500,000 project grant was the first from NIDA received by Dr. Allan Cohen, who founded PIRE in 1974, and Tom Adams was brought on shortly afterward to oversee the work. See Marsha Manatt, *Parents, Peers, and Pot II: Parents in Action* (Rockville, MD: NIDA, 1983), 4; Arnold S. Trebach, *The Great Drug War* (New York: Macmillan, 1987), 137.

10. NIDA, *A Guide to Mobilizing Ethnic Minority Communities for Drug Abuse Prevention*, 7.

11. Ibid., 9.

12. Massing, *The Fix*, 173–174.

13. In May 1981, the NFP did invite one African American parent activist, Vonneva Pettigrew of Washington, DC, to join its board. Pettigrew

created room for five more nonwhite board members during her NFP tenure, though none of them were Joan Brann.

14. Associated Press, "First Lady Fights Drug Abuse," *The* (Oxnard, CA) *Press-Courier,* July 5, 1984, 26.

15. Massing, *The Fix,* 174.

16. United Press International, "First Lady Leads War on Drugs," *Baltimore Afro-American,* July 14, 1984, 3.

17. Jane Wilkie, "Just Say No: How the Most Successful Antidrug Group Got Started—And Why It Grew," *Good Housekeeping,* January 1987, 64. Wilkie's article is by far one of the longest and most complete about the history of the Just Say No program. Though obviously written for a commercial audience, I am nonetheless taking its reportage as fact. Wilkie interviewed Brann and spent time in Oakland, and while I don't always agree with her journalistic voice, I believe that her understanding of the Just Say No phenomenon is valid.

18. Ibid.

19. Ibid., 66, 67.

20. Ibid., 66.

21. Donnie Radcliffe, "Resuming the Battle: First Lady, 'Punky Brewster' Star Assail Drug Use," *Washington Post,* February 23, 1985, G3.

22. Associated Press, "Nancy Tells Kids to Say No to Pushers," *Gadsden* (AL) *Times,* April 27, 1985, A10.

23. Mark A. Stein, "Takes 'Just Say No' Campaign to Oakland: First Lady Warns Children of Drug Peril," *Los Angeles Times,* November 27, 1985.

24. Angel Wiltz, letter to "Dear Abby," "Plug for 'Just Say No' Clubs," *St. Petersburg* (FL) *Evening Independent,* August 30, 1985, 2B.

25. Joan Brann, letter to "Dear Abby," "Kids Across the Country Are Now Saying 'No' to Drugs," *Harlan* (KY) *Daily Enterprise,* February 4, 1986, 5.

26. Sue Rusche, "Straight Talk About Drugs: Kids 'Just Say No' to Drugs," *Nashua* (NH) *Telegraph,* May 8, 1986, 23.

27. Ibid.

28. *Proceedings of the National Conference on Preventing Alcohol and Drug Abuse in Black Communities, May 22–24, 1987* (Rockville, MD: US Department of Health and Human Services, 1987), 33, 91.

29. Associated Press, "Reagan Warms Antidrug Talk," *Beaver County* (PA) *Times,* August 5, 1986, A5.

30. Ronald Reagan, "Address to the Nation on the Campaign Against Drug Abuse," September 14, 1986, in *Public Papers of the President of the*

United States: Ronald Reagan, 1981–1989, vol. 2 (Washington, DC: US Government Printing Office, 1986).

31. Gerald M. Boyd, "Reagans Advocate 'Crusade' Against Drugs," *New York Times,* September 15, 1986.

32. *Pacific Institute for Research and Evaluation, Plaintiff-Appellant v. Procter & Gamble, Co., Defendants-Appellees,* No. 92-15660, US Court of Appeals, Ninth Circuit, November 2, 1993; Tamara Henry, "Procter & Gamble, the Consumer Goods Giant, Was Accused," United Press International, August 12, 1988.

33. Tom Adams, *Grass Roots: Ordinary People Changing America* (New York: Citadel Press, 1991), 262–263.

34. Ibid., 246–250.

35. Massing, *The Fix,* 188.

36. *Pacific Institute for Research and Evaluation, Plaintiff-Appellant v. Procter & Gamble, Co., Defendants-Appellees,* No. 92-15660, US Court of Appeals, Ninth Circuit, November 2, 1993.

37. Jean Bryant, "Just Say No Pledge Cards Distributed in Campaign," *Pittsburgh Press,* September 12, 1987, B1.

38. Adams, *Grass Roots,* 253–258.

39. Rangel's speech is reprinted in Adams, *Grass Roots,* 258–261; see also William Eaton, "Company Accused of Exploiting 'Just Say No' Campaign," *Los Angeles Times,* August 13, 1988.

40. Michelle Locke, "Just Say No Clubs Thrive a Decade After Start," *Beaver County (PA) Times,* August 4, 1996, C2; PR Newswire, "'Just Say No' International Changes Name and Focus to Youth Power," May 14, 1998.

41. Jonathan M. Moses, "Advertisers Plug Products with Antidrug Message," *Washington Post,* September 2, 1988.

42. Lloyd Johnston, Jerald Bachman, and Patrick O'Malley, "Illicit Drug Use by American High School Seniors, College Students and Young Adults Continued to Decline in 1987, but U-M Researchers Say US Usage Still Highest in Industrialized World" (press release), University of Michigan, Institute for Social Research, January 12, 1988.

43. Robert Lindsey, "Oakland Journal: Drug-Related Violence Erodes a Neighborhood," *New York Times,* April 4, 1988.

44. Sharon K. Amatetti, *Prevention Plus II: Tools for Creating and Sustaining Drug-Free Communities* (Rockville, MD: Office for Substance Abuse Prevention, 1989), 238.

45. Adams, *Grass Roots,* 263.

Chapter 11: Crack Update

1. Sue Rusche, *Crack Update* (Atlanta: NFIA, 1986).

2. Craig Reinarman and Harry Gene Levine, eds., *Crack in America: Demon Drugs and Social Justice* (Berkeley: University of California Press, 1997), 3; Jimmie L. Reeves and Richard Campbell, *Cracked Coverage: Television News, the Anti-Cocaine Crusade, and the Reagan Legacy* (Durham, NC: Duke University Press, 1994), 16.

3. Baum, *Smoke and Mirrors*, 277.

4. Alexander, *The New Jim Crow*, 59.

5. Gettman, *Crimes of Indiscretion*, 48.

6. Michael Massing, "Crack's Destructive Sprint Across America," *New York Times*, October 1, 1989.

7. Jefferson Morley, "What Crack Is Like," *The New Republic*, October 2, 1989, 13.

8. Michael Demarest, "Cocaine: Middle Class High," *Time*, July 6, 1981.

9. Craig Reinarman and Harry G. Levine, "The Crack Attack: America's Latest Drug Scare, 1986–1992," in *Images of Issues: Typifying Contemporary Social Problems*, edited by Joel Best (New York: Aldine de Gruyter, 1995), 151.

10. Peter Kerr, "Anatomy of the Drug Issue," *New York Times*, November 17, 1986, A1.

11. Ibid.

12. Ronald Reagan, "Remarks on Signing the Antidrug Abuse Act of 1986," October 27, 1986, The American Presidency Project, http://www.presidency.ucsb.edu/ws/?pid=36654.

13. Joel Brinkley, "Antidrug Law: Words, Deeds, Political Expediency," *New York Times*, October 27, 1986.

14. "NFP President Issues a Call to Action!" *Legislative Update: National Federation of Parents for Drug-Free Youth Newsletter*, Summer 1986, 5.

15. Sue Rusche, "Who Really Killed Len Bias?" *Nashua* (NH) *Telegraph*, September 29, 1986, 18.

16. Marc Fisher, "Drug Abuse Prevention: Schools Bombarded with Bewildering Array of Products," *Washington Post*, April 5, 1987, R1.

17. Pat Sloan, "Too Much? Media Swamped with Antidrug Ads," *Advertising Age*, June 8, 1987, 3.

18. US Department of Health and Human Services, Office of the Inspector General, *National Youth Drug Education Programs* (Washington, DC: US Government Printing Office, 1988), 18.

19. Biff Wilson and Sue Rusche, memo to Charles Rangel and Carlton Turner, August 12, 1986, Folder: "Families in Action Computer Data Base Presentation 02/27/1986—3:00pm (1)," Box 25, Carlton E. Turner Files, Ronald Reagan Library, Simi Valley, CA.

20. Joyce Nalepka, "Message from the President," *NFP Prevention Parent-line,* June 1986, 2.

21. Press News Service, "Saudis Funded Nancy Reagan's Drug War," *Pittsburgh Post-Gazette,* March 7, 1990, A16.

22. Adams, *Grass Roots,* 222, 228.

23. All quotes from Charles Culhane, "National Parent Federation Ousts President," *US Journal of Drug and Alcohol Dependence,* January 1987.

24. Baum, *Smoke and Mirrors,* 235.

25. "Drug Withdrawal," *Time,* January 19, 1987.

26. Though she published these books well after 1986, Schuchard had returned to her interest in literary history by the '80s and was engaged in research for her future work. See Marsha Keith Schuchard, *Restoring the Temple of Vision: Cabalistic Freemasonry and Stuart Culture* (Leiden, The Netherlands: Brill Academic Publishing, 2002); *Why Mrs. Blake Cried: William Blake and the Sexual Basis of Spiritual Vision* (New York: Century, 2006); *William Blake's Sexual Path to Spiritual Vision* (Rochester, VT: Inner Traditions, 2008); and *Emanuel Swedenborg, Secret Agent on Earth and in Heaven: Jacobites, Jews, and Freemasons in Early Modern Sweden* (Leiden, The Netherlands: Brill Publishing, 2011).

27. Gerry Yandel, "Pro-Marijuana Group Changes with the Times," *Atlanta Journal-Constitution,* October 2, 1987.

28. Jon Gettman, "Morality: Actions Speak Louder Than Words," *High Times,* February 1987, 15.

29. Steven Hager, "Tommy, Can You Hear Me? Pot Protestors Rallied by Gettman and Rosenthal," *High Times,* January 1988, 19.

30. Jon Gettman, "Parity: The Drug Paraphernalia Issue," *High Times,* April 1987, 30.

31. Ibid.

32. NORML, "Drugs & Children," Common Sense Series, 1987, provided to the author by Jon Gettman.

33. Burt Neal, "College and Pot: A Subject for Study," *High Times,* March 1987, 28.

34. Jon Gettman, "NORML-izer," *High Times,* March 1987, 30.

35. Leslie Stackel, "Mandatory Minimum Sentences: How Federal Law Forces Judges to Mete Out Justice," *High Times,* July 1993, 46–49, 56.

36. See Don Fiedler, "NORML-IZER," *High Times,* December 1989, 23.

37. Bob Greene, "'70s Magazine Wants to Go to 'Pot,'" *Orlando Sun Sentinel,* April 7, 1987.

38. Jon Gettman, "The Secret Plan to End the War," *High Times,* May 1988, 23.

Chapter 12: "The Florence Nightingale of Medical Marijuana"

1. Peter Gorman, "The *High Times* Interview: Brownie Mary Rathbun," *High Times,* January 1993, 51–54.

2. Graeme Zielinski, "Activist Robert C. Randall Dies," *Washington Post,* June 8, 2001.

3. Michael Pollan, "Living with Medical Marijuana," *New York Times,* July 20, 1997.

4. Lee, *Smoke Signals,* 140–142.

5. Fred Garner, "The Judge Who Ruled Marijuana Is Medicine," *Counterpunch,* March 2, 2009.

6. Ibid.; David E. Anderson, "Robert Randall—America's Only Legal Smoker of Pot," *Ludington* (MI) *Daily News,* January 11, 1977, 11.

7. Garner, "The Judge Who Ruled Marijuana Is Medicine."

8. Zielinski, "Activist Robert C. Randall Dies"; Associated Press, "Robert Randall, 53; Sued for Marijuana," *New York Times,* June 8, 2001.

9. David E. Anderson, "Marijuana for Medical Use," United Press International, September 17, 1981.

10. United Press International, "Brownies Too Hot to Handle," *Spokane* (WA) *Daily Chronicle,* January 15, 1981, 15.

11. Associated Press, "Brownie Mary Is Arrested," *The* (Nashua, NH) *Telegraph,* February 13, 1981, 14.

12. Mary Rathbun and Dennis Peron, *Brownie Mary's Marijuana Cookbook and Dennis Peron's Recipe for Social Change* (San Francisco: Trail of Smoke Publishing, 1993), 38.

13. United Press International, "'Brownie Mary' Ordered to Cook Legal Sweets," *Lodi* (CA) *News-Sentinel,* June 6, 1981, 2.

14. Claudia Wallis, "Medicine: The Deadly Spread of AIDS," *Time,* September 6, 1982; Alex Brummer, "Center of Hope for AIDS Victims," *New Straits Times,* November 19, 1985, 16.

15. Gorman, "The High Times Interview: Brownie Mary Rathbun."

16. Ibid.

17. Associated Press, "Marijuana Booster Busted for Baking," *Lodi* (CA) *News-Sentinel*, July 24, 1992, 5.

18. Rathbun and Peron, *Brownie Mary's Marijuana Cookbook*, 42.

19. Ibid., 40–43.

20. Carey Goldberg, "Wealthy Ally for Dissidents in the Drug War," *New York Times*, September 11, 1996.

21. Larry D. Smith, "Proposition 215—Against," *Palo Verde* (CA) *Valley*, November 1, 1996, 5; "Proposition 215—For," *Palo Verde Valley*, November 1, 1996, 5.

22. Carey Goldberg, "Medical Marijuana Use Winning Backing," *New York Times*, October 30, 1996.

23. Richard Lacayo, "Marijuana: Where There's Smoke, There's Fire," *Time*, October 28, 1996.

24. Lee, *Smoke Signals*, 247.

25. Pollan, "Living with Medical Marijuana."

26. United Press International, "Marijuana Use OK'd for AIDS Sufferer," *Lodi* (CA) *News-Sentinel*, December 19, 1989, 11; Stephen G. Reed, "Medicinal Pot," *Sarasota* (FL) *Herald-Tribune*, February 8, 1999, E1, E4.

27. Sue Rusche, *Guide to the Drug Legalization Movement and How You Can Stop It!* (Atlanta: National Families in Action, 1997), 45–46, 81.

28. Peter Gorman, "Gettman Dumped," *High Times*, July 1989, 19.

29. "Cowan to Resign as NORML Head," *High Times*, August 1995, 33.

30. Steve Bloom, "Keith Stroup: Still NORML After All These Years," *High Times*, October 1997, 65.

31. Francine Prose, "HERS; Trying On the 60's," *New York Times Magazine*, August 11, 1991.

32. Melissa Henneberger, "Ideas and Trends; 'Pot' Surges Back, but It's, Like, a Whole New World," *New York Times*, February 6, 1994.

33. "Number of Legal Medical Marijuana Patients," Pro-Con.Org, March 3, 2016, http://medicalmarijuana.procon.org/view.resource.php?resource ID=005889.

34. Steven Nelson, "Debate Over? 89 Percent Support Medical Pot in New Poll," *US News & World Report*, June 6, 2016.

35. Pete Brady, "Brownie Mary Bakes No More," *Cannabis Culture*, July 1, 1999.

36. Elaine Woo, "'Brownie Mary' Rathbun Dies; Advocated Medical Marijuana," *Los Angeles Times*, April 13, 1999.

37. Marianne Costantinou, "Friends Pay Tribute to Brownie Mary's Life," *San Francisco Examiner*, April 18, 1999.

38. "Marijuana Arrests for Year 2007: 872,721 Tops Record High—Five Percent Increase over 2006," NORML, September 15, 2008, http://norml .org/news/2008/09/15/marijuana-arrests-for-year-2007-872721-tops -record-high-five-percent-increase-over-2006.

Chapter 13: A Social Justice Issue

1. Alexander, *The New Jim Crow*, 2–9.
2. Jennifer Schuessler, "Drug Policy as Race Policy: Best Seller Galvanizes Debate," *New York Times*, March 6, 2012.
3. Ibid., 18, 11.
4. Jesse Wegman, "The Injustice of Marijuana Arrests," *New York Times*, July 28, 2014; Dylan Matthews, "The Black/White Marijuana Arrest Gap, in Nine Charts," *Washington Post*, June 4, 2013.
5. Matt Ferner, "More Americans Than Ever Say They've Tried Marijuana, Gallup Poll Finds," *Huffington Post*, July 22, 2015, http://www.huff ingtonpost.com/entry/marijuana-poll_us_55b010c6e4b07af29d577562.
6. Ricardo Baca, "Colorado Marijuana Sales Skyrocket to More Than $996 Million in 2015," *The Cannabist*, February 9, 2016; Ricardo Baca, "Colorado Marijuana Sales: $1 Billion in First Ten Months of 2016," *The Cannabist*, December 12, 2016.
7. Andrew Blake, "Marijuana Sales in Washington State Top $1 Billion: Report," *Washington Times*, July 8, 2016.
8. Art Swift, "Support for Legal Marijuana Use Up to 60% in US," Gallup, October 19, 2016.
9. Katy Steinmetz, "California Lt. Gov. Gavin Newsom on Marijuana Legalization: 'Our Purpose Is Social Justice,'" *Time*, June 21, 2016.
10. Diane Goldstein, "Marijuana Legalization—A Step Toward Social Justice," *San Francisco Gate*, October 25, 2014.
11. For more information, see Campaign Zero, http://www.join campaignzero.org/solutions/#brokenwindows.
12. Lavanya Ramanathan, "A Bottle of Juice for $55? How One Start-Up Is Testing the Limits of DC's Marijuana Law," *Washington Post*, April 26, 2016.
13. Alexander, *The New Jim Crow*, 6–7.
14. Peter Hermann et al., "DC Police Bust 'Kush Gods' Outfit That Traded Marijuana for 'Donations,'" *Washington Post*, December 23, 2015.
15. Ben Nuchols, "DC Adds Race to Nation's Debate on Legalizing Pot," *Aurora* (CO) *Sentinel*, October 13, 2014.

16. Drug Policy Alliance, "DC Marijuana Initiative Receives Major Civil Rights Endorsements from DC NAACP and the DC Branch of the National Organization for Women" (press release), October 23, 2014.

17. German Lopez, "Washington, DC, Police Chief on Marijuana: 'All Those Arrests Do Is Make People Hate Us,'" *Vox*, March 3, 2015, http://www.vox.com/2015/3/3/8143371/cathy-lanier-marijuana.

18. Nuchols, "DC Adds Race to Nation's Debate on Legalizing Pot."

19. Marc Fisher et al., "With Marijuana Legalization, Green Rush Is On in DC," *Washington Post*, February 25, 2015.

20. Kaitlyn Boecker, "On DC's One-Year Anniversary with Legalized Marijuana, Work Remains," *Washington Post*, February 25, 2016; Drug Policy Alliance, "Friday: One Year Anniversary of Marijuana Legalization in Washington, DC" (press release), February 24, 2016.

21. All of the following *Washington Post* quotes are from John Woodrow Cox, "How DC Pot Legalization Has Become 'the Dealer-Protection Act of 2015,'" *Washington Post*, May 17, 2015.

22. Perry Stein, "More American High School Students Smoke Pot Than Binge Drink, Report Says," *Washington Post*, August 1, 2016.

23. Christopher Ingraham, "What Happened in Washington State After Voters Legalized Recreational Marijuana," *Washington Post*, December 29, 2016; Oregon Health Authority, Public Health Division, *Marijuana Report: Marijuana Use, Attitudes, and Health Effects in Oregon*, January 2016, https://public.health.oregon.gov/PreventionWellness/marijuana/Documents/oha-8509-marijuana-report.pdf.

24. Lloyd Johnston, "Daily Marijuana Use Among College Students Highest Since 1980" (press release), University of Michigan, Institute for Social Research, August 31, 2015.

25. Kevin Sabet, interview with author, May 19, 2016.

26. Josh Sens, "Tilting at Windmills in Berkeley," *San Francisco Gate*, June 1, 2001.

27. Z. Byron Wolf, "Another Battle at the Park," *Berkeley Daily Planet*, April 7, 2000.

28. Kevin Sabet, interview with author, May 19, 2016.

29. German Lopez, "Meet the Man Trying to Halt Marijuana Legalization," *Vox*, March 24, 2016, http://www.vox.com/2015/3/20/8257631/kevin-sabet-marijuana-legalization.

30. John Lavitt, "Policy Advocate Kevin Sabet Believes Big Marijuana Is the Next Big Tobacco," *The Fix*, June 3, 2016, https://www.thefix.com/policy-advocate-kevin-sabet-believes-big-marijuana-next-big-tobacco.

31. Jan Hoffman, "Study Finds Sharp Increase in Marijuana Exposure Among Children in Colorado," *New York Times,* July 25, 2016, A19.

32. Smart Approaches to Marijuana, "Mission and Vision," https://learn aboutsam.org/who-we-are/mission-vision/.

33. Kevin Sabet, interview with author, May 19, 2016.

34. Ibid.

35. Lopez, "Meet the Man Trying to Halt Marijuana Legalization."

36. Ted Hesson, "Why Some of DC's Black Residents Aren't Sold on Marijuana Legalization," *Fusion,* October 17, 2014.

37. Rachel Weiner, "'Two. Is. Enough. DC.' Forms to Oppose Marijuana Legalization Effort in the District," *Washington Post,* September 17, 2014; Mike DeBonis, "DC, Where Blacks Are No Longer a Majority, Has a New African American Affairs Director," *Washington Post,* February 4, 2015.

38. For more information, see http://www.momsstrong.org.

39. Anne Saker, "6 Reasons Marijuana Legalization Failed in Ohio," *USA Today,* November 4, 2015; Keith Stroup, personal communication with author, January 4, 2016.

40. Katie Sola, "Legal US Marijuana Market Will Grow to $7.1 Billion in 2016," *Forbes,* April 19, 2016; Jennifer Kaplan, "Cannabis Industry Expected to Be Worth $50 Billion by 2026," *Bloomberg,* September 12, 2016.

41. Amanda Chicago Lewis, "How Black People Are Being Shut Out of America's Weed Boom: Whitewashing the Green Rush," *BuzzFeed News,* March 16, 2016.

42. Jon Gettman, "Marijuana Arrests in Colorado After the Passage of Amendment 64," Drug Policy Alliance, March 25, 2015, http://www.drugpolicy.org/resource/marijuana-arrests-colorado-after-passage-amendment-64.

43. Carol Rose, "It's Black and White: The Social Justice Case for Legalizing Marijuana," WBUR, November 2, 2016, http://www.wbur.org/cognoscenti/2016/11/02/yes-on-question-4-legalize-marijuana-carol-rose.

44. Spencer Buell, "Massachusetts Votes to Legalize Marijuana," *Boston,* November 8, 2016.

45. Alexander, *The New Jim Crow,* 221, 226, 222.

46. April M. Short, "Michelle Alexander: White Men Get Rich from Legal Pot, Black Men Stay in Prison," *AlterNet,* March 16, 2014, http://www.alternet.org/drugs/michelle-alexander-white-men-get-rich-legal-pot-black-men-stay-prison.

47. Janice Williams, "Legal Pot Hasn't Resulted in More Teens Smoking Marijuana," *Newsweek,* March 22, 2017.

48. National Institute on Drug Abuse, "Overdose Death Rates," January 2017, https://www.drugabuse.gov/related-topics/trends-statistics/overdose -death-rates.

49. Josh Harkinson, "Marijuana Legalization May Be Unstoppable," *Mother Jones,* February 28, 2013, http://www.motherjones.com/mojo /2013/02/new-polls-and-votes-suggest-marijuana-legalization-unstoppable.

Conclusion: Lessons Learned

1. Christopher Ingraham, "One Striking Chart Shows Why Big Pharma Companies Are Fighting Legal Marijuana," *Washington Post,* July 13, 2016.

2. James Hidgon, "Jeff Sessions' Coming War on Marijuana," *Politico,* December 5, 2016.

3. Lanny Swerdlow, interview with author, April 7, 2016.

INDEX

Abbott, Wallace, 182, 183
Abbott Laboratories, 253
Acapulco Gold (brand name), 38, 39, 40
Accessories Digest (magazine), 105–106
ACLU. *See* American Civil Liberties
    Union
ACT. *See* Alliance for Cannabis
    Therapeutics
ACTION, 152, 154, 163, 200
  Bourne's position in, 120–121
  budget cuts in, 160
  founding and purpose of, 153
Ad Council, 174
Adams, W. Thomas ("Tom"), 167,
    169–175, 176
  on conflict within antidrug
    movement, 199
  corporate takeover and, 180–186
  credited with handbook publication,
    177–178
Adam's Apple Distributing Company, 79
Addams, Shay, 85, 86
adolescents
  crack use in, 185, 189
  drug dealing by, 169, 189
  legalization and, 237, 238, 254
  NORML's position on drugs and,
    202–203
  paraphernalia sold to, 75, 86–87
  rates of drug use in, 144, 150–151,
    155, 185, 254
  rates of marijuana use in, 72, 87, 95,
    104–105, 123–124, 125, 136–137,
    144, 150–151, 155, 161–162, 185,
    192, 222, 238

  research on marijuana use in, 95
  See also parent movement
Advertising Age, 197
African American Institute (AAI), 166
African Americans, 3, 17–18, 25, 27
  arrest rates in, 228, 230, 234, 243, 245,
    248, 259
  crack use in, 190, 194
  incarceration rates in, 190, 224,
    225–228, 247, 248
  Just Say No campaign and, 167–172,
    178
  legalization and, 234–235, 242–243,
    244–248
Agnew, Spiro, 76
Agriculture Department, US, 4
Ahmed, Hani, 236
AIDS/HIV, medical marijuana and, 8,
    205, 207, 208, 209, 214–217, 219,
    220, 259
Alaska
  decriminalization in, 69–70
  legalization in, 228
  medical marijuana legalized in, 220
Alaska Supreme Court, 69
alcohol
  adolescents' use of, 237
  prohibition of, 1, 3, 8, 55, 87, 231, 251,
    258
  Shafer Commission on, 54
Aldrich, Michael ("Dr. Dope"), 18, 19,
    39–40, 41
Alexander, Michelle, 225–228, 234,
    245–247, 248, 252
Ali, Akosua, 235

Emily Dufton holds a PhD in American Studies from George Washington University. She lives outside of Washington, DC.

Photograph by Travis S. Pratt